BARRON'S

IELTS

(INTERNATIONAL ENGLISH LANGUAGE TESTING SYSTEM)

Lin Lougheed, Ed.D.

BARRON'S

Acknowledgments
Directions in the Model Tests used with permission of the IELTS partners. Charts on pages 3 and 7 are reprinted from the IELTS Handbook with permission of the IELTS partners.

The author wishes to thank the following organizations, institutions, bloggers, and clearinghouse for their kind permission to use their source material. If we neglected to list your name, please contact us so we can correct that omission.

(p194) Adult Intelligence, by Phillip Ackerman, ED410228, ERIC Clearinghouse on Assessment and Evaluation, Washington, DC, 1996.

(p139) Less Television, Less Violence, TV-Free America, *www.tvturnoff.org/lessviolence.htm*;

(p143) Issues **Affecting the Southern Resident Orcas** from Declining Fish Populations, The Whale Museum (*www.whalemuseum.org*);

All inquiries should be addressed to:
Barron's Educational Series, Inc.
250 Wireless Boulevard
Hauppauge, New York 11788
www.barronseduc.com

Library of Congress Catalog Card No.: 2006040752

ISBN-13: 978-0-7641-7935-8 (Book with audio CD)
ISBN-10: 0-7641-7935-7 (Book with audio CD)

Library of Congress Cataloging-in-Publication Data
Lougheed, Lin, 1946-
Barron's IELTS (International English Language Testing System) / Lin Lougheed.
p. cm.
ISBN-13: 978-0-7641-7935-8 (book with audio CD)
ISBN-10: 0-7641-7935-7 (book with audio CD)
1. International English Language Testing System—Study guides. 2. English language—Textbooks for foreign speakers. 3. English language—Examinations—Study guides. I. Title: How to prepare for the IELTS (International English Language Testing System). II. Title: How to prepare for the International English Language Testing System. III. Barron's Educational Series, Inc. IV. Title.

PE1128.L6436 2006
428.1076—dc22

2006040752

Printed in the United States of America
9 8 7 6 5 4 3

CONTENTS

1

INTRODUCTION

Over half a million people take IELTS each year. There are more than 400 test centers that administer IELTS in over 100 countries around the world. Today it is one of the most accepted international exams for academic qualification. You can learn more about IELTS by visiting the official website at **www.ielts.org**.

Purpose

IELTS is available for people who need to demonstrate their English language proficiency for specific purposes. There are two formats of IELTS to choose from depending on your needs. You should take the Academic Training modules if you are planning to apply to an international university where English is the spoken language. The General Training modules are more suitable if you want to work, live, or study at a secondary institution in an English-speaking country.

Test-takers

International students represent the highest percentage of candidates who take IELTS. An IELTS score is a recognized measurement of English proficiency at over 1200 educational facilities around the world. Government departments and businesses around the globe also require an IELTS or equivalent score for employment or immigration. Medical professionals who want to work overseas in the UK must take IELTS.

Skills Tested

IELTS consists of four modules testing the full range of English language skills—Reading, Writing, Listening, and Speaking. The Listening and Speaking sections are the same for both the Academic and General Training modules. The Reading and Writing modules are different in the Academic and General Training modules.

Language Tested

IELTS is an international test. The English used in the test and heard on the audio can be British, American, Australian, or New Zealand English. The language tested will be comprehensible to any learner of English. Even though IELTS is created in Britain, test-takers who studied another form of English will not be penalized (or *penalised*).

In this book, we have pointed out the common differences between American English and the English used in other parts of the world. We have provided footnotes to show differences in spelling and differences in usage. Whatever spelling you use when writing your test answers, the examiners will accept your spelling as long as you are consistent throughout.

International users of English are aware of differences in usage and spelling. Most international users understand that *colour* is written *color* in American English and that *organize* is written *organise* in British English. Because of films, international magazines, travel, and the Internet, we know that *apartment* and *flat* and *gas* and *petrol*, *city center* and *downtown* are synonyms. We know that an American form is *filled out* and in Britain is *filled in*. In Britain, a family could take a *holiday* at the *sea*. In America, people head toward land: in Florida, *vacationers* go to the *beach* for a *vacation*; in New Jersey, they go to the *shore*. We may use one synonym, but we understand the other without problem.

We know that the cultural institutions of English speaking countries are organized (*organised*) differently. American and Australian students study for a *semester* or a *term*; British students study for a *term*. In Canada and Britain, students get *marks*; in America, they get *grades*. A British *public* school is a *private* school in America. In America, a building begins on the *first* floor. In Britain, one starts at the *ground* floor. We can understand these differences from the context. Their meanings will not be misunderstood.

The common usage differences in this book are:

American	**British**
math	maths
college major	subject
city hall	town hall
pharmacy	chemist
parking garage/lot	car park
movies/film	film
movie theatre	cinema
sidewalk	pavement
cell phone	mobile phone
graduated from college	left college
school/college/university	college/university

The common spelling differences in this book are:

Suffixes		**Doubling of consonants**	
-yze	-yse	traveling	travelling
-ize	-ise	label	labelled
-or	-our		
-am	-amme		
-ck	-que		
-er	-re		
Prefixes		**Use of dipthong *ae***	
co	co-	anesthesia	anaesthesia
re	re-		

Format

The whole test takes 2 hours and 45 minutes. The Listening, Reading, and Writing modules are taken in one sitting. The Speaking module may be taken within 7 days before or after the other modules. It is usually taken the same afternoon or within 2 or 3 days. You will have to arrange for the Speaking module at your test center.

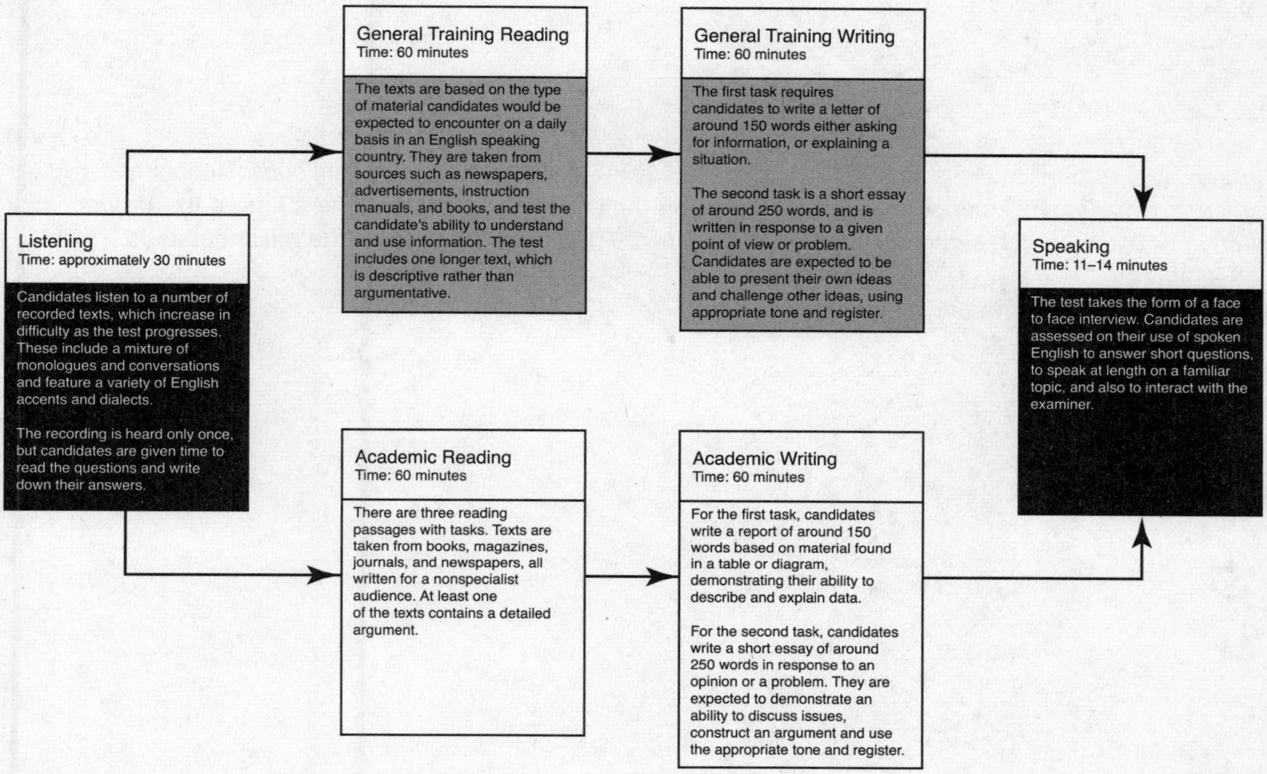

Listening
Time: approximately 30 minutes
Candidates listen to a number of recorded texts, which increase in difficulty as the test progresses. These include a mixture of monologues and conversations and feature a variety of English accents and dialects.
The recording is heard only once, but candidates are given time to read the questions and write down their answers.
General Training Reading
Time: 60 minutes
The texts are based on the type of material candidates would be expected to encounter on a daily basis in an English speaking country. They are taken from sources such as newspapers, advertisements, instruction manuals, and books, and test the candidate's ability to understand and use information. The test includes one longer text, which is descriptive rather than argumentative.
General Training Writing
Time: 60 minutes
The first task requires candidates to write a letter of around 150 words either asking for information, or explaining a situation.
The second task is a short essay of around 250 words, and is written in response to a given point of view or problem. Candidates are expected to be able to present their own ideas and challenge other ideas, using appropriate tone and register.
Academic Reading
Time: 60 minutes
There are three reading passages with tasks. Texts are taken from books, magazines, journals, and newspapers, all written for a nonspecialist audience. At least one of the texts contains a detailed argument.
Academic Writing
Time: 60 minutes
For the first task, candidates write a report of around 150 words based on material found in a table or diagram, demonstrating their ability to describe and explain data.
For the second task, candidates write a short essay of around 250 words in response to an opinion or a problem. They are expected to demonstrate an ability to discuss issues, construct an argument and use the appropriate tone and register.
Speaking
Time: 11–14 minutes
The test takes the form of a face to face interview. Candidates are assessed on their use of spoken English to answer short questions, to speak at length on a familiar topic, and also to interact with the examiner.

*Reprinted from the IELTS Handbook with permission of the IELTS partners.

2

QUESTIONS AND ANSWERS ABOUT IELTS

Should I take the Academic or General Training exam?

If you are planning on taking an undergraduate or postgraduate course at an English college or university, you should take the Academic Training exam. Your entrance to an institution will be based on this exam. The General Training exam tests the English language communication skills or general communication skills that are needed for those who want to live and work in English-speaking countries. Although the Reading and Writing modules of the Academic exam measure the candidate's ability to function in a higher educational institution, a range of educational and social contexts are used in the Listening and Speaking sections of both tests. It is important that you choose the correct test on your application form. The institution or agency that will be receiving your scores will tell you which exam to take.

Where can I take IELTS?

More than 400 test centers around the world administer IELTS. Most test centers are run by the British Council, IELTS Australia, or universities and language schools. Some testing centers also offer off-site testing for large groups by prior arrangement with IELTS. Contact your local examination center or visit **www.ielts.org** to find out where the nearest IELTS test center is located.

Where can I find information about registering for the test?

You can contact your nearest examination center or visit the official IELTS website for more information about application procedures and the location of a test center near you.

How much does it cost to take IELTS?

Test fees are set centrally by the British Council and its partners. The fees are generally set for a year at a time. You can find out the cost to take IELTS in your currency by calling your test center. If for some reason you cannot take the test, contact your test center as soon as possible. A partial refund may be available.

Is this a paper-and-pencil test or is there a computer-based version?

As of May 2005, a computer-based IELTS (CBIELTS) became available at select test centers around the world. These tests are usually administered on alternative dates to the paper test. If you are taking the CBIELTS, you will take the Listening and Reading modules on the computer. If you are worried about your typing abilities, you have the option of doing the Writing section on paper. The Speaking section will still be administered face-to-face. CD-ROM versions of the CBIELTS are available for practice. See **www.ielts.org** for a list of test centers that offer the computer-based version.

How is IELTS different from the TOEIC or TOEFL test?

- IELTS does not rely as heavily on multiple-choice questions.
- Different accents are used in IELTS including British, New Zealand, Australian, and American.
- Two different formats are offered (Academic and General Training), depending on the purposes of the test-taker.
- IELTS is offered more regularly than TOEIC and TOEFL at most test centers.

What can I take into the testing room?

On your desk you will be allowed only pencils and erasers (rubbers). (On the paper-based test, the answer sheet for the Listening and Reading modules must be written in pencil as parts will be scanned by a computer.) You cannot use correction fluid. You also may not borrow or lend writing utensils during the test. There will be a designated area for you to put your other personal belongings. You will not be allowed to have any electronic devices such as pagers and cell (mobile) phones in the testing room.

What identification is required?

You will need to have two forms of identification (such as a valid photo ID card, passport, driver's license, student ID, or national ID) with you when you register, as well as on test day. When you take the Speaking module, you will have to present your photo ID again.

How many times will I hear the recording in the Listening module?

Each Listening section is played only once. You must take notes in the Listening question booklet as you listen. After the 30-minute section, you will be given 10 minutes to transfer your notes to your answer sheet. In Sections 1, 2, and 3, there are pauses so you can review the questions. There are 30 seconds to check answers after each section. The examiner will not see your notes.

What types of things will I have to talk about in the Speaking section?

You will not be asked to talk about anything that you need background information for. All of the questions deal with common experiences that do not require special knowledge. It is not a good idea to try to memorize answers to questions that you think will be asked because you may not address the question exactly as the examiner asks. You may ask the examiner to repeat a question or clarify a word you are unsure of.

Will I have any time to prepare my Speaking answers?

Part 2 is the only section in which you will be given time to prepare. You will have one minute to organize your thoughts and take notes for your speech. You are allowed to refer to these notes when you speak, but you should look at the examiner as much as possible.

What criteria are my Speaking answers based on?

Your ability to communicate in English is measured in two ways:

1. Fluency and coherence: content, delivery, organization
2. Language use: vocabulary, pronunciation, grammar

How can I find out my results?

Your test results will be sent to your home address or your educational institute within 2 weeks of taking the test. Your overall band score will be given on the Test Report Form, as will a breakdown of your scores in the four separate sections. On the IELTS registration form, you can designate up to five institutions, agencies, or individuals to receive your Test Report Form. For additional reports, the fee is $10 per form.

What is a band?

You cannot pass or fail IELTS. The test is scored on a band scale. A band is a level of ability. In each section, you can score anywhere from a band of 0 (nonuser) to a band of 9 (expert user). In the Listening and Reading modules, a mark is given for each correct answer. This number is then converted into a band, with a conversion table. Overall scores are an average of all four sections and can be given in whole or half bands.

How can I interpret my band scores?

A general description of the competency level for each of the nine bands is reprinted from the IELTS website with permission. The overall band requirement for each institution or government body may be different. A band of 6 or 6.5 is a common requirement for university admission.

9	Expert user	Has fully operational command of the language: appropriate, accurate, and fluent with complete understanding.
8	Very good user	Has fully operational command of the language with only occasional unsystematic inaccuracies and inappropriacies. Misunderstandings may occur in unfamiliar situations. Handles complex detailed argumentation well.
7	Good user	Has operational command of the language, though with occasional inaccuracies, inappropriacies, and misunderstandings in some situations. Generally handles complex language well and understands desired reasoning.
6	Competent user	Has generally effective command of the language despite some inaccuracies, inappropriacies, and misunderstandings. Can use and understand fairly complex language, particularly in familiar situations.
5	Modest user	Has partial command of the language, coping with overall meaning in most situations, though likely to make many mistakes. Should be able to handle basic communication in own field.
4	Limited user	Basic competence is limited to familiar situations. Has frequent problems in understanding and expression. Is not able to use complex language.
3	Extremely limited user	Conveys and understand only general meaning in very familiar situations. Frequent breakdowns in communication occur.
2	Intermittent user	No real communication is possible except for the most basic information using isolated words or short formulae in familiar situations and to meet immediate needs. Has great difficulty understanding spoken and written English.
1	Nonuser	Essentially has no ability to use the language beyond possibly a few isolated words.
0	Did not attempt the test	No assessable information provided.

How long is my score valid?

An IELTS score is generally recognized for two years. Some institutions may accept your score after 2 years if you can provide proof that you have maintained your English language proficiency. If you are applying for admission to a post secondary institution, your last test score will be used.

When can I retake the test?

You may repeat the test whenever and as often as you wish. However, some studies suggest that 3 months may be the minimum amount of time that average learners need to improve their band score. During these 3 months, candidates must continue their efforts to improve their English through class study or self-study.

How can I improve my score on each of the test sections?

Most importantly you must read, write, speak, and listen to English on a regular basis. *Barron's IELTS* will help you achieve your goal.

3

PREPARING FOR IELTS

- **A Study Plan**
- **Using This Book**
- **Tips for Success**
  - Listening Tips
  - Reading Tips
  - Writing Tips
  - Speaking Tips
  - Exam Day Tips

A Study Plan

It takes a lot of self-discipline to learn English. Only you can make yourself do it. These suggestions will help you improve your discipline and your English.

- Study on a regular basis. Study at the same time of day. Make your study habits part of your routine. You must develop good study habits. Tell yourself that you can't surf the Internet, because you must study for IELTS. If you miss your scheduled time, do it later. Make a contract with yourself. For example, I will study English for 2 hours a day after lunch. And don't break that contract.
- Write out your study contract. If your plan is on paper, you are more likely to do it later.
- Don't give yourself unreasonable goals. For example, if you can't study 4 hours a day, tell yourself you will study 30 minutes after you wake up and 30 minutes before you go to bed.
- Budget your time. The IELTS is a timed test so time your study sessions.
- Use your time effectively. If you only have 10 minutes to study, learn to take advantage of these short periods.
- Listen, read, write, and speak as much English as you can. The best way to improve any skill is by practicing it.
- Write down new words in a notebook. Study and then review these words frequently.
- Develop a positive attitude. It is difficult to learn a language, but not impossible. Other people have done it; many people have done it well. You, too, can learn to speak, read, and write English as a native speaker does.

Using This Book

You can study the material in this book in many ways. You can study it in a class; you can study it by yourself starting with the first page and going all the way to the end; or you can study only those parts where you know you need extra help.

Here are some suggestions for getting the most out of *Barron's IELTS.*

- Look over the Table of Contents so you have an idea of what is in the book.
- Take a Model Test so you understand where you need more help.
- Become familiar with the directions for IELTS. Get to know what the task is. This will help you move quickly through the test.
- Study efficiently. If you don't have much time, only study where you need extra help.
- Use the strategies. These strategies will help you score well on IELTS.
- Use the explanatory answers. These answers will explain why an answer choice is wrong. For many of the items, the answers will only be approximate. Your answer need not match the one provided as a sample.
- Study a little every day. Don't fall behind. Keep at it.

Tips for Success

Listening Tips

- Make sure that you know what the question is asking.
- Practice listening for a full half-hour. Concentrate. Do not let your mind wander. Can you repeat what you heard? Can you summarize what you heard?
- Use the time before each Listening section to underline key words in the question, such as *who, where, when,* and *what.*
- Mark your answers carefully. If you are asked to give a letter (A), don't put the phrase.
- Look out for speakers who correct themselves. Their second statement is the one that is usually asked for.
- Be careful not to make simple spelling mistakes. These will be penalized.
- Incomplete or shortened answers (i.e., times and dates) will be marked as incorrect.
- A variety of accents are used including British, Australian, and American. Practice listening to different native English speakers.
- Remember that answers that exceed word limits (even use of *a* or *the*) will be marked as incorrect.

Reading Tips

- Time management is key. Remember that you won't be given ten extra minutes of transfer time at the end of the Reading module as you are in the Listening module. Also, be prepared for the passages to get progressively difficult and demand more of your time.
- Skimming and scanning are important comprehension skills. You must learn and practice these skills.
- Learn to analyze titles and headings and to predict paragraph subject matter from subtitles and topic sentences.
- Always read twice the section that is relevant to the question.
- Underline important parts as you read. Do this when you are practicing and when you are doing the test.
- If the instructions ask you to use no more than three words to complete an answer, do not write more than three words. You will lose points.
- Be careful not to mix up *True/False* with *Yes/No*. These are considered by many to be the most difficult questions on the test. Practice them often so you will be confident during the test.

Writing Tips

- Don't underestimate the planning stage. It is very important to plan your writing carefully.
- Manage your time carefully. You should spend about 20 minutes on Task 1 and 40 minutes on Task 2. Leave about 5 minutes to proofread your work.
- Answer all parts of the question, and underline key points in it.
- Learn the words and phrases used to link sentences and paragraphs.
- Add personal experiences and details whenever possible.
- Read as much and as often as you can.
- Learn to look at your writing and estimate how many words it is. Precious time is wasted counting words.

Speaking Tips

- Imagine that the examiner is a friend.
- Practice introducing yourself and answering typical "getting to know you" questions.

- Don't waste preparation time writing out full sentences. Make notes of just your key ideas.
- Practice turning short notes into a short speech.
- Record your voice and listen to it.
- Practice giving opinions and supporting them with examples and details. You are being marked on your opinions and speaking abilities, not your knowledge.
- Pay attention to verb tenses. You may need to talk about the past, present, and future in the same topic.
- Ask the examiner to repeat or explain a question if you are unclear about a task.

Exam Day Tips

- Read all communication from the test center carefully. You may receive directions or advice on nearby hotels.
- Be early. Don't be anxious about being late. Give yourself more than enough time to get to the test center. If you live far away, you may want to arrive the night before. Then you can relax without worrying about being late.
- Be comfortable. Don't wear clothes that don't fit or don't feel good.
- Don't take more than the necessary items with you to the testing center. The only things you will be allowed to take into the testing room are pencils and erasers (rubbers), your identification, and possibly a bottle of water. Everything else, including handbags, coats, jackets (even blazers or other jackets normally worn indoors), and cell (mobile) phones, will have to be left outside the testing room.
- You will have to bring two forms of identification with you to the testing site. The test administrators normally ask for a passport and a secondary form of identification such as a driver's license or a student ID card. You will be asked to arrive at the testing center at least 30 minutes ahead of time for check-in and identification check. Anyone who arrives late will not be admitted to the test.
- The Listening, Reading, and Writing parts of the test last about 3 hours altogether. You will have to remain in your seat in the testing room during this entire period of time, even if you finish the test early.
- You will be permitted to leave the room to go to the toilet if necessary. Raise your hand and quietly ask the person in charge for permission to leave the testing room. Do not disturb the other test-takers.
- The last part of the test is the Speaking Part. It takes up to 20 minutes. This is a face-to-face interview, so each test-taker will be assigned a time for his or her interview. You probably won't know the time for your interview until the day of the test, so you need to be prepared to spend most of the day at the testing center.

4

LISTENING MODULE

- **QUICK STUDY**
  - Overview
  - Question Types
  - Listening Tips
  - Completing the Blanks
- **LISTENING SKILLS**
  - Target 1—Making Assumptions
  - Target 2—Understanding Numbers
  - Target 3—Understanding the Alphabet
  - Target 4—Listening for Descriptions
  - Target 5—Listening for Time
  - Target 6—Listening for Frequency
  - Target 7—Listening for Similar Meanings
  - Target 8—Listening for Emotions
  - Target 9—Listening for an Explanation
  - Target 10—Listening for Classifications
  - Target 11—Listening for Comparisons and Contrasts
  - Target 12—Listening for Negative Meaning
  - Target 13—Listening for Chronology

QUICK STUDY

Overview

There are four sections to the Listening module. There are 40 questions altogether. The audio will last approximately 30 minutes.

During the test, you will be given time to read the questions *before* you hear the audio. As you listen, you should write your answers in your test booklet. Do not wait until the end. The answers in the audio follow the order of the questions. If you hesitate and think about one question, you may miss the next question. The audio keeps going.

At the end of each section, you will be given 30 seconds to check your answers. You will have an additional 10 minutes to transfer your answers from your test booklet to the official answer sheet. You must transfer your answers. If you don't transfer your answers, your answers will not be counted. If you don't transfer your answers, you will not receive a listening score.

The Listening modules are the same for both the Academic and the General Training versions of the IELTS.

Listening Module

Sections	Topics	Speakers
1	General, everyday topics	Conversation between two people
2	General, everyday topics	One person
3	School or training-related topics	Conversation between two or more people
4	School or training-related topics	One person

Questions Types

There are a variety of question types on the IELTS Listening module. You will find examples of these types in this chapter.

- Multiple-choice
- Short answer
- Sentence completion
- Chart completion
- Flowchart completion
- Graphs
- Tables
- Making notes
- Summarizing[1]
- Labeling[2] diagrams, plans, and maps
- Classification
- Matching
- Selecting from a list

[1]BRITISH: Summarising

[2]BRITISH: labelling

Listening Tips

These tips will help you improve your listening score.

1. Learn and understand the directions now. You will want to use your time during the test to study the questions, not the directions.
2. Study the different types of questions. Be prepared for what the question might ask you to do. Be prepared to complete a sentence, check[1] a box, or choose a letter.
3. You should take notes in your question booklet as you listen. You can circle possible answers and change your mind later when you transfer your answers to the answer sheet.
4. If you don't know an answer, you can guess. However, there is a penalty for wrong answers. Make sure you think you are right. If you guess wrong, you will lose a point.
5. Anytime you have a chance, study the next set of questions. Make assumptions about what you think you will hear.
6. When you make assumptions, ask yourself: *Who? What? When? Where?* and *How?*
7. The correct answer is often repeated, but the words will not be written exactly as they are heard. The test will use paraphrases and synonyms.
8. There is a lot of information given in the dialogues and lectures that is not tested. Try to listen only for answers to the questions.
9. Don't get stuck on a question. If you didn't hear the answer, go on.
10. The answers are given in order. For example, if you hear the answer to Question 10, but didn't hear the answer for Question 9, you missed Question 9. You will not hear the answer later. Guess the answer to Question 9 and move on.
11. Be sure to read the instructions you receive from the test center. Some supply pencils; some ask you to bring your own. If you are given an IELTS pencil at the start of the exam, you will probably not be allowed to bring you own pen or pencil into the examining room. You could bring a number 2 pencil, a soft lead pencil, to make sure you have something to write with. You may have to leave it outside the test center, but it's better to have a pencil than not.
12. When you write a word in a blank, you must spell the word correctly. It doesn't matter if you use British or American spelling. It must be spelled correctly. You will get a lower score if you did not spell correctly.

Completing the Blanks

Number of Words and Spelling

Many IELTS test-takers do not correctly complete the blanks. Some test-takers use more than the suggested number of words, or they do not spell the answer correctly.

If you make these mistakes, you will lose points. Be careful when you complete blanks. You may know the correct answer but if you don't spell it correctly or if you add additional words, you will get a lower score.

[1]BRITISH: Tick a box

Number of Words

Complete the sentence below. Write **NO MORE THAN THREE WORDS** *for each answer.*

Incorrect: The scientists discovered *a new cure/treatment*.

Correct: The scientists discovered *a cure*.

The incorrect answer above counts as four words. Four words will count against you. You can use fewer than three words, but you cannot use more than three words. Do not use a slash.

Number of Words

Complete the sentence below. Write **NO MORE THAN THREE WORDS** *for each answer.*

Incorrect: The scientists discovered *a new cancer treatment*.

Correct: The scientists discovered *a cancer treatment*.

The incorrect answer above counts as four words. Four words will count against you. Use no more than three.

Spelling

Complete the sentence below. Write **NO MORE THAN THREE WORDS** *for each answer.*

Incorrect: The scientists discovered *a cancer treetment*.

Correct: The scientists discovered *a cancer treatment*.

You must spell the words correctly. A misspelled word will count against you. You can use British or American spelling, but you must spell the word correctly.

You can practice your spelling by taking dictation. Listen to the audio in this book. Write down everything you hear. Check your spelling in the audio script in the back of this book.

Questions 1–10

The following statements are not completed correctly. Write the correct answer. Write **NO MORE THAN THREE WORDS** *for each answer.*

1 The shelves were filled with *with fruts and fresh vegetables*.

The shelves were filled with *fruits and vegetables*.

In the incorrect sentence, *with* is repeated, *fruits is* misspelled, the adjective *fresh* is not necessary to the statement, and there are five words instead of three.

2 Cynthia lives near *to the train stattion*.
Cynthia lives near ....

3 If you return a library book late, you must *pay a fine of 25 cents*[1] *a day*.
If you return a library book late, you must ....

4 Their trip was spoiled because of *they had very bad weather*.
Their trip was spoiled because of ....

[1]US Currency: 100 cents in one dollars.

5 The fountain is in the center of the *beautiful, sunny roses garden.*
The fountain is in the center of the ....
6 Students *usually can to choose* the topic for their essay.
Students .... the topic for their essay.
7 *More or less ten thousend of* visitors come to the museum each year.
.... visitors come to the museum each year.
8 If you don't understand the assignment, you should *have to ask the professor* for help.
If you don't understand the assignment, you should .... for help.
9 Roberto was excited about *about taking a trip to Alaska.*
Roberto was excited about ....
10 Many northern song birds *spend the long witer* in Mexico.
Many northern song birds .... in Mexico.

Gender and Number

You must pay attention to the grammar of the sentence when completing a blank. You must also pay attention to the grammar of the sentence. The words you put in the blank must match the tense, gender, and number of the rest of the sentence. Don't use a singular verb when a plural verb is required. Don't use a singular noun when a plural noun is required. Don't use a masculine pronoun to refer to a feminine or neutral antecedent.

If you make these mistakes, you will loose points. Be careful when you complete blanks. You may know the correct answer but if you don't spell it correctly or add additional words, you will get a lower score.

Verb Agreement

Incorrect: The scientists at the research hospital *is looking* for a cure.
Correct: The scientists at the research hospital *are looking* for a cure.

The incorrect answer above uses a singular verb *is*. A plural verb *are* refers to the plural subject *scientists*. The singular noun *hospital* is the object of the preposition *at* not the subject of the sentence.

Singular/Plural Noun

Incorrect: They ordered five *shirt*.
Correct: They ordered five *shirts*.

The incorrect answer above uses a singular noun *shirt*. A plural noun *shirts* is needed because of the plural number *five*.

Pronoun Agreement

Incorrect: The patients have confidence *in his doctors*.
Correct: The patients have confidence *in their doctors*.

The incorrect answer above uses a singular pronoun *his*. A plural pronoun *their* refers to the plural subject *patients*.

Questions 1–10

The following statements are not completed correctly. Write the correct answer. Write **NO MORE THAN THREE WORDS** for each answer.

1. Unlike most other ducks, wood ducks *build thier nest* in trees.
   Unlike most other ducks, wood ducks .... in trees.
2. The new compact laptop computer is very popular among *busines traveler*.
   The new compact laptop computer is very popular among ....
3. Bananas grow in *in a tropicale climates*.
   Bananas grow in ....
4. Fruit *cost moor* in the winter than in the summer.
   Fruit .... in the winter than in the summer.
5. Mrs. Smith donated *his old close* to charity.
   Mrs. Smith donated .... to charity.
6. Students in this class have to *must take two exam* this semester[1].
   Students in this class have to .... this semester.
7. The college professor bought *new house*.
   The college professor bought ....
8. Mr. and Mrs. Rodgers *took his vacations*[2] in August this year.
   Mr. and Mrs. Rogers .... in August this year.
9. Every house *have a garden* in the back.
   Every house .... in the back.
10. The female dragonfly *likes to lay their eggs* under water.
    The female dragonfly .... under water.

[1]BRITISH: term
[2]BRITISH: holiday

LISTENING SKILLS

Target 1—Making Assumptions

In order to understand a conversation, you should focus on two things: the speakers and the topic. To score well on the IELTS, you should determine what you know and what you need to know.

As you listen to a conversation, you must make some assumptions about the speakers.

Who are they?
What is their relationship?
Where are they?
What do they plan to do?
What did they do?
What are their feelings?

You must also make some assumptions about the topic.

What are they talking about?
What happened?
What might happen?

You want to know *who*, *what*, *when*, *where*, *why*, and *how*.

To help you make these assumptions, you should scan the questions in your Listening Test booklet quickly and ask yourself: *Who? What? When? Where? Why?* and *How?* By looking for the answers to these general questions, you will discover what you know and what you need to know.

You will have about 20 seconds to look over these questions. Use that time to make assumptions about the listening passage. Read the question first. Then read the exercise on "Assumptions" on the following page. Do the exercises. Finally, listen to the conversation and test your assumptions.

CD TRACK 1

SECTION 1—Questions 1–10

Questions 1–5

Complete the form below. Write **NO MORE THAN THREE WORDS AND/OR A NUMBER** *for each answer.*

Woodside Apartments[1]
Tenant Application Form

EXAMPLE

Type of apartment requested: ***One bedroom***

Last name[2] **1** ______________________ First name James

Address 1705 **2** ____________ Street , Apt. **3** ________

Phone: Home 721 - 0584 Work: **4** _________

Date of birth **5** _________ 12, 1978[3]

Questions 6–8

Choose three letters, ***A–G****.*

What features will James get with his apartment?

A study
B balcony
C garage parking space[4]
D storage space
E exercise club
F fireplace
G washing machine

Questions 9–10

Complete the sentences. Write **NO MORE THAN THREE WORDS** *for each answer.*

9 The apartment will be ready next ____________.

10 James will have to pay __________ of the first month's rent as a deposit.

[1]BRITISH: flats
[2]BRITISH: surname
[3]BRITISH: day month year; AMERICAN: month day, year
[4]BRITISH: parking place

Assumptions

Find the answers to: Who? What? When? Where? Why? and How?

Who are the speakers?
What are they talking about?
When is something happening?
Where is something happening?
Why are they having a conversation?

We know this:
James wants to rent an apartment at the Woodside Apartments. He is a prospective tenant. The apartment is not ready yet. He will have to pay a deposit.

Answer these questions. Write **NO MORE THAN THREE WORDS** *for each answer.*

Who: *James*
What: *renting an apartment*
When: *Not ready*
Where: *Woodside Apartments*
Why: *Apartment deposit*

Circle the clues in Questions 1–10 that help you make these assumptions.
James wants to rent a one-bedroom apartment at the Woodside Apartments.

How do we know his first name is James?
How do we know he wants to rent?
How do we know he wants a one-bedroom apartment?
How do we know the name of the building?

He is a prospective tenant.
How do we know he is a prospective tenant?

The apartment is not ready yet.
How do we know the apartment is not ready?

He will have to pay a deposit.
How do we know there is a deposit?

We don't know this:
Write the number in Questions 1–10 next to the question you have to answer.

What is James' last name? Question ______
What street does he live on? Question ______
What is his work telephone number? Question ______
What month was he born? Question ______
What features will he get with his apartment? Question ______
When will the apartment be ready? Question ______
How much is the deposit? Question ______

Now listen to the conversation. Listen for the answers you don't know.

CD TRACK 2

SECTION 2—Questions 11–20

Questions 11–13

Complete the information about the museum. Write **NO MORE THAN THREE WORDS AND/OR A NUMBER** *for each answer.*

Jamestown Museum of Art
Information for Visitors

Entrance Fees: Adults $ **11** ____________
Children $ **12** ____________
Entrance is free for senior citizens on **13** ____________.

Hours
Tues–Thur 11:00 A.M.–5:00 P.M.
Fri 11:00 A.M.–7:00 P.M.
Sat–Sun 10:00 A.M.–6:00 P.M.
Mondays and holidays closed

Questions 14–18

Fill in the missing information on the map of the museum. Write **NO MORE THAN THREE WORDS** *for each answer.*

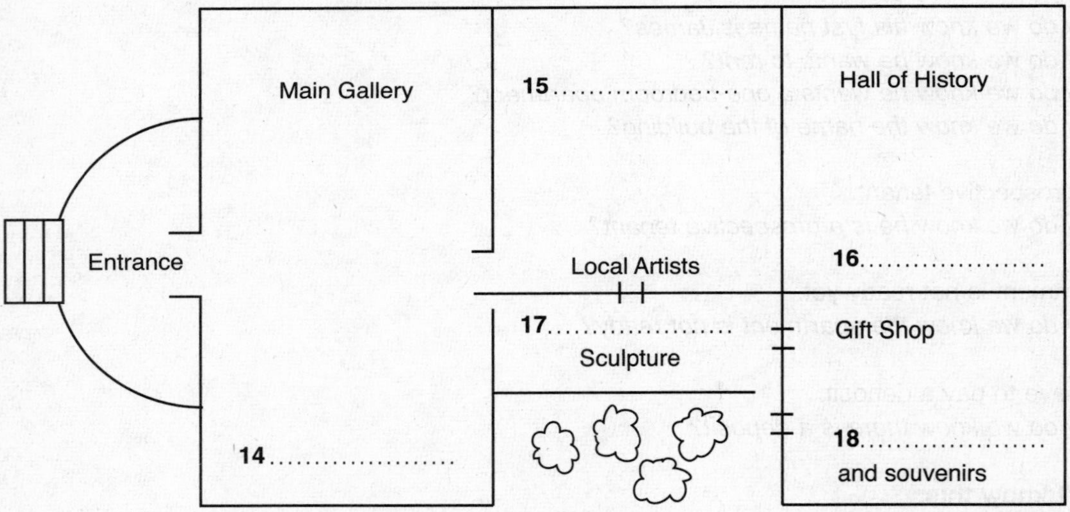

Questions 19–20

Complete the notice below. Write **NO MORE THAN THREE WORDS** *for each answer.*

Notice to museum visitors.

The following areas are restricted.

Hall of History: Closed for **19** ____________. Will reopen in April.

20 ____________: Museum staff offices. Employees only. All others must have an appointment.

Assumptions

Find the answers to: Who? What? When? Where? and Why?

Who are the speakers?
What are they talking about?
When is something happening?
Where is something happening?
Why are they having a conversation?

We know this:

The Jamestown Museum of Art has varied hours of operation, but it is closed on Monday and holidays. There are four galleries. One gallery has local art. The other has sculpture. There is a gift shop. The Hall of History will reopen in April. The Museum staff offices are open only by appointment to non-staff members.

Answer these questions Write **NO MORE THAN THREE WORDS** for each answer.

Who: ______________
What: ______________
When: ______________
Where: ______________
Why: ______________

Circle the clues in Questions 11–20 that help you make these assumptions.

We do not know this:

Write the number in Questions 11–20 next to the question you have to answer.

What is the admission price for adults?	Question ______
What is the admission price for children?	Question ______
When is there no admission fee for senior citizens?	Question ______
What kind of art is in the Hall of History?	Question ______
In which gallery is local art located?	Question ______
What kind of art is in the Main Gallery?	Question ______
In which gallery is sculpture located?	Question ______
What besides souvenirs is sold in the gift shop?	Question ______
Why is the Hall of History closed?	Question ______
Where are the staff offices located?	Question ______

Now listen to the conversation. Listen for the answers you don't know.

Target 2—Understanding Numbers

Many of the questions on the IELTS Listening Module ask you to remember, identify, and/or write numbers that you hear. This is an easy skill to practice, but a difficult one to perfect.

EXAMPLE

CD TRACK 3

You will see: *Write the number you hear.*
What is the flight number? ....

You will hear: Flight 33 leaves from Gate 13 Concourse C3

Many numbers sound alike. Here are a few easily confused numbers.

3	13	30	33
4	14	40	44
6	16	60	66

Try to use the context to make a guess about what you are hearing. When you look over the questions to make assumptions about the topic, pay attention to those questions that ask for specific numbers. Listen carefully for those numbers.

Questions 1–5

Listen for the numbers and answer the questions. Write a number in the blank or *choose the correct letter, **A**, **B**, or **C**.*

1

Credit Card Charge Form

Card Holder: Roger Wilcox

Address: 13 High Street

Card Number : ....

2 How many seats are there in the new theater?

A 200
B 250
C 500

3

Name	Phone
Roberts, Sherry	....

4 How much will the woman pay for the hotel room?

A $255
B $265
C $315

5

Lost Luggage Report
Passenger name: Richard Lyons
Flight number: ....

CD TRACK 4

Questions 6–10

Listen to these telephone numbers. Pay attention to the way three different speakers say the same number.

1 703–6588
2 744–1492
3 202–9983
4 671–4532
5 824–1561

Now write the numbers you hear.

6 ....
7 ....
8 ....
9 ....
10 ....

Target 3—Understanding the Alphabet

Many of the questions on the IELTS Listening Module ask you to remember, identify, and/or write letters of the alphabet that you hear. This is a good skill to practice for the test and for real life.

CD TRACK 5

EXAMPLE

You will see: *Write the name you hear.*
What is the person's name? ....

You will hear:
Speaker 1: Is your name spelled[1] L - i - n or L - y - n - n?
Speaker 2: Actually, it's Lynne with an e.

Questions 1–6

Circle the correct spelling of the name you hear.

1	Tomas	Thomas
2	Maine	Main
3	Patty	Patti
4	Roberts	Robertson
5	Springfield	Springvale
6	Nixon	Dixson

[1]BRITISH: spelt

CD TRACK 6

Questions 7–12

*Complete the statements. Write **NO MORE THAN THREE WORDS AND/OR A NUMBER** for the answer.*

7

Order Form

Name **A** .... *Green*
Credit Card Number **B** ....

8

Telephone Directory

Barney's Discount Store 673–0982
A .... Theater **B**................

9

Hotel Serenity

Albert Street (Private Bag 91031)
Auckland 1, New Zealand
Tel: (9) 309-6445

Reservations

Name: *Roberta* **A** ....
Room number *304*
Price **B** £..........................

10

Royale Theater
Ticket Order Form

Name: *Peter Park*
Address: *75* **A** .... *Street*
City: *Riverdale*
Seat number: **B** ....

11

Professor: Dr.[1] **A** ....
Office hours: T, Th 3:00–5:00
Office number: **B** ....

12

Addresses

W
Name: Wild Flower Society
Address: **A** .... State Street
City: **B** ....

[1]BRITISH: No period after Dr

Target 4—Listening for Descriptions

When you listen to a conversation or a lecture, you see in your mind what the speaker is discussing. If the speaker talks about a garden, you will see in your mind some plants, trees, and walkways. As the speaker continues and talks about a fountain in the garden, you will add a fountain in your mind's eye. You might think the fountain is made of cement, but the speaker describes one made of marble. You can change the image easily in your mind.

On the IELTS, you will have to listen to descriptions and match them to a drawing in your test booklet.

EXAMPLE

Look at the following houses. Write a short description of each.

A

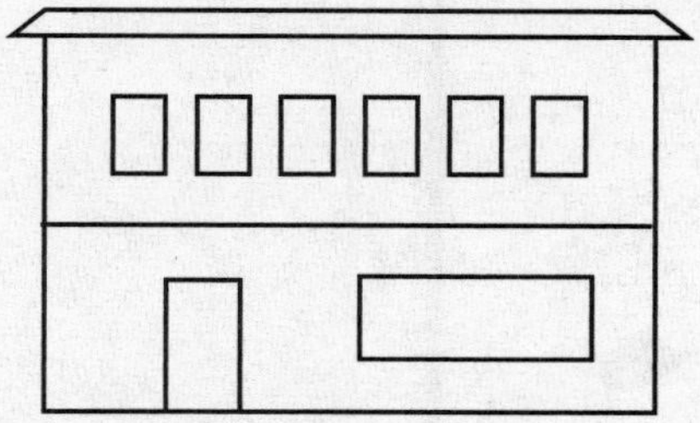

____

____

____

____

B

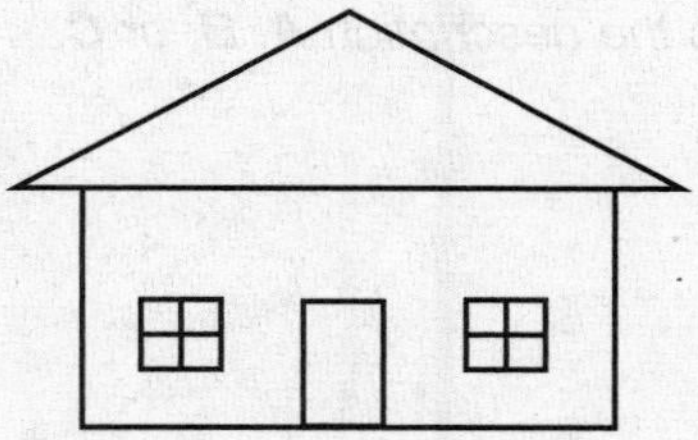

____

____

____

____

C

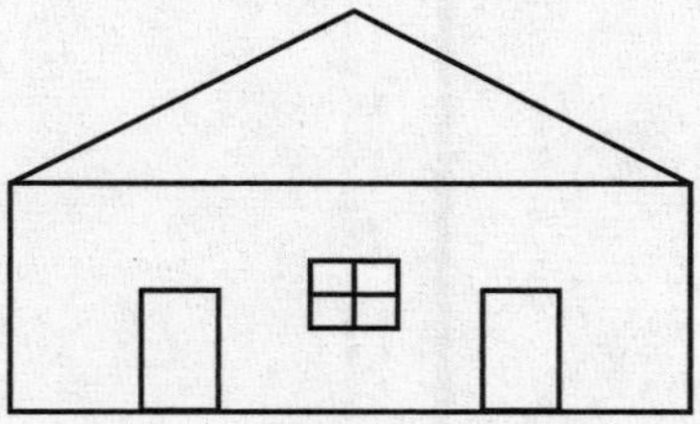

____

____

____

____

CD TRACK 7

*Now listen to the conversation. Where does the woman live? Choose the correct letter, **A**, **B**, or **C**.*

Questions 1–2

1 *Look at the following men. Write a short description of each.*

*Now listen to the news bulletin. Choose the letter that matches the description **A, B**, or **C**.*

2 *Look at the following women. Write a short description of each.*

*Now listen to the conversation. Choose the letter that matches the description **A, B**, or **C**.*

Target 5—Listening for Time

Listening for time is a very important skill. You must know when something happened. You must listen for a date, a day, a month, a year, or a time.

CD TRACK 8

EXAMPLE

You will see: *Choose the correct letter,* ***A***, ***B***, *or* ***C***.

A

B

C

You will hear: The train was almost thirty minutes late. It didn't arrive until five o'clock.

Common Words and Phrases for Time

10:00 A.M. noon 5:00 P.M. Midnight	In January In February May 3 November 14	1912 1925 2005 2007	This week This month Next week Next month
At 4:00 Before 6:30 to 3:30 After 7:00 Half-past two Quarter-past three Quarter to four	March 5 of this year April 12 of next year	In the spring In the summer In the autumn[1]	On weekday mornings Any afternoon from 1:00
Sunday Monday Tuesday	On June 10th On August 3rd	Yesterday Tomorrow Day after tomorrow	

[1]AMERICAN: Fall

TIME—QUESTIONS 1–6

Listen for the correct time.

Questions 1 and 2

*Choose the correct letter, **A**, **B**, or **C**.*

1 What time does the class usually begin?

A 2:00
B 2:30
C 4:00

2 What time will the final exam begin?

A 1:45
B 3:15
C 4:05

Questions 3 and 4

*Choose the correct letter, **A**, **B**, or **C**.*

3 What time will the next train leave for Chicago?

A 
B 
C 

4 What time will it arrive in Chicago?

A 
B 
C 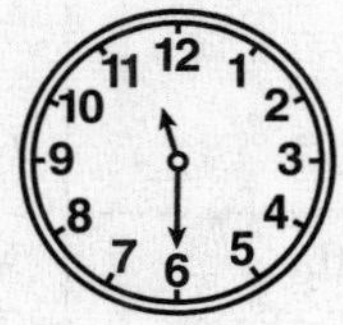

Questions 5 and 6

Complete the schedule with the correct times.

Cindy's Schedule

	Monday
9:00	Spanish class
11:30	haircut
5.........	lunch with Jeannine
1:30	job interview
6.........	exercise class

CD TRACK 9

DATE—QUESTIONS 1–6

Most of the world writes the date as month/day/year (mm/dd/yy). Americans use both the "American" form and the International form: dd/mm/yy.

American:	May 15, 2010	April 23rd, 2009
International:	15 May 2010	23rd April 2009

Both forms are included in these exercises.

Listen for the correct date.

Questions 1 and 2

Complete these notes with the correct date and month.

Notes

City Museum of Art
Opened: August **1** ...., *1898*
Opening celebration: **2** *1, 1898*

Questions 3 and 4

Complete the form with the correct month and date.

Insurance Application

Applicant name: *Priscilla Katz* .... Date of birth: **3** *22*
Spouse: *Georges Katz* .... Date of birth: *July* **4** ....

Questions 5 and 6

*Choose the correct letter, **A**, **B**, or **C**.*

5 Which is the most popular time to visit Silver Lake?
A August
B September
C October

6 What day will the man leave for Silver Lake?
A 7 November
B 11 November
C 17 November

CD TRACK 10

DAY—QUESTIONS 1–6

Listen for the correct day.

Questions 1 and 2

Complete the schedule with the correct days.

Class Schedule for Jim McDonald

English: **1** .... and Wednesday

History: **2** ....

Questions 3 and 4

Complete each sentence with the correct day.

There are tennis lessons at the club every **3** .... and Saturday.
The steam room is closed every **4** ....

Questions 5 and 6

*Choose the correct letter, **A**, **B**, or **C**.*

5 When is the final exam?
A Thursday
B Friday
C Saturday

6 When is the essay due?
A Monday
B Tuesday
C Wednesday

CD TRACK 11

YEAR—QUESTIONS 1–6

Listen for the correct year.

Questions 1 and 2

Complete the time line with the correct year.

Life of John James Audubon

1785	**1**	1842	**2** ....
Born in Haiti	Left Haiti for the United States	*Birds of America* published in the United States	Died

Questions 3 and 4

Choose the correct letter, ***A****,* ***B****, or* ***C****.*

3 When was Maria Mahoney born?
A 1808
B 1908
C 1928

4 When did she become governor?
A 1867
B 1957
C 1967

Questions 5 and 6

Complete the sentences with the correct years.

5 Library construction was begun in ....
6 The construction was finished in ....

CD TRACK 12

SEASON—QUESTIONS 1–6

Listen for the correct season.

Questions 1 and 2

Complete the table with the correct seasons.

Season	Weather
1	cool, rainy
2	hot, dry

Questions 3 and 4

Choose the correct letter, ***A****,* ***B****, or* ***C****.*

3 When did Josh begin his hiking trip?
A Late winter
B Early spring
C Late spring

4 When did he finish his trip?
A Late summer
B Late autumn[1]
C Early winter

[1] AMERICAN: Fall or autumn

Questions 5 and 6

Complete the sentences with the correct years.

5 The busiest time of year at the language school is ....
6 The least busy time of year at the language school is ....

Target 6—Listening for Frequency

There are certain adverbs that tell you when something might happen. These two groups of adverbs will help you determine the time.

CD TRACK 13

EXAMPLE

You will see: *Choose the correct letter,* ***A****,* ***B****, or* ***C****.*
Sam goes to the gym
(A) every day.
(B) often.
(C) occasionally.

You will hear: Sam works out at the gym several days a week.

Common Adverbs of Frequency	Common Adverbial Time Words or Phrases
always usually often sometimes occasionally seldom hardly ever rarely never	every day daily twice a week once a month on occasion every year, yearly every other week from time to time once in a while

Questions 1–6

Listen to the conversations. Put a check[1] (✓) by the frequency of the action.

	always	often	sometimes	seldom	never
1					
2					
3					
4					
5					
6					

[1]BRITISH: tick

Questions 7–12

CD TRACK 14

Listen to the conversations. Put a check (✓) by the frequency of the action.

	daily	twice a week	once a month	every other week	from time to time
7					
8					
9					
10					
11					
12					

Target 7—Listening for Similar Meanings

CD TRACK 5

The words that you hear are not always the words that you see in your test booklet. You will have to listen for similar meanings. You could hear a synonym or you could hear a paraphrase.

EXAMPLE

You will see: *Write the answer.*

Who are the respondents? ....

You will hear: The survey participants who wrote answers to the questions are all college graduates.

Questions 1–6

Look at the underlined words or phrases in the questions below. Listen to the audio. Write the synonym or paraphrase that you hear.

1 How many people are in the group? ....
2 When is the work corrected? ....
3 How fast is the population increasing? ....
4 What happened to the plants in the region? ....
5 When will the apartment be ready? ....
6 What kind of work does the woman do? ....

Target 8—Listening for Emotions

Can you tell if someone is excited to do something or is not looking forward to something? While listening, try to determine a speaker's emotion? How is that emotion expressed?

CD TRACK 16

EXAMPLE

You will see: *Choose the correct letter, **A**, **B**, or **C**.*

What is Mark's attitude toward the debate?

A He's nervous.
B He's looking forward to it.
C He's more excited than Jane.

You will hear: Jane: I can't wait to debate the team from Oxford.
Mark: I'm more apprehensive than excited. In fact, I'm not looking forward to it at all.

Common Words That Express Emotion

afraid	ecstatic	nervous
angry	embarrassed	pleased
annoyed	exhausted	proud
ashamed	frustrated	sad
bored	happy	shocked
confused	jealous	surprised
disappointed	mad	unhappy
disgusted	miserable	upset
		worried

Questions 1–6

Listen to the conversation and answer the questions about emotions.

1 How did local residents feel about the millionaire's donation?
A angry
B surprised
C excited

2 How does the man feel about his science experiment?
A frustrated
B glad
C eager

3 What confuses students?
A foreign languages
B language lab equipment
C class assignments and tests

4 What is the man's attitude towards the contest?
A He's upset.
B He's disappointed.
C He's indifferent.

5 How did people at the school feel about the mayor's visit?
A They were surprised.
B They were bored.
C They were annoyed.

6 How does the woman feel about her research project?
A nervous
B bad
C happy

Target 9—Listening for an Explanation

On the IELTS exam, a speaker may explain how something is done or made. You will have to listen and remember the steps of the process.

CD RACK 17

EXAMPLE

You will see: *Match the letter in the diagram with one of these labels.*

1 ____ Electrical socket[1]
2 ____ Metal loops of wires
3 ____ Cord
4 ____ Appliance
5 ____ Your toast is ready to eat!
6 ____ Plug

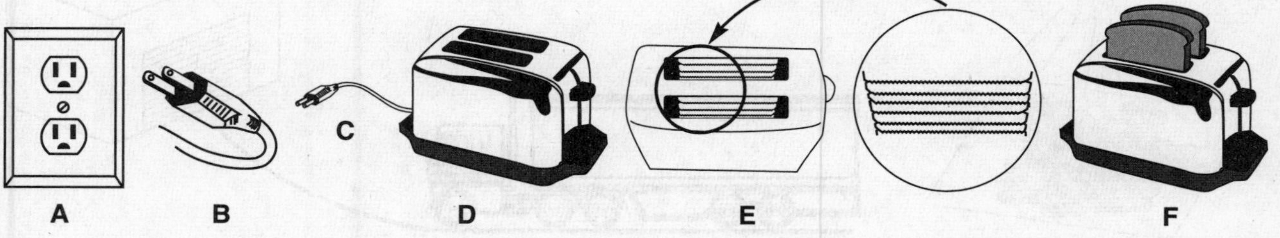

You will see: *Complete these sentences describing the process to make toast. Write* **NO MORE THAN THREE WORDS** *for each answer.*

7 Electricity runs from ____________.
8 Electricity runs down ____________.
9 Electricity runs to ____________.
10 Electricity is slowed by ____________.
11 When resistance to metal is high, metal will get ____________.

[1]AMERICAN: outlet, also socket

12 The wires turn ______________.
13 The bread ______________.
14 You eat the ______________.

You will hear: How does a toaster brown your toast every morning? Like all household appliances that heat up, a toaster works by converting electrical energy into heat energy. The electrical current runs from the electrical outlet in your kitchen wall, through the toaster plug, to the toaster cord. It travels down the cord to the appliance itself. Inside the toaster are wire loops. The wires are made of a special type of metal. Electricity passes slowly through this metal, creating friction. This friction causes the wires to heat up and glow orange. When the wires have sufficiently heated, your toast pops ready to eat.

Questions 1–12

Label the process diagram below based on what you hear.

1 ______________ **2** ______________ **3** ______________ **4** ______________

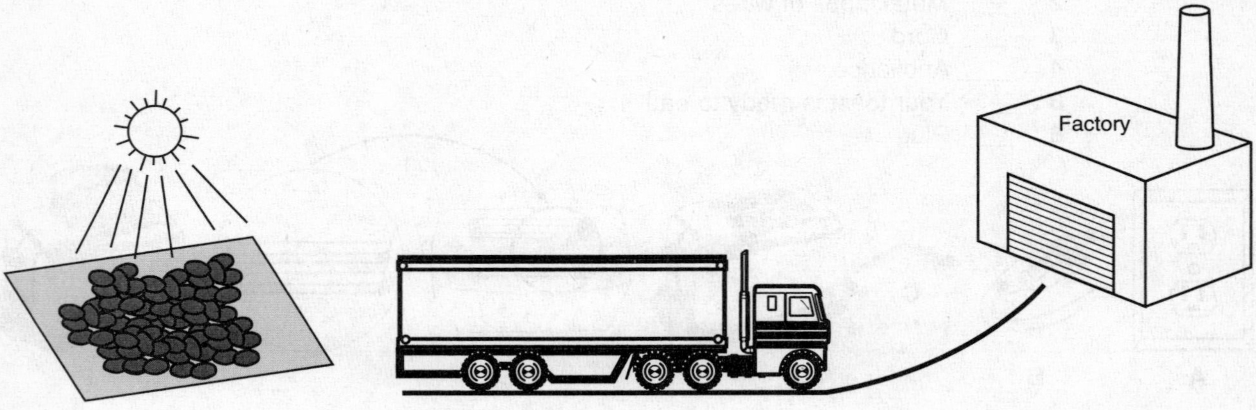

5 ______________ **6** ______________

Complete the sentences. Write **NO MORE THAN THREE WORDS** *for each answer.*

7 When the fruit is ripe, it ....
8 Then the seeds ....
9 The cocoa[1] beans are fermented in vats for ....
10 Then the beans .... in the sun.
11 The cocoa beans .... the factory.
12 At the factory, the cacao beans are turned into ....

[1]Cacao refers to the tree. Cocoa is the drink. Cocoa is often used for both the tree and the beverage.

Target 10—Listening for Classifications

You will have to group similar objects or ideas on the IELTS Listening section. You will have to determine how to classify objects or ideas.

CD TRACK 18

EXAMPLE

You will see: *When would these courses most likely be offered? Write them under the appropriate program[1] below.*

Project Management	Literature of the 21st Century
History of Africa	Labor[2] Negotiations
The Art of Negotiating	International Relations
Creativity in the Workplace	Introduction to Philosophy

Course Offerings

1 .... Program	**2** ....
Introduction to Art	Organizational[3] Behavior
Basic Chemistry	Commercial Law
Beginning Spanish	Compensation and Benefits
....	....
....	....
....	....
....	....

You will hear: The school offers two types of courses. One during the day is designed for students who are pursuing their academic degree full time. The night courses are designed for students who work during the day and are taking specific courses for an advanced business certificate.

These words and phrases are often used when classifying something.

Classification Words and Phrases

Can be divided into Can be categorized[4] as Can fit into this category	Types Kinds Ways

[1]BRITISH: programme
[2]BRITISH: labour
[3]BRITISH: organisational
[4]BRITISH: categorised

Questions 1–5

Complete the classifications below based on what you hear.

1 *Which of the following are offered to first class passengers only? Choose three letters,* ***A–E****.*

A pillows and blankets
B snacks
C full meals
D magazines
E free movies

2 *Complete the chart. Write* **ONE WORD** *for each answer.*

Royal Theater	Deluxe Theater
War films	**B** .... films
A .... films	Classic films

3 *Complete the chart. Write* **ONE WORD** *for each answer.*

	A	**B** ....
Time to fly	Day	Night
Wing position	Folded back	Horizontal
Antennae	Thin	Feathery

4 *Check the things that the woman has already done to get ready for the party.*

To Do List

A Clean house __
B Cook __
C Go shopping __
D Plan decorations __
E Mail invitations __

5 *Complete the chart. Write* **NO MORE THAN THREE WORDS** *for each answer.*

Tree Type	Description
A	Beautiful flowers, interesting leaves
B	Tall, broad leaves
C	Cones, needles

Target 11—Listening for Comparisons and Contrasts

Speakers often compare or contrast objects or ideas to help describe something. On the IELTS Listening section, you will have to determine what is being compared and what is being contrasted.

D ACK 9

EXAMPLE

You will see: Put a check (✓) to show if these items are alike or different.

		Same	Different
A	Nationality		
B	Sex		
C	Age		
D	Given name		
E	Present occupation		
F	Future occupation		
G	Sports		
H	Love of dancing		

You will hear:

Speaker 1: I've been corresponding by letter with a French student.

Speaker 2: In English? You don't speak French, do you?

Speaker 1: No, unfortunately, but she writes English well. We have a lot in common.

Speaker 2: Like what, your age?

Speaker 1: Well, I'm actually about two years older than she is. But we do have the same first name.

Speaker 2: And you're both students.

Speaker 1: Yes, and we both are studying to be doctors, although she wants to be a pediatrician[1], and I want to be a neurosurgeon.

Speaker 2: It seems the only similarities are your sex and your given name.

Speaker 1: Well, we both like to swim. She likes to dance, too, but you know how little I like dancing.

These words and phrases are often used with comparison and contrast.

Comparison		**Contrast**	
almost the same as	in common	although	more than
also	just as	but	nevertheless
as	like, alike	differ from	on the other hand
at the same time as	neither/nor	different from	otherwise
correspondingly	resemble	even though	still
either/or	similar to	however	unlike
in a like manner	similarly	in contrast to	while
in the same way	than	instead	yet
		less than	

[1]British: paediatrician

Questions 1–4

Complete the chart below based on what you hear.
Put a check (✓) to show if these items are alike or different.

1 Jobs

	Alike	Different
A Salary		
B Schedule		
C Responsibilities		
D Location		
E Transportation		

2 Libraries

	Alike	Different
A Location		
B Size		
C Parking facilities		
D Number of books		
E Services		

3 Club Memberships

	Alike	Different
A Cost		
B Use of club facilities		
C Access to fitness classes		
D Locker room privileges		
E Individual fitness plan		

4 Frogs and Toads

	Alike	Different
A Place for babies to live		
B Place for adults to live		
C Type of skin		
D Shape		
E Way to make sounds		

Target 12—Listening for Negative Meaning

On the IELTS, you may have to determine whether a statement is positive or negative. Listen to the statement carefully to determine whether the sense of the statement is positive or negative.

CD TRACK 20

EXAMPLE

You will see: *Choose the correct letter, **A**, **B**, or **C**.*

What does the woman say about the book?

A She couldn't read it.
B She was able to read it.
C She enjoyed reading it.

You will hear: It was a very dense book, but it wasn't impossible to read.

A negative prefix can contradict the word it joins. This usually results in a negative meaning. For example, *unfriendly* contradicts *friendly* and had the negative meaning *not friendly.* But when a negative meaning is added to a negative word, the resulting meaning can be positive. For example, *unselfish* contradicts *selfish* and has the positive meaning *not selfish.*

You can also put a negative word before a verb or clause to change the meaning of the sentence.

These are common negative markers.

Before verbs/clauses	**Before nouns/ phrases**	**Negative prefixes**	**Positive meanings from negative prefixes**	
not	no	un	undone	unlimited
isn't/can't/won't/shouldn't/ couldn't/hasn't/mustn't	nowhere	im	impossible	unparalleled
	nothing	il	illegal	invaluable
		in	indefinite	nonrestrictive
rarely/only rarely	at no time	non	nonsense	nonviolent
hardly	not at this time			
scarcely	in no case			
seldom	by no means			
never				
barely				
not since				
not until				
and neither				

Questions 1–6

Put a check (✓) next to the correct paraphrase of each sentence.

1 I can't wait to start the class.
__ **A** I'm looking forward to the class.
__ **B** I'm not looking forward to the class.

2 The teacher is not only my favorite[1] teacher, she's also my neighbor[2].
__ **A** I like my teacher a lot.
__ **B** I don't like my teacher very much.

3 I can't say that it was a particularly comfortable hotel.
__ **A** The hotel was comfortable.
__ **B** The hotel wasn't comfortable.

4 We'll never find a book as interesting as this.
__ **A** The book is very interesting.
__ **B** The book isn't very interesting.

5 That was not an illegal action.
__ **A** The action was legal.
__ **B** The action wasn't legal.

6 We could scarcely understand him.
__ **A** It was easy to understand him.
__ **B** It wasn't easy to understand him.

Questions 7–12

*Listen to the conversation. Choose the correct letter, **A**, **B**, or **C**.*

7 What describes the weather in the region?
A rainy
B dry
C cloudy

8 When taking the exam, the students can
A take as much time as they need.
B use a dictionary.
C bring several things into the testing room.

9 When will the car be fixed?
A today
B before the end of the week
C on the weekend[3]

[1] BRITISH: favourite
[2] BRITISH: neighbour
[3] BRITISH: at the weekend

10 What is the woman's opinion of the restaurant?
- **A** The food is good.
- **B** The service is bad.
- **C** The wait is too long.

11 Which type of flower is not common in the area?
- **A** violets
- **B** roses
- **C** irises

12 What homework does the man have to do this week?
- **A** write papers and read books
- **B** write papers only
- **C** study for exams

Target 13—Listening for Chronology

Listening for the order that events occur is an important skill. You will need to listen to what happened first, second, and so on.

EXAMPLE

D ACK 1

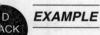

You will see: *Complete the Class Assignment Sheet, putting the assignments in the correct order. Write* **NO MORE THAN THREE WORDS** *for each answer.*

Class Assignment Sheet

A. **1** ....

B. **2** ....

C. Papers submitted

D. Student Presentations

E. **3** ....

You will hear: Before you do your research, we'll have an orientation session in the library so you can become familiar with the various sources of information available there. Each student will give a presentation on his or her research topic after all the papers have been submitted. All of this will have to be completed prior to the date of the final exam.

Common Words and Phrases That Indicate Chronological Order

before after while during between ____ and _____ in (year) on (day) at (time) since ______ later earlier formerly every (number) (years, months, days) at the turn of the century (decade) in the first half of the century in the 20s, 1980s, . . .	at birth, in childhood, in infancy, as an adult, in adulthood, in old age simultaneously, at the same time as former, latter previous previously prior to first, second, third, etc. in the first place, second place to begin with next, then, subsequently in the next place at last in conclusion finally

Questions 1–5

*Listen to the audio and put these actions in the correct chronological order. Write **1** for the first action, **2** for the second, and so forth.*

1

____ Fill in application
____ Submit application
____ Get references
____ Pay a deposit
____ Receive notification of apartment
____ Sign lease

2

____ Leopold Mozart published a book.
____ Wolfgang Mozart began to compose music.
____ Leopold began taking Wolfgang on tours of Europe.
____ Wolfgang Mozart settled in Vienna.
____ Wolfgang's mother died.

3

____ Left home
____ Had picnic
____ Made sandwiches
____ Went swimming
____ Checked into motel

4

____ Find partner
____ Choose topic
____ Get professor's approval
____ Design research
____ Start research

5

____ Walk through rose garden
____ Show tickets
____ View pond area
____ Visit greenhouse
____ Photograph butterfly garden

5

READING MODULE

- **QUICK STUDY**
  - Overview
  - Question Types
  - Reading Tips
- **READING SKILLS**
  - Target 1—Using the First Paragraph to Make Predictions
  - Target 2—Using the Topic Sentence to Make Predictions
  - Target 3—Looking for Specific Details
  - Target 4—Analyzing the Questions and Answers
  - Target 5—Identifying the Tasks

QUICK STUDY

Overview

The Reading module lasts 60 minutes. The reading passages and the questions will be given to you on a Question Paper. You can write on the Question Paper, but you can't take it from the room.

You will write your answers on the Answer Sheet. Unlike the Listening module, you will have no time to transfer your answers. You will have only 60 minutes to read the passages, answer the questions, and mark your answers.

The Reading modules on the Academic and the General Training versions of the IELTS are different.

Reading Module: Academic Reading

Time	Tasks	Topics	Sources
60 minutes	Read three passages and answer 40 questions	General interest topics written for a general audience	Journals, magazines, books, newspapers

Reading Module: General Training Reading

Time	Tasks	Topics	Sources
60 minutes	Read three passages and answer 40 questions	Basic social English Training topics General interest	Notices, flyers, timetables, documents, newspaper articles, instructions, manuals

Question Types

There are many types of questions used in the Reading module. You should be familiar with these types.

- Multiple-choice questions
- Short-answer questions
- Completing sentences
- Completing notes, summary, tables, flowcharts
- Labeling a diagram
- Choosing headings for paragraphs or sections of a text
- Locating information
- Identifying points of view
- Identifying writer's claims
- Classifying information
- Matching lists or phrases

You will have a chance to practice the tasks of these different question types in Target 5.

Reading Tips

Before You Take the Test

1. Read as much as you can in English.
2. Keep a notebook of the words you learn.
3. Try to write these words in a sentence. Try to put these sentences into a paragraph.
4. Learn words in context—not from a word list.
5. Know the types of questions found on the IELTS test.
6. Know the type of information sought on the IELTS test.
7. Know how to make predictions.
8. Know how to skim and scan, to look quickly for information.

During the Test

1. Read the title and any headings first. Make predictions about the topic.
2. Look over the questions quickly. Make predictions about content and organization.
3. Read the passage at a normal speed. Don't get stuck on parts you don't understand.
4. When you answer the questions, don't spend too much time on the ones you don't feel sure about. Make a guess and go on.
5. After you have answered all the questions, you can go back and check the ones you aren't sure about.
6. Don't spend more than 20 minutes on each passage.

READING SKILLS

In order to understand a reading passage, you need to understand the context of a passage. You need to have a clue about the topic. When you pick up a paper to read, you scan the headlines and choose an article that interests you. The clues in the newspaper (headlines, graphics, photos) catch your eye and give you a context.

A passage on the IELTS is given to you; you did not choose to read it. There are few clues. You do not know what it is about. It may or may not interest you. Yet in order to understand it, you need some clues to help you understand the passage. Without the clues, you will not understand it very well. To score well on the IELTS, you should determine what you know and what you need to know.

When you look at a passage, you must make some predictions about the passage.

What is the passage about?
What is the main idea?
Who are the characters?
When are things taking place?
Where is it happening?
Why is it important?

You want to know *who*, *what*, *when*, *where*, and *why*.

In this section you will learn how the following can give you the answers to: *Who? What? When? Where?* and *Why?*

Using the first paragraph
Using the topic sentences
Using specific details
Using the questions and answers

Target 1—Using the First Paragraph to Make Predictions

The first paragraphs of a passage can help you make predictions about the context of a passage.

The first paragraph often contains

the topic sentence (a summary of the main idea of the passage)
a definition of the topic
the author's opinion
clues to the organization of the passage

If you understand the first paragraph, you will understand the topic, the author's opinion (if any), and where to look for information within the passage.

Read this first paragraph of a passage on the illness, obsessive-compulsive disorder.

> Obsessive-compulsive disorder (OCD) is clinically diagnosed as an anxiety disorder. This disorder affects up to 4 percent of adults and children. People who suffer from this debilitating disorder have distressing and obsessive thoughts, which usually cause them to perform repetitive behaviors[1] such as counting silently or washing their hands. Though OCD sufferers understand that their obsessions are unrealistic, they find it stressful to put these intrusive thoughts out of their minds. Those who suffer from obsessive-compulsive disorder develop strict behavioral[1] patterns that become extremely time-consuming and begin to interfere with daily routines. Many people with OCD delay seeking treatment because they are ashamed of their own thoughts and behavior.

Topic Sentence
Obsessive-compulsive disorder (OCD) is clinically diagnosed as an anxiety disorder.

Definition of Topic
People who suffer from this debilitating disorder have distressing and obsessive thoughts, which usually cause them to perform repetitive behaviors.

Author's Opinion
None given.

[1]British: Behaviour/behavioural

Organizational Clues
The author may discuss

- Obsessive behavior,
- Stress of sufferers, and/or
- Treatment

PRACTICE 1

Read these introductory paragraphs to other passages. Make predictions about the topics using these first paragraphs.

1 The spread of wildfire is a natural phenomenon that occurs throughout the world and is especially common in forested areas of North America, Australia, and Europe. Locations that receive plenty of rainfall but also experience periods of intense heat or drought are particularly susceptible to wildfires. As plant matter dries out, it becomes brittle and highly flammable. In this way, many wildfires are seasonal, ignited by natural causes, most specifically lightning. However, human carelessness and vandalism also account for thousands of wildfires around the globe each year. To gain a clear understanding of how wildfires spread, it is necessary to analyze what it takes to both create and control these fires.

2 The term "bird brain" has long been a common means of expressing doubts about a person's intelligence. In reality, birds may actually be a great deal more intelligent than humans have given them credit for. For a long time, scientists considered birds to be of lesser intelligence because the cerebral cortex, the part of the brain that humans and other animals use for intelligence, is relatively small in size. Now scientists understand that birds actually use a different part of their brain, the hyperstriatum, for intelligence. Observations of different species of birds, both in the wild and in captivity, have shown a great deal of evidence of high levels of avian intelligence.

3 In 1834, a little girl was born in New Bedford, Massachusetts. She would grow up to become one of the richest women in the world. Her name was Hetty Green, but she was known to many as the Witch of Wall Street.

Target 2—Using the Topic Sentence to Make Predictions

Every paragraph has a key sentence called a topic sentence. This topic sentence explains what a paragraph is about. It is the general idea of a paragraph. If you understand the general idea, you can look for the specific details which support the idea.

Read the second paragraph of the passage on OCD. The first sentence happens to be the topic sentence.

> OCD sufferers experience worries that are both unreasonable and excessive and that act as a constant source of internal stress. Fear of dirt and contamination are very common obsessive thoughts. The obsession with orderliness and symmetry is also common. In other cases, persistent thoughts are centered on doubts, such as whether or not a door is locked or a stove is turned off. Impulses, such as the urge to swear in public or to pull a fire alarm, are other types of OCD symptoms. In order to be diagnosed with OCD, a sufferer must exhibit obsessions and/or compulsions that take up a considerable amount of time (at least one hour per day).

Topic Sentence

OCD sufferers experience worries that are both unreasonable and excessive and that act as a constant source of internal stress.

Questions to Ask Yourself

What are unreasonable worries?
What are excessive worries?

PRACTICE 2

Read these paragraphs. Underline the topic sentence. Ask one or two questions about the topic sentence.

1 To combat excessive thoughts and impulses, most OCD sufferers perform certain repetitive rituals that they believe will relieve their anxiety. These compulsions can be either mental or behavioral in nature. Common rituals include excessive checking, washing, counting, and praying. Over time, OCD sufferers attach strict rules to their compulsions. For example, a woman who is obsessed with cleanliness might wash her hands three times before having a meal in order to get the thought of the dirty dishes or silverware out of her mind. However, in many cases, the compulsions aren't related to the obsession at all. A man obsessed with the image of dead animals might count silently up to 500 or touch a specific chair over and over in order to block the images. Holding onto objects that would normally be discarded, such as newspapers and empty containers, is another common compulsion.

2 OCD symptoms generally begin between the age of 10 and 24 and continue indefinitely until a person seeks treatment. A child's upbringing does not seem to be part of the cause of the disorder, though stress can make the symptoms stronger. The underlying causes of OCD have been researched greatly and point to a number of different genetic factors. While studies show that OCD and its related anxiety disorders are often passed down through families, the specific symptoms for each family member are rarely the same. For example, a mother who is obsessed with order may have a son who can't stop thinking about a single word or number.

3 Research on OCD sufferers has found certain physiological trends. In particular, many studies show an overactivity of blood circulation in certain areas of the brain. As a result of this increase in blood flow, the serotoninergic system, which regulates emotions, is unable to function effectively. Studies have also shown that OCD sufferers have less serotonin than the average person. This type of abnormality is also observed in Tourette syndrome and Attention Deficit Hyperactive Disorder. People who developed tics as children are found to be more susceptible to OCD as well. Many reports of OCD point to infections that can trigger the disorder, namely streptococcal infections. It is believed that a case of childhood strep throat can elicit a response from the immune system that produces certain neuropsychiatric disorders, such as OCD.

Target 3—Looking for Specific Details

When you read, you first want to know the general idea. Next you read for specific ideas. The author supplies specific details to support his or her ideas. Knowing where to look for these supporting statements will help you answer questions on the IELTS.

When you identified the topic sentences in Practice 2, you found the general idea of the paragraph. When you asked your questions about the topic sentence, you expected the specific details would be the answers.

Read the second paragraph of a passage. The specific details follow the topic sentence.

> OCD sufferers experience worries that are both unreasonable and excessive and that act as a constant source of internal stress. Fear of dirt and contamination are very common obsessive thoughts. The obsession with orderliness and symmetry is also common. In other cases, persistent thoughts are centered on doubts, such as whether or not a door is locked or a stove is turned off. Impulses, such as the urge to swear in public or to pull a fire alarm, are other types of OCD symptoms. In order to be diagnosed with OCD, a sufferer must exhibit obsessions and/or compulsions that take up a considerable amount of time (at least one hour per day).

Topic Sentence

OCD sufferers experience worries that are both unreasonable and excessive and that act as a constant source of internal stress.

Questions to Ask Yourself

What are unreasonable worries?
What are excessive worries?

Supporting Details

Fear of dirt and contamination
The obsession with orderliness and symmetry
Persistent doubts
Impulses

PRACTICE 3

Read the three paragraphs from Practice 2 again. Pay attention to the topic sentence. Underline the details that support the topic sentence.

Target 4—Analyzing the Questions and Answers

You made predictions about the content based on the first paragraph, the topic sentences, and the specific details. Now let's look at how the questions or statements in your Reading test booklet can help you narrow these predictions and choose the correct answer.

To help you answer the questions in your Reading test booklet, take a few seconds to look over the questions or statements. Sometimes the questions are before the passage; sometimes they come after the passage. Ask yourself: *Who? What? When? Where?* and *Why?* By looking for the answers to these general questions, you will discover what you know and what you need to know. When you read the passage, you can test the predictions you made.

As you look at the question or statement and answer options, look for the key words. Key words may give you a clue to the context. They may help you predict what the passage is about.

Look at these typical IELTS comprehension questions.

Questions 1–8

Complete the summary of the reading passage below.

Choose your answers from the box below and write them in boxes 1–8 on your answer sheet. There are more words than spaces so you will not use them all.

People who suffer from obsessive-compulsive disorder have **1** .... thoughts, doubts, and fears that they cannot **2** .... OCD sufferers develop certain ways of acting in order to **3** .... their fears. For example, being afraid of dirt is a common **4** ...., which may lead to excessive hand washing. Or, an OCD sufferer who worries about a locked door may engage in excessive **5** .... Some OCD sufferers keep things that other people would **6** .... Research shows that OCD may be a disorder that is **7** ...., though members of the same family don't always show the same symptoms. It is also possible that certain infections may **8** .... the disorder.

checking
doctor
upbringing
inherited
reduce
cause
treatment
throw away
unreasonable
obsession
control
compulsive
diagnosis
counting

First identify the key words. (These are circled above to help you.) Then look for these words in the passage. You will know where to look because you have made predictions using topic sentences and specific details.

Notice the words close to the circled words in the passage. Do they help you complete the summary above?

PRACTICE 4

Identify the key words in these questions and circle them in the questions and in the reading passage on the next page. Notice the words close to the circled words in the passage. Do they help you complete the questions below?

Questions 9–16

Do the following statements agree with the information in the reading passage?

In boxes 9–16 write

TRUE	if the statement is true according to the passage
FALSE	if the statement contradicts the passage
NOT GIVEN	if there is no information about this in the passage

9 OCD often results from the way a child is raised.

10 Stress can have an effect on OCD.

11 OCD sufferers are deficient in serotonin.

12 Obsessive-compulsive disorder usually begins after the age of 17.

13 Many OCD patients prefer psychotherapy to medication.

14 OCD is very difficult to treat.

15 Many OCD sufferers keep their problem a secret.

16 Antibiotics can be used to treat OCD.

You should spend 20 minutes on Questions 9–16, which are based on the reading passage below.

Obsessive-compulsive Disorder

Obsessive-compulsive disorder (OCD) is clinically diagnosed as an anxiety disorder and affects up to 4 percent of adults and children. People who suffer from this debilitating disorder have distressing and obsessive thoughts, which usually cause them to perform repetitive behaviors such as counting silently or washing their hands. Though OCD sufferers understand that their obsessions are unrealistic, they find it stressful to put these intrusive thoughts out of their minds. Those who suffer from obsessive-compulsive disorder develop strict behavioral patterns that become extremely time-consuming and begin to interfere with daily routines. Many people with OCD delay seeking treatment because they are ashamed of their own thoughts and behavior.

OCD sufferers experience worries that are both unreasonable and excessive and that act as a constant source of internal stress. Fear of dirt and contamination are very common obsessive thoughts. The obsession with orderliness and symmetry is also common. In other cases, persistent thoughts are centered on doubts, such as whether or not a door is locked or a stove is turned off. Impulses, such as the urge to swear in public or to pull a fire alarm, are other types of OCD symptoms. In order to be diagnosed with OCD, a sufferer must exhibit obsessions and/or compulsions that take up a considerable amount of time (at least one hour per day).

To combat excessive thoughts and impulses, most OCD sufferers perform certain repetitive rituals that they believe will relieve their anxiety. These compulsions can be either mental or behavioral in nature. Common rituals include excessive checking, washing, counting, and praying. Over time, OCD sufferers attach strict rules to their compulsions. For example, a woman who is obsessed with cleanliness might wash her hands three times before having a meal in order to get the thought of the dirty dishes or silverware out of her mind. However, in many cases, the compulsions aren't related to the obsession at all. A man obsessed with the image of dead animals might count silently up to 500 or touch a specific chair over and over in order to block the images. Holding onto objects that would normally be discarded, such as newspapers and empty containers, is another common compulsion.

OCD symptoms generally begin between the age of 10 and 24 and continue indefinitely until a person seeks treatment. A child's upbringing does not seem to be part of the cause of the disorder, though stress can make the symptoms stronger. The underlying causes of OCD have been researched greatly and point to a number of different genetic factors. While studies show that OCD and its related anxiety disorders are often passed down through families, the specific symptoms for each family member are rarely the same. For example, a mother who is obsessed with order may have a son who can't stop thinking about a single word or number.

Research on OCD sufferers has found certain physiological trends. In particular, many studies show an overactivity of blood circulation in certain areas of the brain. As a result of this increase in blood flow, the serotoninergic system, which regulates emotions, is unable to function effectively. Studies have also shown that OCD sufferers have less serotonin than the average person. This type of abnormality is also observed in Tourette syndrome and Attention Deficit Hyperactive Disorder. People who developed tics as children are found to be more susceptible to OCD as well. Many reports of OCD point to infections that can trigger the disorder, namely streptococcal infections. It is believed that a case of childhood strep throat can elicit a response from the immune system that produces certain neuropsychiatric disorders, such as OCD.

Because OCD sufferers tend to be so secretive about their symptoms, they often put off treatment for many years. The average OCD sufferer waits about 17 years before receiving medical attention. As with many anxiety disorders, early diagnosis and proper medication can lessen many of the symptoms and allow people to live fairly normal lives. Most treatment plans for OCD involve a combination of medication and psychotherapy. Both cognitive and behavioral therapies are used to teach patients about their disorder and work through the anxiety. Serotonin reuptake inhibitors are prescribed to increase the brain's concentration of serotonin. This medication successfully reduces the symptoms in many OCD sufferers in a short amount of time. For cases when OCD is linked to streptococcal infection, antibiotic therapy is sometimes all that is needed.

Target 5—Identifying the Tasks

There are many types of questions on the IELTS Reading Test. It is important to know what the question is asking you to do.

Question types:

- Multiple-choice questions
- Short-answer questions
- Completing sentences
- Completing notes, summary, tables, flowcharts
- Labeling a diagram
- Choosing headings for paragraphs or sections of a text
- Choosing three or four answers from a list
- Yes, No, True, False, or Not Given questions
- Classifying information
- Matching lists or phrases

The questions for the practice reading passages on the next page are labeled. Be familiar with the question types so you can quickly complete the task and answer the question correctly.

PRACTICE 5

READING PASSAGE 1

Read the passage and answer the questions. Use your predicting skills. Note the type of questions.

Zulu Beadwork

The South African province of KwaZulu-Natal, more commonly referred to as the Zulu Kingdom, is named after the Zulu people who have inhabited the area since the late 1400s. KwaZulu translates to mean "Place of Heaven." "Natal" was the name the Portuguese explorers gave this region when they arrived in 1497. At that time, only a few Zulu clans occupied the area. By the late 1700s, the AmaZulu clan, meaning "People of Heaven," constituted a significant nation. Today the Zulu clan represents the largest ethnic group in South Africa, with at least 11 million people in the kingdom. The Zulu people are known around the world for their elaborate glass beadwork, which they wear not only in their traditional costumes but as part of their everyday apparel. It is possible to learn much about the culture of the Zulu clan through their beadwork.

The glass bead trade in the province of KwaZulu-Natal is believed to be a fairly recent industry. In 1824, an Englishman named Henry Francis Fynn brought glass beads to the region to sell to the African people. Though the British are not considered the first to introduce glass beads, they were a main source through which the Zulu people could access the merchandise they needed. Glass beads had already been manufactured by the Egyptians centuries earlier around the same time when glass was discovered. Some research points to the idea that Egyptians tried to fool South Africans with glass by passing it off as jewels similar in value to gold or ivory. Phoenician mariners brought cargoes of these beads to Africa along with other wares. Before the Europeans arrived, many Arab traders brought glass beads down to the southern countries via camelback. During colonization[1], the Europeans facilitated and monopolized[2] the glass bead market, and the Zulu nation became even more closely tied to this art form.

The Zulu people were not fooled into believing that glass beads were precious stones but, rather, used the beads to establish certain codes and rituals in their society. In the African tradition, kings were known to wear beaded regalia so heavy that they required the help of attendants to get out of their thrones. Zulu beadwork is involved in every realm of society, from religion and politics to family and marriage. Among the Zulu women, the craft of beadwork is used as an educational tool as well as a source of recreation and fashion. Personal adornment items include jewelry, skirts, neckbands, and aprons. Besides clothing and accessories, there are many other beaded objects in the Zulu culture, such as bead-covered gourds, which are carried around by women who are having fertility problems. Most importantly, however, Zulu beadwork is a source of communication. In the Zulu tradition, beads are a part of the language with certain words and symbols that can be easily read. A finished product is considered by many artists and collectors to be extremely poetic.

The code behind Zulu beadwork is relatively basic and extremely resistant to change. A simple triangle is the geometric shape used in almost all beaded items. A triangle with the apex pointing downward signifies an unmarried man, while one with the tip pointing upward is worn

[1]BRITISH: colonisation

[2]BRITISH: monopolised

by an unmarried woman. Married women wear items with two triangles that form a diamond shape, and married men signify their marital status with two triangles that form an hourglass shape. Colors are also significant, though slightly more complicated since each color can have a negative and a positive meaning. Educated by their older sisters, young Zulu girls quickly learn how to send the appropriate messages to a courting male. Similarly, males learn how to interpret the messages and how to wear certain beads that express their interest in marriage.

The codes of the beads are so strong that cultural analysts fear that the beadwork tradition could prevent the Zulu people from progressing technologically and economically. Socio-economic data shows that the more a culture resists change the more risk there is in a value system falling apart. Though traditional beadwork still holds a serious place in Zulu culture, the decorative art form is often modified for tourists, with popular items such as the beaded fertility doll.

MATCHING

Questions 1–3

Match each definition in List A with the term it defines in List B.

*Write the correct letter **A–E** in boxes 1–3 on your answer sheet. There are more terms than definitions, so you will not use them all.*

List A	Definitions
1	It means *Place of Heaven*.
2	It is the Portuguese name for southern Africa.
3	It means *People of Heaven*.

List B	Terms
A	Phoenician
B	Natal
C	AmaZulu
D	Explorer
E	KwaZulu

SHORT-ANSWER QUESTIONS

Questions 4–6

Answer the questions below.

*Write **NO MORE THAN THREE WORDS** for each answer.*

Write your answers is boxes 4–6 on your answer sheet.

4 Which country does the Zulu clan reside in?

5 When did the Portuguese arrive in KwaZulu-Natal?

6 How many members of the Zulu kingdom are there?

TRUE–FALSE–NOT GIVEN QUESTIONS

Questions 7–11

Do the following statements agree with the information given in the passage? In boxes 7–11 on your answer sheet, write

TRUE if the statement is true according to the passage
FALSE if the statement contradicts the passage
NOT GIVEN if there is no information about this in the passage

7 The British were the first people to sell glass beads in Africa.

8 Henry Frances Flynn made a lot of money selling glass beads to the Zulu people.

9 The Zulu people believed that glass beads were precious stones.

10 The Zulu people use glass beads in many aspects of their daily lives.

11 Zulu women believe that bead-covered gourds can help them have babies.

LABELING A DIAGRAM

Label the diagram below. Choose one or two words from the reading passage for each answer. Write your answers in boxes 12–15 on your answer sheet.

Zulu Beadwork Code

READING PASSAGE 2

Read the passage and answer the questions. Use your predicting skills. Note the type of questions.

CHOOSING HEADINGS

Questions 1–5

The following reading passage has five sections ***A–E****.*

Choose the correct heading for each section from the list of headings on the next page.

Write the correct number ***i–viii*** *in boxes 1–5 on your answer sheet. There are more headings than sections, so you will not use them all.*

1 Section **A**

2 Section **B**

3 Section **C**

4 Section **D**

5 Section **E**

List of Headings	
i	Colorblindness[1] in different countries
ii	Diagnosing colorblindness
iii	What is colorblindness?
iv	Curing colorblindness
v	Unsolved myths
vi	Animals and colorblindness
vii	Developing the ability to see color
viii	Colorblindness and the sexes

Colorblindness

A

Myths related to the causes and symptoms of "colorblindness" abound throughout the world. The term itself is misleading, since it is extremely rare for anyone to have a complete lack of color perception. By looking into the myths related to color blindness, one can learn many facts about the structure and genetics of the human eye. It is a myth that colorblind people see the world as if it were a black and white movie. There are very few cases of complete colorblindness. Those who have a complete lack of color perception are referred to as monochromatics, and usually have a serious problem with their overall vision as well as an inability to see colors. The fact is that in most cases of colorblindness, there are only certain shades that a person cannot distinguish between. These people are said to be dichromatic. They may not be able to tell the difference between red and green, or orange and yellow. A person with normal color vision has what is called trichromatic vision. The difference between the three levels of color perception have to do with the cones in the human eye. A normal human eye has three cones located inside the retina: the red cone, the green cone, and the yellow cone. Each cone contains a specific pigment whose function is to absorb the light of these colors and the combinations of them. People with trichromatic vision have all three cones in working order. When one of the three cones does not function properly, dichromatic vision occurs.

B

Some people believe that only men can be colorblind. This is also a myth, though it is not completely untrue. In an average population, 8% of males exhibit some form of colorblindness, while only 0.5% of women do. While there may be some truth to the idea that more men have trouble matching their clothing than women, the reason that color vision deficiency is predominant in males has nothing to do with fashion. The fact is that the gene for color blindness is located on the X chromosome, which men only have one of. Females have two X chromosomes, and if one carries the defective gene, the other one naturally compensates. Therefore, the only way for a female to inherit colorblindness is for both of her X chromosomes to carry the defective gene. This is why the incidence of color deficiency is sometimes more prevalent in extremely small societies that have a limited gene pool.

C

It is true that all babies are born colorblind. A baby's cones do not begin to differentiate between many different colors until he is approximately four months old. This is why many of the modern toys for very young babies consist of black and white patterns or primary colors, rather than traditional soft pastels. However, some current research points to the importance of developing an infant's color visual system. In 2004, Japanese researcher Yoichi Sugita of the Neuroscience Research Institute performed an experiment that would suggest that color vision deficiency isn't entirely genetic. In his experiment, he subjected a group of baby monkeys to monochromatic lighting for one year. He later compared their vision to normal monkey who had experienced the colorful world outdoors. It was found that the test monkeys were unable to perform the color-matching tasks that the normal monkeys could. Nevertheless, most cases of colorblindness are attributed to genetic factors that are present at birth.

[1]BRITISH: colour, colourblindness, colourful

D

Part of the reason there are so many inconsistencies related to colorblindness, or "color vision deficiency" as it is called in the medical world, is that it is difficult to know exactly which colors each human can see. Children are taught from a very young age that an apple is red. Naming colors allows children to associate a certain shade with a certain name, regardless of a color vision deficiency. Someone who never takes a color test can go through life thinking that what they see as red is called *green*. Children are generally tested for colorblindness at about four years of age. The Ishihara Test is the most common, though it is highly criticized[1] because it requires that children have the ability to recognize[2] numerals. In the Ishihara Test, a number made up of colored dots is hidden inside a series of dots of a different shade. Those with normal vision can distinguish the number from the background, while those with color vision deficiency will only see the dots.

E

While many of the myths related to colorblindness have been busted by modern science, there are still a few remaining beliefs that require more research in order to be labeled as folklore. For example, there is a longstanding belief that colorblindness can aid military soldiers because it gives them the ability to see through camouflage. Another belief is that everyone becomes colorblind in an emergency situation. The basis of this idea is that a catastrophic event can overwhelm the brain, causing it to utilize[3] only those receptors needed to perform vital tasks. In general, identifying color is not considered an essential task in a life or death situation.

Multiple-Choice Questions

Questions 6–8

*Choose the correct letter, **A, B, C,** or **D.** Write your answers in boxes 6–8 on your Answer Sheet.*

6 People who see color normally are called

A monochromatic.
B dichromatic.
C trichromatic.
D colorblind.

7 Children usually begin to see a variety of colors by the age of

A one month.
B four months.
C one year.
D four years.

8 Children who take the Ishihara Test must be able to

A distinguish letters.
B write their names.
C read numbers.
D name colors.

[1] BRITISH: criticised

[2] BRITISH: recognise

[3] BRITISH: utilise

Completing a Summary

Questions 9–12

Complete the summary using words from the box below.

Write your answers in boxes 9–12 on your Answer Sheet. There are more answers than spaces, so you will not use them all.

It is a common **9** .... that only men suffer from colorblindness. On average **10** .... than ten percent of men have this problem. Women have two **11** .... For this reason it is **12** .... for a woman to suffer from colorblindness.

myth	a little less
X chromosomes	defective genes
fact	slightly more
exactly	less likely
more probable	

READING PASSAGE 3

Read the passage and answer the questions. Use your predicting skills. Note the type of question.

Antarctic Penguins

Though penguins are assumed to be native to the South Pole, only four of the seventeen species have evolved the survival adaptations necessary to live and breed in the Antarctic year round. The physical features of the Adelie, Chinstrap, Gentoo, and Emperor penguins equip them to withstand the harshest living conditions in the world. Besides these four species, there are a number of others, including the yellow feathered Macaroni penguin and the King penguin that visit the Antarctic regularly but migrate to warmer waters to breed. Penguins that live in Antarctica year round have a thermoregulation system and a survival sense that allows them to live comfortably both on the ice and in the water.

In the dark days of winter, when the Antarctic sees virtually no sunlight, the penguins that remain on the ice sheet sleep most of the day. To retain heat, penguins huddle in communities of up to 6,000 of their own species. When it's time to create a nest, most penguins build up a pile of rocks on top of the ice to place their eggs. The Emperor penguin, however, doesn't bother with a nest at all. The female Emperor lays just one egg and gives it to the male to protect while she goes off for weeks to feed. The male balances the egg on top of his feet, covering it with a small fold of skin called a brood patch. In the huddle, the male penguins rotate regularly so that none of the penguins have to stay on the outside of the circle exposed to the wind and cold for long periods of time. When it's time to take a turn on the outer edge of the pack, the penguins tuck their feathers in and shiver. The movement provides enough warmth until they can head back into the inner core and rest in the warmth. In order to reduce the cold of the ice, penguins often put their weight on their heels and tails. Antarctic penguins also have complex nasal passages that prevent 80 percent of their heat from leaving the body. When the sun is out, the black dorsal plumage attracts its rays and penguins can stay warm enough to waddle or slide about alone.

Antarctic penguins spend about 75 percent of their lives in the water. A number of survival adaptations allow them to swim through water as cold as –2 degrees Celsius. In order to stay warm in these temperatures, penguins have to keep moving. Though penguins don't fly in the air, they are often said to fly through water. Instead of stopping each time they come up for air, they use a technique called "porpoising," in which they leap up for a quick breath while swiftly moving forward. Unlike most birds that have hollow bones for flight, penguins have evolved hard solid bones that keep them low in the water. Antarctic penguins also have unique feathers that work similarly to a waterproof diving suit. Tufts of down trap a layer of air within the feathers, preventing the water from penetrating the penguin's skin. The pressure of a deep dive releases this air, and a penguin has to rearrange the feathers through a process called "preening." Penguins also have an amazing circulatory system, which in extremely cold waters diverts blood from the flippers and legs to the heart.

While the harsh climate of the Antarctic doesn't threaten the survival of Antarctic penguins, overheating can be a concern, and therefore, global warming is a threat to them. Temperate species have certain physical features such as fewer feathers and less blubber to keep them cool on a hot day. African penguins have bald patches on their legs and face where excess heat can be released. The blood vessels in the penguin's skin dilate when the body begins to overheat, and the heat rises to the surface of the body. Penguins who are built for cold winters of the Antarctic have other survival techniques for a warm day, such as moving to shaded areas, or holding their fins out away from their bodies.

Classifying Information

Questions 1–5

Classify the following facts as applying to

A *Antarctic penguins*
B *Temperate-area penguins*

Write the appropriate letter, ***A*** *or* ***B****, in boxes 1–5 on your answer sheet.*

1 stand in large groups to keep warm

2 spend about three quarters of its time in the water

3 have feathers that keep cold water away from its skin

4 have areas of skin without feathers

5 have less blubber

Completing Sentences

Questions 6–9

Complete each of the following sentences with information from the reading passage. Write your answers in boxes 6–9 on your Answer Sheet. Write **NO MORE THAN THREE WORDS** *for each answer.*

6 Most penguins use .... to build their nests.

7 While the male emperor penguin takes care of the egg, the female goes away to ....

8 A .... is a piece of skin that the male emperor penguin uses to protect the egg.

9 Penguins protect their feet from the cold of the ice by standing on their ....

Choosing Answers from a List

Questions 10–13

The article mentions many facts about penguins.

Which four of the following features are things that enable them to survive in very cold water?

Write the appropriate letters ***A–H*** *in boxes 10-13 on your Answer Sheet.*

A They move through the water very quickly.

B They hold their flippers away from their bodies.

C They choose shady areas.

D When necessary, their blood moves away from the flippers and toward the heart.

E They breathe while still moving.

F The blood vessels in their skin dilate.

G They waddle and slide.

H Their feathers hold in a layer of air near the skin.

6

WRITING MODULE

- **QUICK STUDY**
  - Overview
  - Question Types
  - Writing Tips
- **WRITING SKILLS**
  - Target 1—Writing for a Specific Audience
  - Target 2—Completing the Task
  - Target 3—Determining the Task
  - Target 4—Developing a Thesis Statement
  - Target 5—Organizing Your Writing
  - Target 6—Writing a Paragraph
  - Target 7—Writing the Introduction
  - Target 8—Writing with Variety

QUICK STUDY

Overview

There are two writing tasks in both the Academic and General Training Writing modules.

Academic Writing Module

	Time	Number of Words	Task
Task 1	20	150	Describe a chart or graph.
Task 2	40	250	Give an opinion on a subject. or Propose a solution to a problem.

General Training Writing Module

	Time	Number of Words	Task
Task 1	20	150	Write a letter asking for assistance with a problem.
Task 2	40	250	Give an opinion on a subject. or Propose a solution to a problem.

Question Types

You should be familiar with the variety of tasks on the IELTS Academic Writing Module and on the General Training Writing module.

Academic Writing Module
Describe a chart
Give an opinion
Propose a solution to a problem

General Training Writing Module
Write a letter asking for assistance

The following activities will help you become familiar with these question types.

Writing Tips

1. Make sure you organize[1] your writing *before* you begin. Use the back of your answer sheet to create a concept map.
2. The examiners judge your writing on its clarity. Make sure you have supported your ideas with specific details.
3. You can write more than 150 words for Task 1 or more than the 250 words for Task 2, but you can't write less. You will lose points if you have less than the assigned number of words in your essay.
4. In the introductory paragraph, paraphrase your ideas. Do not use the exact words in the introduction that you use in the body of the essay. This gives your writing more variety and more interest.
5. You must answer the question completely. Do not leave any part out or you will lose points.
6. Organize your time carefully. Leave time for planning, writing, and revising.

WRITING SKILLS

Target 1—Writing for a Specific Audience

You write for someone to read what you write. But who is this someone? Your classmate in the seat next to you at school? Your aunt who lives in another city? Strangers in a distant place?

Before you write, you should ask yourself some questions:

Who am I writing to?
What will he or she find interesting about my subject?
What does he or she already know about my subject?
How can I explain my subject effectively to him or her?

An IELTS examiner will read your writing. Who is this examiner?

Write the letter that you think matches the IELTS examiner.

YES (Y) NO (N) POSSIBLE (P)

A high school student	
An experienced teacher	
A native speaker of English	
A kindly grandmother	
A strict grammarian	
A famous author	
A fair grader	

[1]BRITISH: organise

There are all types of examiners. It is safe to say they are not in high school. But they could be any of the other types. Whoever they are, they have been very well trained to read your writing and to grade you fairly.

The instructions for the writing tasks sometimes ask you to write to a specific person. The examiner will read your writing as if she or he were that person. Here are some of the types:

a university lecturer
an educated reader
your teacher
an airline employee
a librarian
a supermarket manager
a landlord or landlady
a bank manager

You should imagine a reader and write to that person. Imagine what they already know about your subject and what they would like to know. Then tell them in a very interesting way.

Target 2—Completing the Task

It is very important that you do the task completely. For each task, you will be given a limited amount of time and a minimum number of words. Do not spend more than the given time, and do not write fewer than the minimum number of words. You can write more words, but be careful that you work within the time limit.

These are the instruction lines for each task.

Task 1

- You should spend about 20 minutes on this task.
- You should write at least 150 words.

Task 2

- You should spend about 40 minutes on this task.
- You should write at least 250 words.

PRACTICE

Complete this table.

	Time	Words
Task 1		
Task 2		

Target 3—Determining the Task

ACADEMIC WRITING

There are two principle tasks in the Academic Writing module. In Task 1 you will be asked to describe something and in Task 2 you will be asked to make an argument and support your opinion.

Look at the following examples.

Task 1—Describe Something

Example

You should spend about 20 minutes on this task.

> ***The chart below shows the results of a survey that sampled a cross section of travelers at a major metropolitan airport about the purpose of their trip. The survey was carried out during four different months in 2002.***
>
> ***Summarize the information by selecting and reporting the main features, and make comparisons where relevant.***

Write at least 150 words.

Purpose of Travel

	March 2002	June 2002	September 2002	December 2002
Business	73%	29%	53%	34%
Holiday	18%	54%	31%	35%
Visit family	6%	13%	11%	26%
Other	3%	4%	5%	5%

Task 2—Support Your Opinion

Example

You should spend about 40 minutes on this task.

Write about the following topic:

> ***Most schools offer some type of physical education program to their students. Why is physical education important? Should physical education classes be required or optional?***

Give reasons for your answer and include any relevant examples from your own knowledge or experience.

Write at least 250 words.

GENERAL TRAINING WRITING

There are two tasks in the General Training Writing module. In Task 1 you will be asked to write to someone, explain a problem, and ask for the solution; in Task 2 you will be asked to give and support your opinion.

Task 1—Write to Someone, Explain a Problem, and Ask for the Solution

Example

You should spend about 20 minutes on this task.

Write about the following topic:

> ***You and a friend had dinner at an expensive restaurant last night. The waiter was incompetent, and the food was not good. Write a letter to the restaurant manager, and describe what happened. Ask for your money back.***

Write at least 150 words.

Task 2—Support Your Opinion

Example

You should spend about 40 minutes on this task.

Write about the following topic:

> ***More and more people are relying on the Internet as their major source of news and information.***
>
> ***What advantages does the Internet have for the average person? What disadvantages could it have now or in the future?***

Give reasons for your answer. Write at least 250 words.

Target 4—Developing a Thesis Statement

Before you begin writing, you must think about your thesis statement. A thesis statement is your main idea. It will set the stage for the rest of your writing. You have a thesis statement both for descriptions and for opinions.

GIVE A DESCRIPTION

Example

Write about the following topic:

> ***The diagram on the next page shows the steps in the hiring process at a large corporation.***
>
> ***Summarize the information by selecting and reporting the main features, and make comparisons where relevant.***

Acme Corporation: Recruitment Process

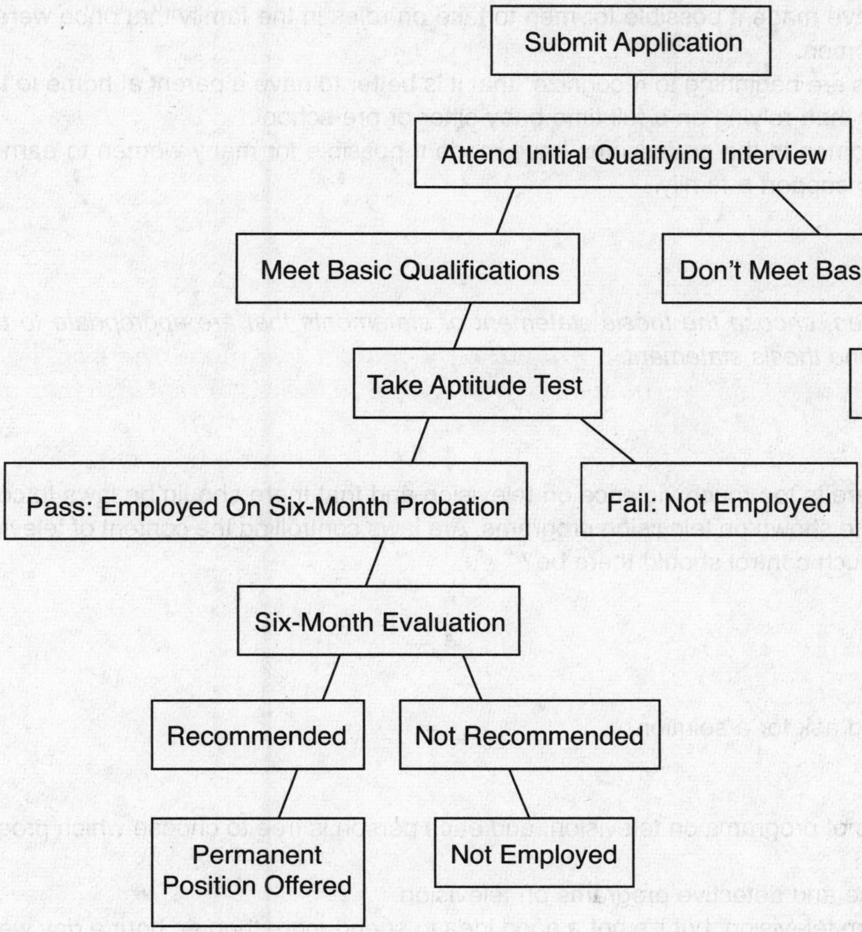

Possible Thesis Statements

1. There are several steps one must go through before being employed by the Acme Corporation.
2. Getting a job at the Acme Corporation is not a simple process.
3. The Acme Corporation wants to make sure that all potential employees are well-qualified before being offered a permanent position at the company.

Support Your Opinion

Example

Write about the following topic:

> ***More and more fathers are taking a break from their careers so that they can stay home and take care of their children while their wives work. This is better for the family than having both parents work full-time. To what extent do you agree or disagree.***

Give reasons for your answer and include any relevant examples from your own knowledge or experience.

Possible Thesis Statements

1. Changing customs have made it possible for men to take on roles in the family that once were considered to be only for women.
2. Many modern couples are beginning to recognize[1] that it is better to have a parent at home to take care of the children, rather than relying on a full-time baby sitter or pre-school.
3. Changing views of women in the professions have made it possible for many women to earn a salary that is high enough to support a family.

PRACTICE

First, identify the task. Then, choose the thesis statement or statements that are appropriate to the topic. There can be more than one thesis statement.

Topic 1

Many people think that there is too much violence on television and that there should be laws to control the amount and type of violence shown on television programs. Are laws controlling the content of television programs necessary? How much control should there be?

Task

(A) Give a description.
(B) Support your opinion.
(C) Explain a problem and ask for a solution.

Thesis Statement

(A) There are many types of programs on television, and each person is free to choose which programs he or she wants to watch.
(B) I enjoy watching police and detective programs on television.
(C) We can learn a lot from television, but it's not a good idea to spend more than an hour a day watching it.

Topic 2

More and more families have computers in their homes. What advantages and disadvantages do home computers have for children? Should parents restrict the amount of time their children spend using the computer?

Task

(A) Give a description.
(B) Support your opinion.
(C) Explain a problem and ask for a solution.

Thesis Statement

(A) Computers have become very inexpensive in recent years.
(B) Computers can contribute a lot to a child's education, but they can be overused.
(C) Computers today can do much more than the computers of just a few years ago.

[1] BRITISH: recognise

Topic 3

The graphs below show the figures for population distribution in the northwest for 1900–2050.

Summarize the information by selecting and reporting the main features, and make comparisons where relevant.

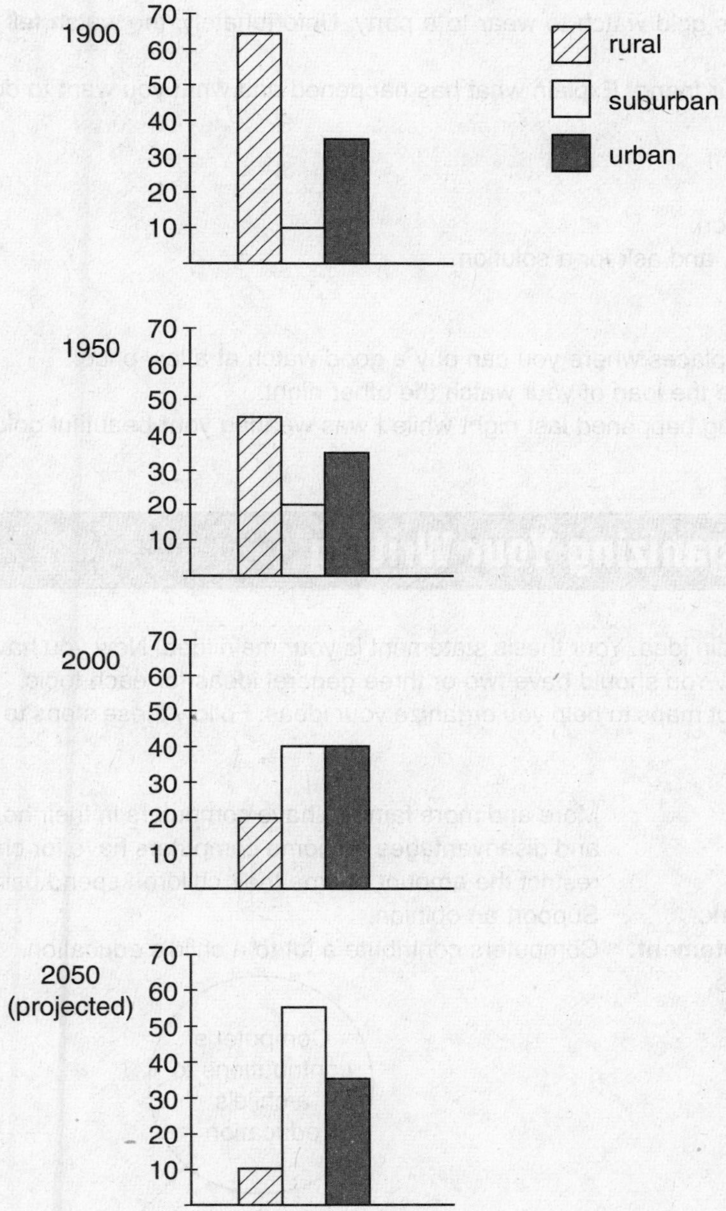

Task

(A) Give a description.
(B) Support your opinion.
(C) Explain a problem, and ask for a solution.

Thesis Statement
(A) Although the cost of living is high in urban areas, cities also have many advantages.
(B) Some people like to live in rural areas because they offer a peaceful and pleasant way of life.
(C) Over the past century, the population in the Northwest has been shifting from largely rural to mostly suburban and urban.

Topic 4

You borrowed a friend's gold watch to wear to a party. Unfortunately, the watch fell off your wrist, and you lost it.

Write a letter to your friend. Explain what has happened and what you want to do about it.

Task
(A) Give a description.
(B) Support your opinion.
(C) Explain a problem, and ask for a solution.

Thesis Statement
(A) There are several places where you can buy a good watch at a low price.
(B) I greatly appreciate the loan of your watch the other night.
(C) An unfortunate thing happened last night while I was wearing your beautiful gold watch.

Target 5—Organizing Your Writing

Your writing needs a main idea. Your thesis statement is your main idea. Now you have to support your main idea with general ideas. You should have two or three general ideas for each topic.

You can use concept maps to help you organize your ideas. Follow these steps to help you organize your writing.

1. **Read the topic.** More and more families have computers in their homes. What advantages and disadvantages do home computers have for children? Should parents restrict the amount of time their children spend using the computer?
2. **Determine the task.** Support an opinion.
3. **Write a thesis statement.** Computers contribute a lot to a child's education.
4. **Add general ideas.**

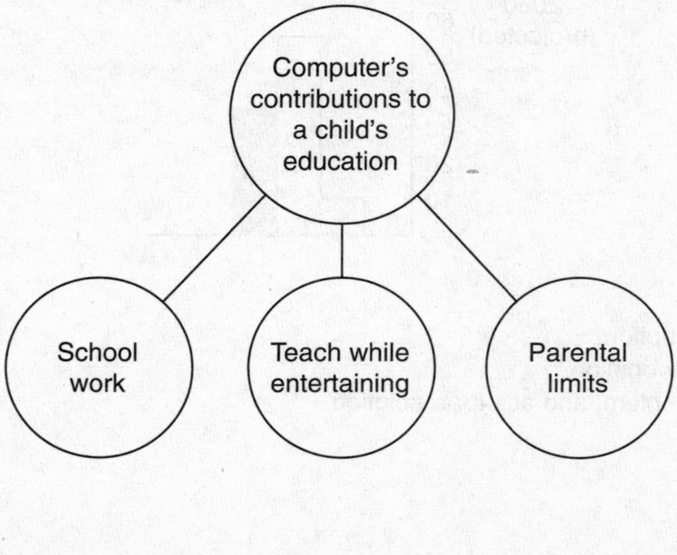

5. Add supporting details.

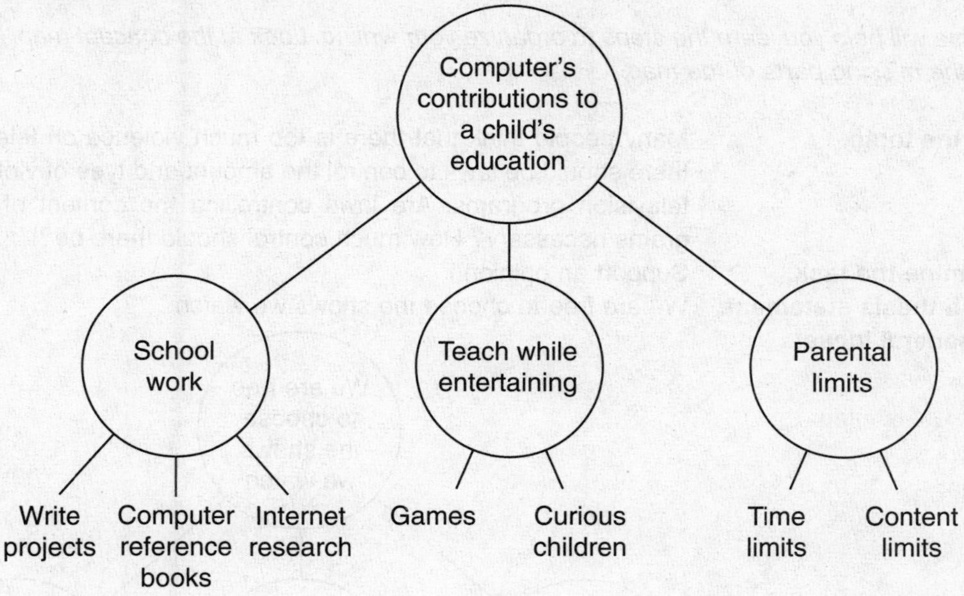

Compare this passage with the concept map above.

Home computers offer many advantages to the average family. One of the most important of these is the contribution computers can make to a child's education. With parental guidance, children can learn a lot by using a computer.

A computer is a useful tool for school work. Computers make it very easy to keep notes and write up school projects. Reference books on computer CDs make it convenient for children to research their school projects. In addition, the Internet makes research on any subject possible from the comfort of one's own home. Children can do all this work independently, without asking their parents to take them to the library or buy expensive reference books for them.

Computers keep children entertained in an educational way. There are many computer games that both attract children and teach them something. The Internet offers the curious child a way to find information about anything that he is interested in. A child can stay gainfully occupied for hours at a time with a computer.

Parents don't need to limit their children's computer time, although they should pay close attention to what a child does with a computer. Using a computer is not a passive activity like watching television is. The more time a child spends on a computer, the more he can learn. However, parents should control which web sites their children visit and which computer games they play. Then the computer is a safe learning tool for children.

Computers contribute a lot to a child's education. Every family should have one.

PRACTICE 1

This exercise will help you learn the steps to organize your writing. Look at the concept map. Read the essay. Complete the missing parts of the map.

1. **Read the topic.** Many people think that there is too much violence on television and that there should be laws to control the amount and type of violence shown on television programs. Are laws controlling the content of television programs necessary? How much control should there be?
2. **Determine the task.** Support an opinion
3. **Write a thesis statement.** We are free to choose the shows we watch.
4. **Add general ideas.**

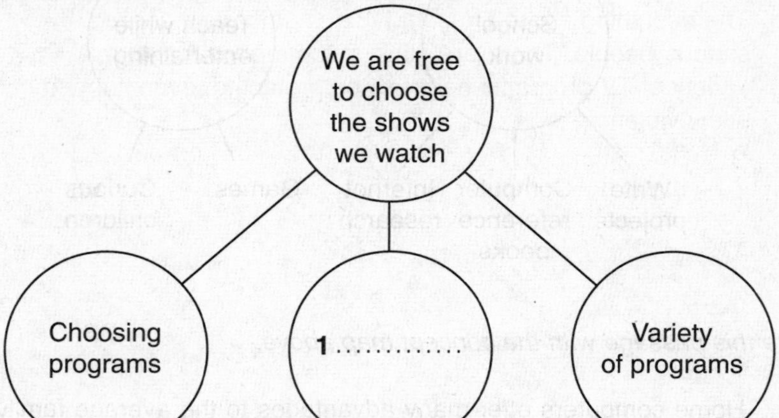

5. **Add supporting details.**

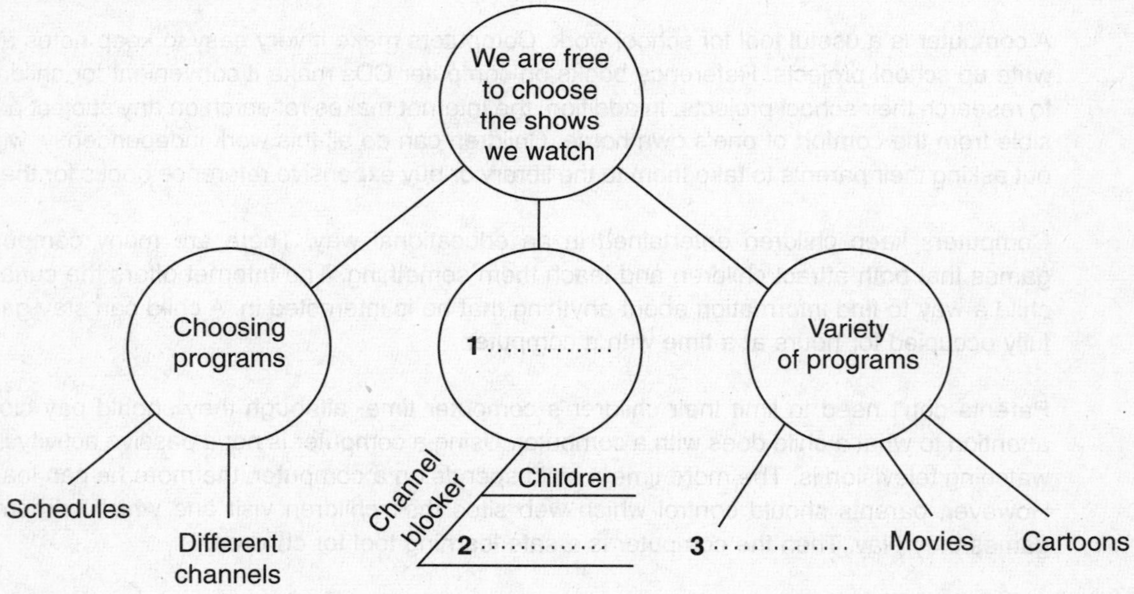

While it is true that there is violence on television, each individual has his or her own idea about how much is too much. Fortunately, we are all free to choose which TV programs we want to watch. Laws are not necessary to help us decide.

It isn't difficult to find out which programs are on TV at any given time. Most newspapers publish a schedule of TV programs everyday. Also, anyone who watches TV regularly knows which programs she likes and which she doesn't like. She knows what kinds of programs each different channel tends to have. It's easy for everyone to avoid violent programs if they want to.

Modern technology has given us a tool for controlling the TV programs we see. Most TVs can be programmed to block certain channels. Parents use this technology to protect their children from seeing shows[1] that are too violent. Adults can also use this technology to avoid seeing programs that they don't want to see.

The best thing about TV is that there is a variety of programs. There are news programs for serious people. There are films and cartoons for people who want to be entertained. The variety of TV programs needs to be protected, even if that means allowing some of them to show violence.

We each have our own ideas about what is too violent and what isn't. It would be difficult to make laws about violence on TV that would satisfy everybody. It is better to let each individual make his or her own choice about what to watch.

PRACTICE 2

This exercise will help you learn the steps to organize your writing. Look at the concept map. Read the essay. Complete the missing parts of the map.

1. **Read the topic.** ***The 3 maps on the next page show Palm Grove is a coastal town about 450 kilometers from the nearest city. It has recently become a major resort.***

   Summarize the information by selecting and reporting the main features, and make comparisons where relevant.

[1]BRITISH: programmes

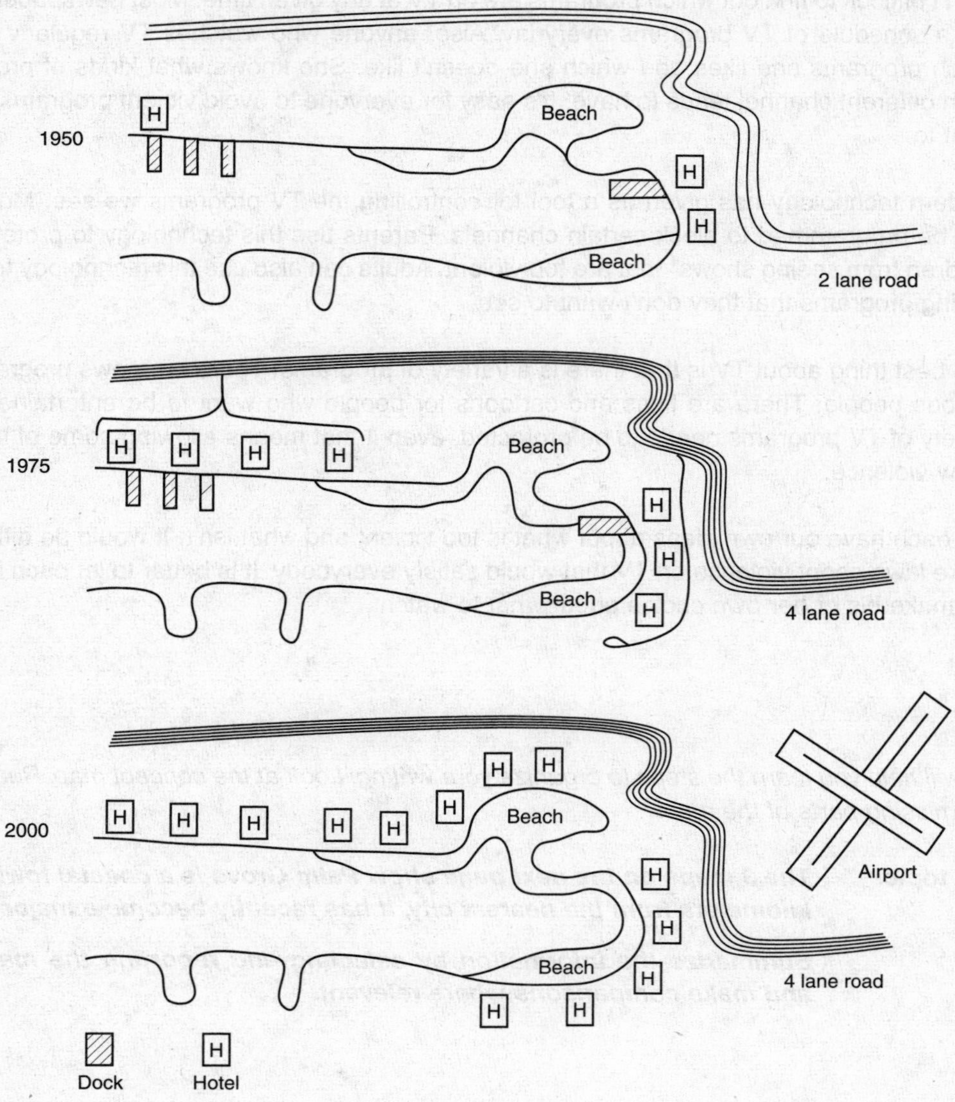

2. **Determine the task.** Describe something.
3. **Write a thesis statement.** Palm Grove became a resort when accessibility from the outside improved.
4. **Add general ideas.**

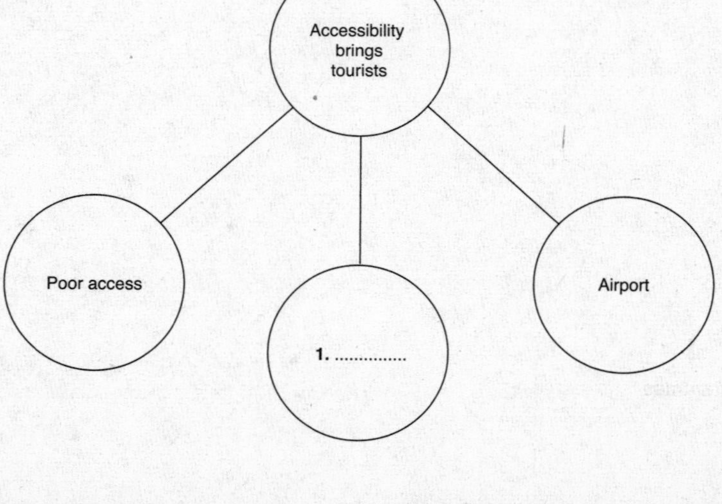

5. Add supporting details.

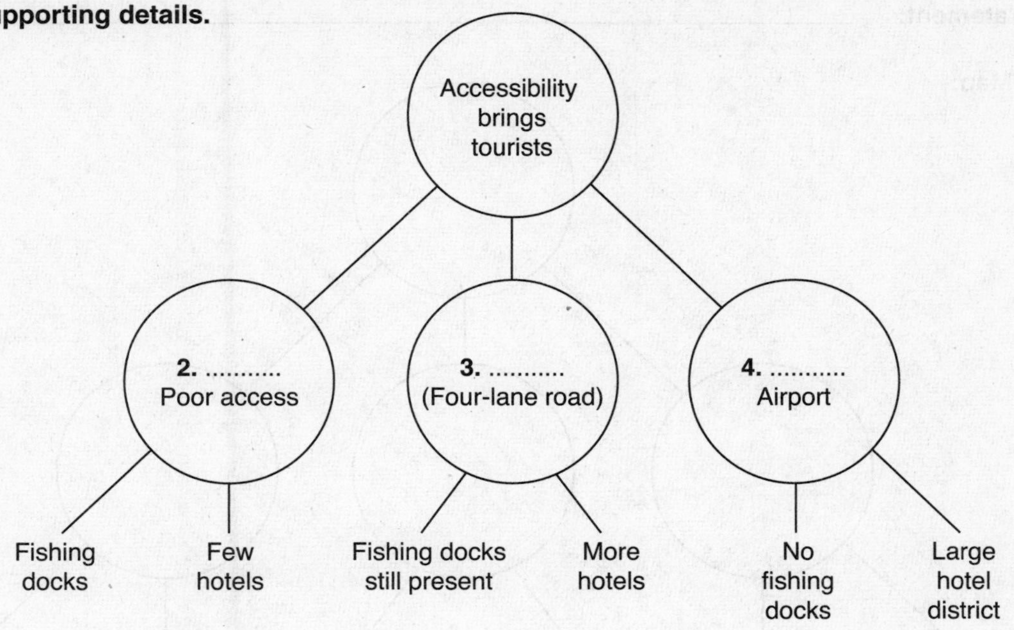

The three maps representing changes in Palm Grove between 1950 and 2000 show that the town became a resort as accessibility from the outside improved.

In 1950, Palm Grove was a small fishing village with few hotels. It lies 450 kilometers from the nearest city. Since the only access to the village in 1950 was by a two-lane road[1], most tourists probably didn't want to make the long trip to get there.

By 1975, a new four-lane highway had brought changes to Palm Grove. It was still a fishing village, but it appears that the new road made it easier for tourists to get there. Several new hotels had been built for them along the beach.

By 2000, an airport had been built just outside Palm Grove. This apparently changed the town into a resort. The hotel district was greatly expanded and the fishing docks removed. Probably most local residents now work in the tourist industry.

PRACTICE 3

Identify the tasks for the following topics. Create a concept map for each. On a separate piece of paper, write an essay or letter using the concept map as a guide. Compare your essays or letters with those in the Answer Key.

Topic 1 Most schools offer some type of physical education program to their students. Why is physical education important? Should physical education classes be required or optional?

Task: ______________________________

[1] BRITISH: Single carriageway or two-way traffic. In America a four-lane highway (road) is in England, a dual carriageway.

Thesis Statement: ______________________________

Concept Map:

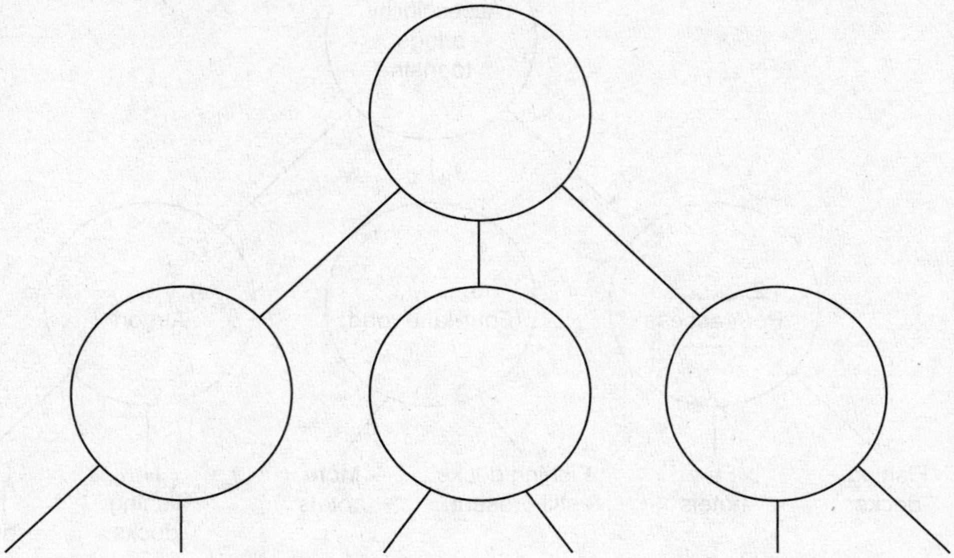

Topic 2 You have had a credit card with the same company for several years, and you always pay your bill on time. Your most recent bill included a $35 charge for late payment because, according to the company, you didn't pay the previous month. You know that you paid on time.

Write a letter to the credit card company. Explain what has happened, and say what you would like them to do about it.

Task: ______________________________

Thesis Statement: ______________________________

Concept Map:

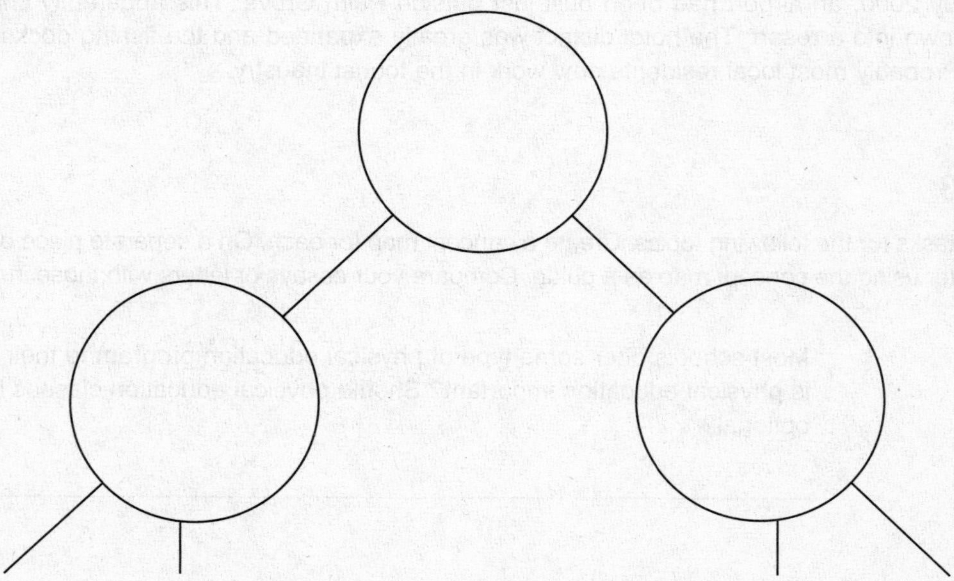

<u>*Topic 3*</u> ***The graph below shows the figures for population distribution in the Northwest Region for 1900–2050.***

Summarize the information by selecting and reporting the main features, and make comparisons where relevant.

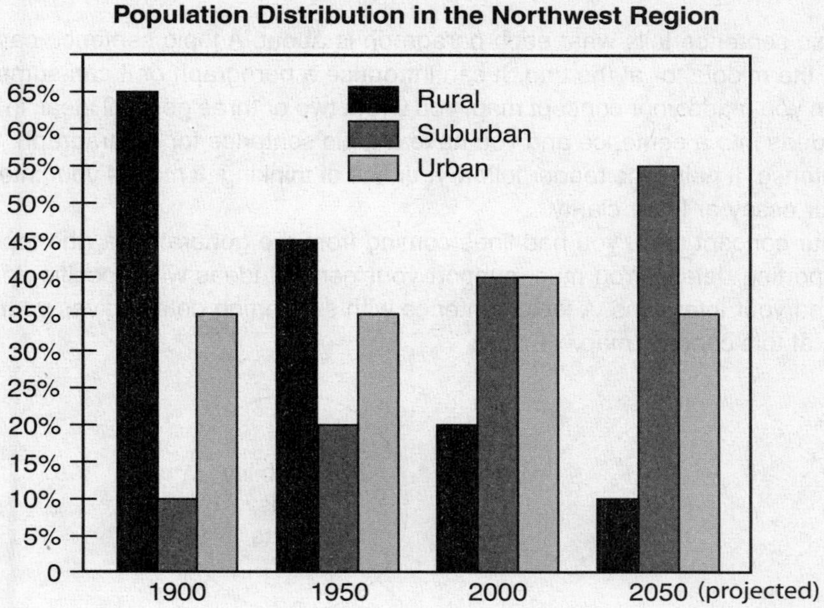

Task: ______________________________

Thesis Statement: ______________________________

Concept Map: (Use a separate sheet of paper for your concept map.)

Target 6—Writing a Paragraph

In the last section, you learned to write your thesis statement. The thesis statement is what your essay or letter is about. An essay is made up of paragraphs. Each paragraph has a topic sentence and supporting details.

A topic sentence tells what each paragraph is about. A topic sentence can come at the start of a paragraph, in the middle, or at the end. It can introduce a paragraph or it can summarize a paragraph.

When you made your concept map, you wrote two or three general ideas in words or phrases. Turn those general ideas into a sentence and you have a topic sentence for a paragraph. It is important to write a good topic sentence. It helps the reader follow your line of thinking. It makes your intentions clear. A topic sentence gives your essay or letter clarity.

In your concept map, you had lines coming from the general idea (the topic sentence). These lines are your supporting details. You must support your general ideas with specific details. This too helps a reader understand your intentions. A topic sentence with supporting details gives your essay or letter clarity.

Look at this concept map.

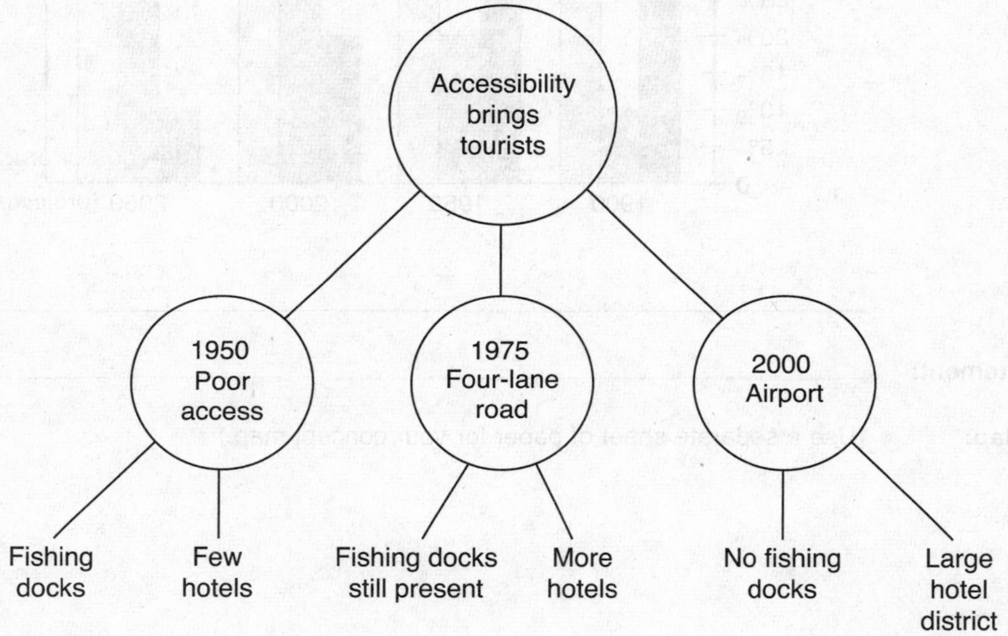

Read the paragraph for the general idea "four-lane road."

> By 1975, a new four-lane highway had brought changes to Palm Grove. It was still a fishing village, but it appears that the new road made it easier for tourists to get there. Several new hotels had been built for them along the beach.

Topic Sentence By 1975, a new four-lane highway had brought changes to Palm Grove.

Supporting Details It was easier for tourists to get there.
Several new hotels had been built.

Look at these examples.

Example 1

A computer is a useful tool for school work. Computers make it very easy to keep notes and write up school projects. Reference books on computer CDs make it convenient for children to research their school projects. In addition, the Internet makes research on any subject possible from the comfort of one's own home. Children can do all this work independently, without asking their parents to take them to the library or buy expensive reference books for them.

Topic Sentence A computer is a useful tool for school work.

Supporting Details Computers make it very easy to keep notes and write up school projects.

Reference books on computer CDs make it convenient for children to research their school projects.

In addition, the Internet makes research on any subject possible from the comfort of one's own home.

Example 2

It isn't difficult to find out which programs are on TV at any given time. Most newspapers publish a schedule of TV programs every day. Also, anyone who watches TV regularly knows which programs she likes and which she doesn't like. She knows what kinds of programs each different channel tends to have. It's easy for everyone to avoid violent programs if they want to.

Topic Sentence It isn't difficult to find out which programs are on TV at any given time.

Supporting Details Most newspapers publish a schedule of TV programs every day.

Also, anyone who watches TV regularly knows which programs she likes and which she doesn't like.

She knows what kinds of programs each different channel tends to have.

PRACTICE

Read the following paragraphs. Write the topic sentence and the supporting details.

1. Modern technology has given us a tool for controlling the TV programs we see. Most TVs can be programmed to block certain channels. Parents use this technology to protect their children from seeing shows that are too violent. Adults can also use this technology to avoid seeing programs that they don't want to see.

Topic Sentence: 1.1 ____________________

Supporting Details: 1.2 ____________________

1.3 ____________________

1.4 ____________________

2. The best thing about TV is that there is a variety of programs. There are news programs for serious people. There are films and cartoons for people who want to be entertained. The variety of TV programs needs to be protected, even if that means allowing some of them to show violence.

   Topic Sentence: 2.1 ____________________

   Supporting Details: 2.2 ____________________

   2.3 ____________________

   2.4 ____________________

3. Physical education classes teach children important skills that they need in life. They teach children how to work together on a team. They teach children how to set a goal and work to achieve it. They teach children about the importance of looking after their health.

   Topic Sentence: 3.1 ____________________

   Supporting Details: 3.2 ____________________

   3.3 ____________________

   3.4 ____________________

Target 7—Writing the Introduction

Once you have developed your concept map, you know what you are going to say and how you are going to write it. You are now ready to write the introduction to your essay or letter.

Some writers wait until they have written the body of the essay before they write the introduction. You don't have that much time. You must be organized from the beginning. The introduction will be easy to write once you have your general ideas and your topic sentences in mind.

Look at these three topic sentences from the topic on computers of the future:

Topic sentences: A computer is a useful tool for school work.

Computers keep children entertained in an educational way.

Parents don't need to limit their children's computer time, although they should pay close attention to what a child does with a computer.

Now let's combine these topics sentences into one paragraph, the introduction. This will tell the reader what we are going to talk about in this essay.

Introduction Home computers offer many advantages for the average family. One of the most important of these is the contribution computers can make to a child's education. With parental guidance, children can learn a lot by using a computer.

Look at the original topic.

Topic: More and more families have computers in their homes. What advantages and disadvantages do home computers have for children? Should parents restrict the amount of time their children spend using the computer?

Notice how in the introduction we show that we will discuss every aspect of the question.

Topic Question	Introduction
More and more families have computers in their homes.	Home computers offer many advantages for the average family.
What advantages and disadvantages do home computers have for children?	One of the most important of these is the contribution computers can make to a child's education.
Should parents restrict the amount of time their children spend using the computer?	With parental guidance, children can learn a lot by using a computer.

The introduction guides the reader. It shows how you plan to develop the topic. It must show that you plan to write about each part of the topic.

Read the following topics and compare the introductions.

Topic 1

Write about the following topic:

> ***Art museums should support themselves mainly by charging admission and by receiving donations from private individuals who are interested in art. That is, museums should receive most of their support from the people who are interested in using them, and not from public funds.***
>
> ***To what extent do you agree or disagree with this statement?***

Give reasons for your answer and include any relevant examples from your own knowledge or experience.

Introduction A

> Art museums are public places and should be funded by the government.

Introduction B

> I don't agree that art museums should be funded by private instead of public money. It is difficult to raise enough private money to run a museum well. In addition, charging high entrance fees will keep many people away from museums. Most important, art is a valuable part of culture and should receive support from society as a whole through government funding.

With Introduction A, the reader knows what the writer believes, but not why. Introduction B gives detailed reasons to support his or her opinion. Note that both Introduction A and B directly address the question "To what extent do you agree or disagree with this statement."

Topic 2

Write about the following topic:

> ***Most schools offer some type of physical education program to their students. Why is physical education important? Should physical education classes be required or optional?***

Give reasons for your answer and include any relevant examples from your own knowledge or experience.

Introduction A

Children can learn a lot of important things in physical education classes.

Introduction B

Physical education is an important part of every child's education. In physical education classes, children learn how to stay healthy. They also learn valuable social skills. Because physical education classes offer so much, they should be required for all children throughout their school years.

The author of Introduction A does not address all parts of the topic. The author of Introduction B guides the reader into the essay. We know what his or her opinion is and how the essay will develop.

PRACTICE

Read these topics. Determine the task. Write your thesis statement. Do a concept map. Write your topic sentences. (You can have between two and four topic sentences.) Then write the introduction to your essay. Be sure you answer all parts of the topic.

Topic 1

Some people believe that the best way to learn anything is "learning by doing." Others would rather learn through books and from teachers. Think of learning a language. Which way do you think is a better way to learn a language?

Task: ______________________________

Thesis Statement: ______________________________

Concept Map: Use a separate sheet of paper to draw a web concept map, if you need more space.

Topic Sentences: 1.1 ______________________________

1.2 ______________________________

1.3 ______________________________

1.4 ______________________________

Introduction:

____

____

____

____

____

____

Topic 2

In many parts of the world and throughout history, governments have moved their capitals. Why would they do this? What are the potential problems and benefits? Would you vote for moving your capital?

Task: ____

Thesis Statement: ____

Concept Map: Use a separate sheet of paper to draw a web concept map, if you need more space.

Topic Sentences: 2.1 ____

2.2 ____

2.3 ____

2.4 ____

Introduction:

____

____

____

____

____

____

Target 8—Writing with Variety

You can know about and read the topic, determine the task, map out your organization, create topic sentences, and write an introduction. You've done the hard part. Writing the body of the essay is easy.

However, you need to show you have command of a variety of styles of written English and can choose the appropriate one for the task. You need to show that you can write cohesively and accurately.

In this section, we will examine different approaches for these tasks.

Task	**Approach**
Describe something	Chronological order Spatial order Classification Definition
Support an opinion	Comparison and contrast Cause and effect Prediction

DESCRIBE SOMETHING

Chronological Order

Chronological order organizes your writing around the sequence of time. You write about what happens first, then what happens second, what happens after that, and what finally happens.

Useful words for time

after at *(time)* at birth, in childhood, in infancy, as an adult, in adulthood, in old age at last at the turn of the century (decade) before between ____ and ____ during earlier every *(number) (years, months, days)* finally first, second, third, etc. former, latter formerly in *(year)*	in conclusion in the 20s, 1980s . . . . in the first half of the century in the first place, second place in the next place later next, then, subsequently on *(day)* previous previously prior to simultaneously, at the same time as since ______ to begin with while

PRACTICE 1

Combine the pairs of sentences using after, while, *or* before. *There may be more than one way to combine these sentences. You may have to change pronouns and verb tenses.*

1. The audience left the concert hall. The orchestra played the last note.
2. Look at the menu. Order your meal.
3. The lights went out. We lit a candle.
4. We were waiting for you in the coffee shop. You were waiting for us at the bookstore.
5. They filled the car with gas[1]. The car ran out of gas.

PRACTICE 2

Put these sentences into chronological order.

1. __ In the future, the town hopes to build an art museum next to the old factory.
2. __ Once the factory opened, river traffic increased bringing raw materials to the factories and taking munitions downstream to the major river port at the mouth of the river.
3. __ In the early 1900s, Winston on Hudson was just a small town on the Hudson River.
4. __ Soon Winston on Hudson became a tourist destination.
5. __ Today, the town's munitions factory has been turned into artist studios.
6. __ Nothing happened in the town until after the start of the First World War when a munitions factory opened.
7. __ Within ten years, cargo boats were followed by passenger boats bringing weekend sightseers.

PRACTICE 3

Write the sentences in Practice 2 as a paragraph. Circle the words that show chronological order.

____

____

____

____

____

____

[1]BRITISH: petrol, filled up with petrol.

aphs about your life describing the important dates and times of events in your life.

Spatial Order

Spatial order organizes your writing around the position of things. You write about where things are in relation to one another.

Useful Words for Spatial Relations

across	adjacent
across from	midpoint
where	halfway
in which, to which, from which	interior
under	diagonal
over	edge
inside	limit
beside	parallel, parallel to
on top of	perpendicular to
along	opposite
through	overlapping
as far as	exterior
north, south, east, west	intersection
northern, southern, eastern, western	rectangle
to the left/on the left-hand side	square
to the right/on the right-hand side	circle
to the north	vertical
in back/in the back of the _____ / behind the	horizontal
in front/in front of the _____	
in the middle	

PRACTICE 5

Look at this diagram of the first floor of a suburban house. Complete the blanks with these prepositions of place:

around	east	north
behind	in front of	right
beside	left	south
between	next to	west

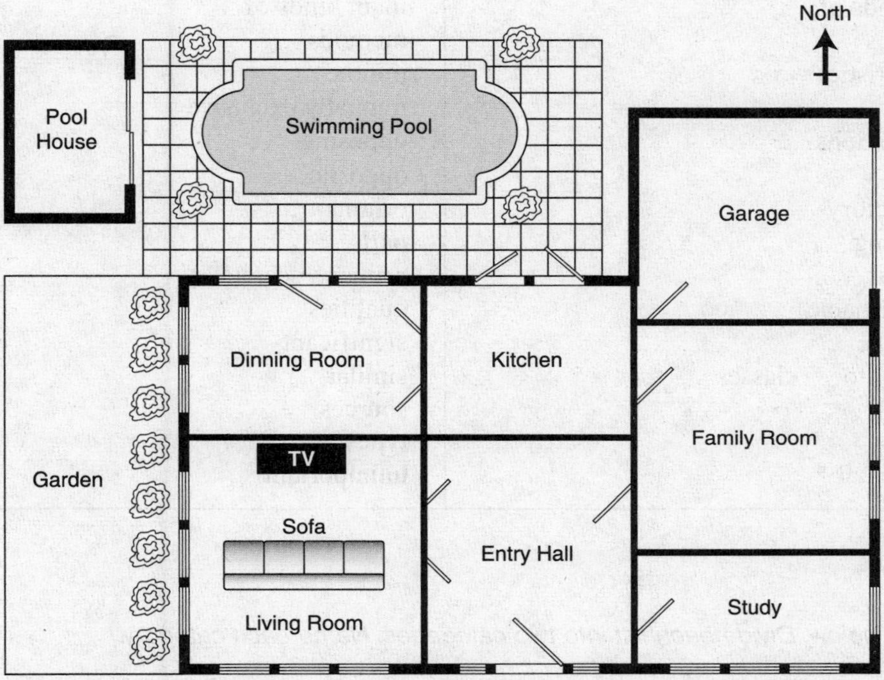

1. The entry hallway is ________ the living room and the study.
2. The dining room is ________ the kitchen.
3. The garage is to the ________ of the house.
4. The pool house is _______ the garden.
5. The living room sofa is ___________ the TV.
6. The garden is on the _________side of the house.
7. The living room windows are on the _________ and _________ walls.
8. The swimming pool is _______ the house.
9. The family room is ________ the kitchen.
10. There are trees ________ the swimming pool.

Classification

Classification organizes your writing around the grouping or classification of things. You write about how things are similar to one another.

Useful Words for Classification

aspects	important
attributes	insignificant
bases	kinds of
basic kinds of	main kinds of
categories	methods
characteristics	minor
classes	mutually exclusive
classifications	opposing
classify	opposite
contradictory	origins
contrasting	parts
dissimilar	primary, secondary
distinguishable	qualities
divide	significant
divided into __ classes	similar
factors	sources
falls into	types of
fundamental	unimportant

PRACTICE 6

Classify the lists below. Divide each list into two categories. Name each category.

Word List	____________	____________
table		
boy		
frog		
car		
chair		
butterfly		
pencil		
teacher		

Word List	______________	______________
doctor		
nurse		
contractor		
hospital		
building plans		
plumber		
patient		
architect		

PRACTICE 7

There are both positive and negative values. What some people see as positive values others see as negative. Match these values with the example sentences. Then, classify these values as either positive or negative. Finally, write a paragraph about either a positive or negative value using the phrases as examples.

Positive Values	Negative Values

A anger
B charity
C envy
D gluttony
E greed
F hope
G humility
H justice
I kindness
J laziness
K patience
L pride

1 _____ I am proud that I am richer than my friends.

2 _____ I am kind to everyone, even those who hate me.

3 _____ I wish I had a house as big as a palace.

4 _____ I eat even though I am not hungry.

5 _____ I do not have to be the first in every line[1].

6 _____ It makes me mad when I don't win.

[1]BRITISH: queue

7 _____ I will never have enough money.

8 _____ I never brag about myself.

9 _____ Tomorrow is another day.

10 _____ It's too hot to work.

11 _____ I always look on both sides of an argument.

12 _____ I give 10 percent of my income to the poor.

DEFINITION

You can write a simple definition of an object like a mobile phone in one sentence. To define a more abstract term like *virtue*, you may need several sentences, perhaps several paragraphs.

Useful Words for Definition

aspect category characteristic clarification clarify class condition define definition	explain explanation form in other words kind method paraphrase type

PRACTICE 8

Concrete objects like a computer can be defined in one sentence. Abstract objects like humility *may take several sentences. Classify these words.*

Words	Concrete	Abstract
printer		
success		
loyalty		
sidewalk		
freedom		
love		
black		
swimming		

Practice 9

Write a definition for each concrete term and each abstract term. Try to be very specific in each. When defining abstract terms, it is helpful to use concrete terms as examples.

EXAMPLES

A printer is a computer peripheral (either laser or ink jet) that enables you to have a paper record of the data in your computer.

Success to me is defined as my own 30-seat jet plane and a ten-bedroom yacht.

SUPPORT AN OPINION

Comparison and Contrast

You can define an object or describe a person by comparing or contrasting the object with something else. You can define a pear by comparing it with a peach or contrasting it with a banana. This is a very useful way to organize your material.

Useful Words for Comparison and Contrast

Comparison	Contrast
almost the same as	different from
common with	differ from
correspond to	even so
in the same way	however
just as	in contrast to
like, alike	in opposition to
resemblance	less than
resemble	more than
similar to	otherwise
similarly	slower than, etc.
to be parallel to	still

Practice 10

Read these questions. Write CON if it's a question asking for contrast. Write COMP if it's a question asking for comparison.

1. ____ How is greed different from envy?
2. ____ How does a mobile[1] phone differ from a landline phone?
3. ____ How are dogs and cats alike?
4. ____ In what ways are trains and planes different?
5. ____ What are the similarities between a chair and a stool?
6. ____ Can you list three ways a restaurant and a cafeteria are alike?
7. ____ What are the differences between classical music and hip hop?
8. ____ How are Japan and Madagascar the same?

[1]AMERICAN: cell or mobile

PRACTICE 11

Complete the blanks with words that show comparison or contrast. Use the words in the list below. Some words may be used more than once. Don't forget to add capitals where necessary.

A

Landline phones and cell phones are devices used for communicating with people in other places. The biggest ______(1)______ between a landline phone and a mobile phone is that a landline phone stays in one place ______(2)______ a mobile phone can go everywhere. A landline phone always stays in your home or office. A mobile phone, ______(3)______, can go wherever you go. There is a disadvantage to this. You always know where your landline phone is—on your desk, on the kitchen wall, by the bed, or wherever you keep it. ______(4)______ a landline phone, a mobile phone is easily misplaced[1].

in contrast to
while
difference
however

B

A restaurant is a place where you order food and it is brought to your table. A cafeteria is ______(5)______ a restaurant, except that in a cafeteria you serve yourself. There are several ways in which a restaurant and a cafeteria are ______(6)______. In ______(7)______ places you can eat a good meal without cooking it yourself. In a restaurant you select your meal from a menu. In a cafeteria you can also choose your meal from among several different possibilities, ______(8)______ in a restaurant. Finally, in ______(9)______ a restaurant and a cafeteria, you have to pay for what you eat.

both
alike
similar to
just as

PRACTICE 12

When you write a compare/contrast paragraph, you begin by defining one item and then comparing or contrasting it with the other item.

Read the example below, then write a passage comparing dogs and cats.

EXAMPLE

A greedy person is someone who wants more of what he or she already has. An envious person is someone who wants what someone else has. For example, I may envy your car, but a greedy person will want a bigger car than you have plus a big garage to put the car in.

[1]BRITISH: mis-placed

PRACTICE 13

Look at the graph and table below. Describe them by comparing and contrasting the information.

1. The graph below shows the average cost of housing in three different areas.

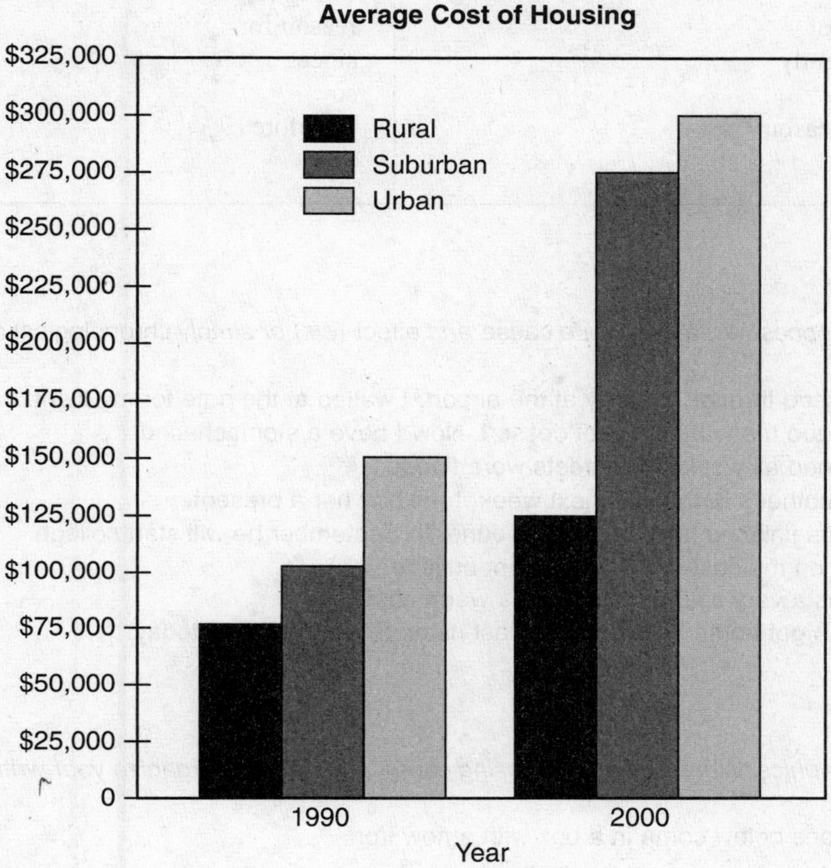

2. The table below shows information about three different types of restaurants.

	Sit-Down Restaurant	Cafeteria	Fast Food Restaurant
Average cost of lunch	$10.00	$7.00	$4.50
Average time spent eating lunch	45 min.	30 min.	20 min.
Average cost of dinner	$17.00	$9.50	$5.00
Average time spent eating dinner	60 min.	45 min.	20 min.

Cause and Effect

A cause and effect relationship is a very useful organizational style. Something happens because something else happened. I turned on the air conditioner and the room became cooler.

Cause and effect is similar to chronological order. First something happens followed by something else. But in cause and effect, there is a definite relationship between the two.

Useful Words for Cause and Effect

accordingly	have an effect on
as a result	hence
because	owing to
because of	reason for
consequently	since
due to	so
for this reason	therefore
	thus

PRACTICE 14

Read these sentences. Write if they are cause *and* effect *(C/E) or simply* chronological order *(CO).*

1. _____ I passed through security at the airport. I waited at the gate for my flight.
2. _____ I ate too many helpings of dessert. Now I have a stomachache.
3. _____ It rained all week. The streets were flooded.
4. _____ My mother's birthday is next week. I will buy her a present.
5. _____ James finished high school last June. In September he will start college.
6. _____ I put on my coat and scarf. I went outside.
7. _____ It was a very cold day. I put on a warm coat.
8. _____ Sarah got home after midnight last night. She's very tired today.

PRACTICE 15

Look at these graphics. Write a paragraph using cause *and* effect *to organize your writing.*

1. The instructions below come in a box with a new iron.

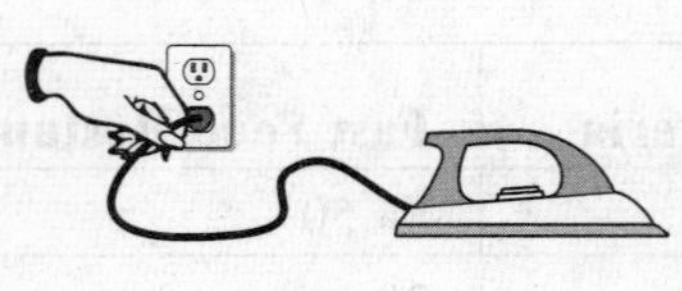

1

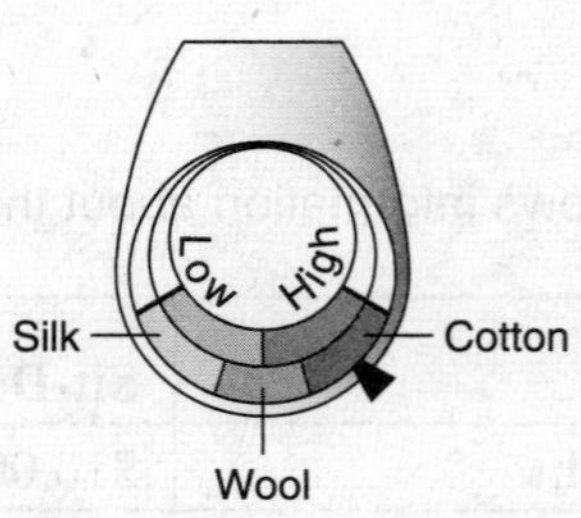

2

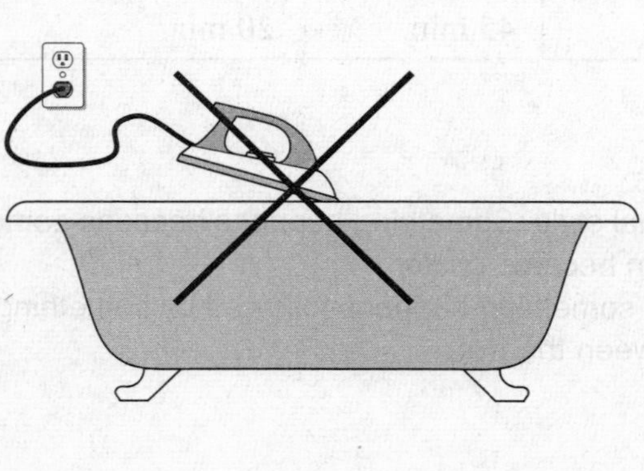

3

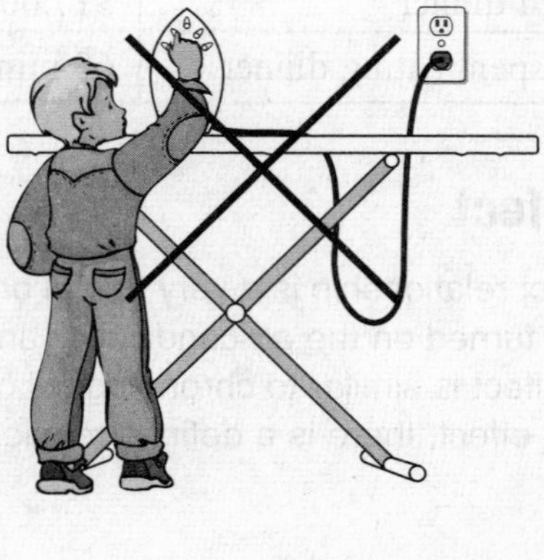

4

2. The graph below shows the average salaries earned by people with different levels of education.

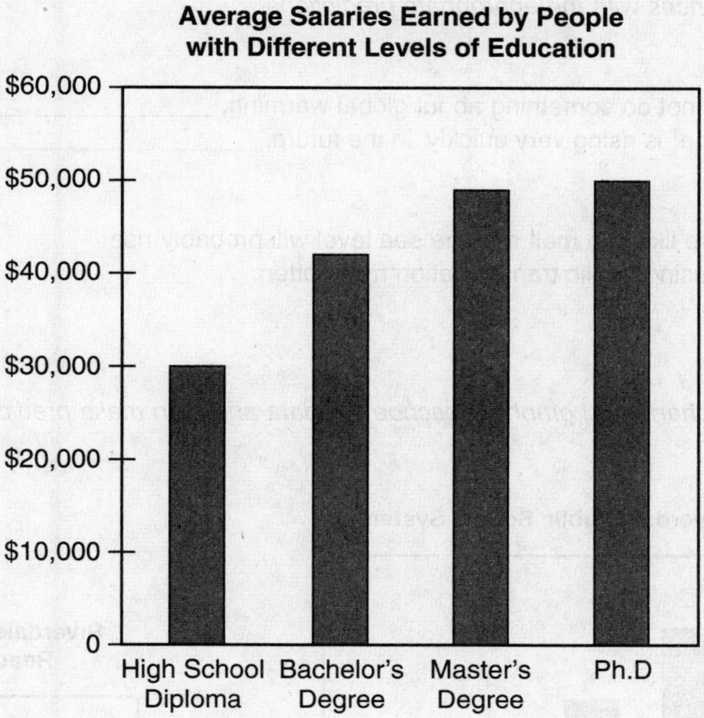

Prediction

A prediction is your guess about what will happen in the future. You base this prediction on the facts you know. A prediction is similar to an inference. It is an educated guess that you deduced from the evidence.

Useful Words for Prediction

forecast	predict
foresee	predictable
future	presume
in the future	probable result
infer	projection
likely	the end result
make a prediction about	the future implications of
most likely	the most likely outcome
plan	the next step
plan to	

PRACTICE 16

Complete these sentences with the appropriate predictions.

Statements

1. If governments do not do something about global warming, ______________________
2. The cost of gasoline[1] is rising very quickly. In the future, ______________________

Predictions

A. The ice shelves are likely to melt and the sea level will probably rise.
B People may start using public transportation more often.

PRACTICE 17

Look at the following charts and graphs. Describe the data and then make predictions about what will happen next.

1.

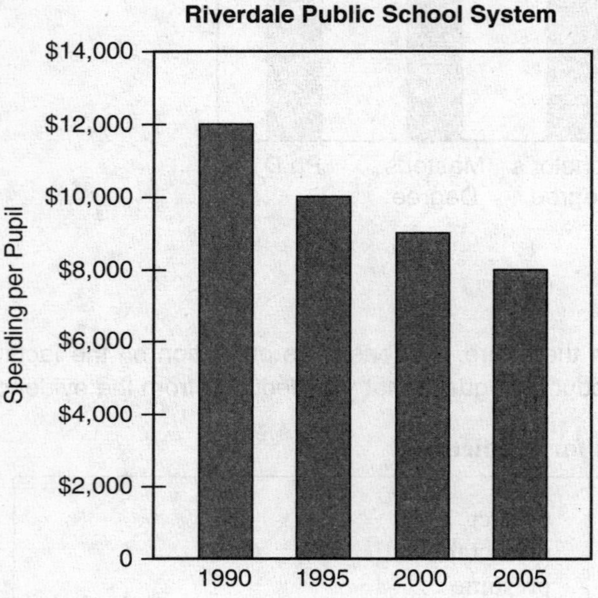

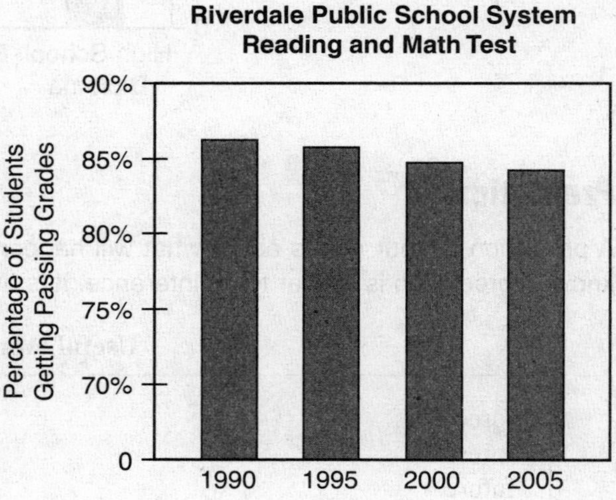

By 2010, the schools will likely ______________________

By 2010, the pupils will probably ______________________

2.

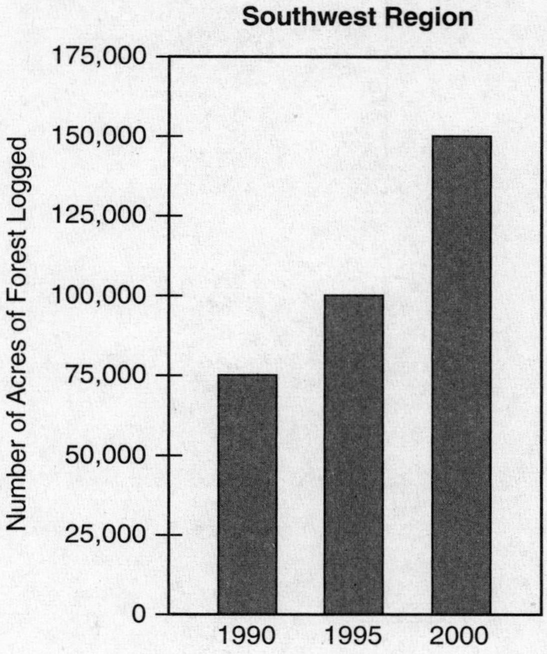

Number of Forest-Dwelling Species in the Southwest

Animals	***1998***	***2002***
Mammals	3	2
Birds	7	5
Amphibians	5	3

By 2005, the number of acres of forest logged will likely ______________________________.

By 2007, the number of forest-dwelling species will likely ______________________________.

7

SPEAKING MODULE

- **QUICK STUDY**
  - Overview
  - Question Types
  - Speaking Tips
- **SPEAKING SKILLS**
  - Target 1—Describing Yourself
  - Target 2—Describing Your Family
  - Target 3—Describing Your Home or Hometown
  - Target 4—Describing Your Occupation or School
  - Target 5—Describing Your Hobbies or General Interests
  - Target 6—Discussing a Topic
  - Target 7—Responding to Follow-up Questions
  - Target 8—Discussing an Issue in Depth

QUICK STUDY

Overview

There are three parts to the Speaking module, which lasts between 11 and 14 minutes. You will be alone in a room with one examiner who will ask you questions and ask you to talk on certain topics. The interview will be recorded. You will be able to make notes in Part 2 only.

The Speaking modules are the same for both the Academic and the General Training versions of the IELTS. Topics include discussions about you, your family, etc.

Speaking Module

Parts	Time	Tasks
Part 1	4–5 minutes	Introductions Identify self Answer questions
Part 2	3–4 minutes: 1 minute preparation, 1–2 minute speaking, 1 minute follow-up questions	Talk on a topic given on a task card
Part 3	4–5 minutes	Discuss with examiner the issues related to the topic in Part 2

Question Types

There are a variety of questions and prompts the examiner will use to get you to talk during the IELTS Speaking module. You should be familiar with these types.

Part 1 *Wh-* questions
Yes/No questions

Part 2 Describe and explain
Wh- questions
Yes/No questions

Part 3 *Wh-* questions
Yes/No questions

The following activities will help you become familiar with these question types.

Part 1

PRACTICE A

Write the answers to the examiner's questions for Part 1.

1. What is your name?
____
2. How do you spell it?
____
3. Do you have your proof of identification? May I see it?
____
4. Let's talk about where you live. Can you describe your neighborhood?
____
5. What is an advantage of living there?
____
6. What is a disadvantage of living there?
____
7. Let's talk about jobs. What kind of job do you have?
____
8. What is the best thing about your job?
____
9. Let's talk about free time. What is one activity you enjoy doing in your free time?
____
10. How did you become interested in this activity?
____

PRACTICE B

Pretend you are taking the Speaking module. The examiner asked you the questions in Practice A. Now give your answers aloud to the examiner's questions for Part 1.

Part 2

Practice C

Make notes to answer the questions on the Task Card for Part 2. Try to do this in one minute.

Task card

Describe a place that you like to go.

You should say:
where the place is
how you get there
what it looks like

and explain why you like this place.

Notes:
Place ______________________
Location ______________________
Transportation ______________________
Appearance ______________________

Why I like it ______________________

____

Practice D

Pretend you are taking the Speaking module. The examiner gave you the Task Card in Practice C. Now give your answers out loud to the examiner's questions for Part 2.

Practice E

Write the answers to the examiner's follow-up questions for Part 2.

1. Do you go on your own to this place?

____

2. Are there similar places you like to go?

____

Practice F

Pretend you are taking the Speaking module. The examiner asked you the questions in Practice E. Now give your answers out loud to the examiner's questions for Part 2 follow-up.

Part 3

Practice G

Write the answers to the examiner's questions for Part 3. Note that these questions are related to the theme of Part 2.

1. Let's consider why people need to vary their surroundings.
   - What kinds of vacations[1] do most people take?
   - Are these different places than people used to go in the past?

____

____

____

2. Finally, let's talk about leisure time.
   - Why is leisure time important?

____

____

____

Speaking Tips

Tips to Help You While Taking the Test

1. **Focus on the task.** Think what the examiner is asking you. Respond precisely to the question or topic.
2. **Speak clearly.** Sit up straight. Talk directly to the examiner. Do not be afraid to make eye contact.
3. **Speak loudly.** Make sure you are heard, but do not yell.
4. **Bring a watch.** You will have one minute to prepare your answer for Part 2. Glance at your watch to make sure you have enough time to complete your task.
5. **Laugh.** Do this before you meet the examiner. Before the speaking test begins, tell yourself a joke or think of something funny. Start to laugh. Laugh harder. Laugh louder. Laughter will make you feel better and more relaxed. It will also push air into your lungs and help you speak better. People around you may think you're crazy[2], but you're there to do well on the IELTS, not to impress people with your sanity.
6. **Smile.** Smile at the examiner. This will put both of you at ease and make you both more comfortable.

Tips to Help You Study for the Speaking Test

1. **Talk to yourself.** When you walk down the street, pay attention to the things around you. What do the buildings look like? Is there a lot of traffic? How is the weather? Is this a typical day and scene in your city? In your mind, describe the scene to someone in English. Imagine a person who has never visited your city, and describe the scene to that person.

   You can do the same thing at school, at work, or anywhere you go. Imagine describing the scene to a person from another country. Explain the customs of people in your country: how they dress, act, and talk in the different situations that you describe.

[1]BRITISH: holidays

[2]BRITISH: mad

2. **Make up stories.** Use your imagination. Look around you on the street, on the bus, on the elevator, wherever you are. Who are those people? Where are they going and why? What are they carrying? What will they do with what they are carrying? Imagine yourself in the story. What would you say to these people?
   Ask yourself questions about everything and everyone you see. How did it get here? Why is it here? What will happen to it next?
3. **Make your daily plans.** Do you talk to yourself about your plans for the day when you get up in the morning? Do this in English. If you have to decide what clothes to wear, what to have for breakfast, if you will walk or take the bus, think about these decisions in English. If you make a shopping list or a reading list or a list of chores, you can do this in English too.
4. **Think about your job.** Imagine you are at a job interview. Talk about your educational and work background. What kind of training and experience do you have? What can you do well? How do you see your future? In your mind, try to sell yourself to a future employer by talking about your strengths and good qualities.
5. **Explain your interests.** Choose a hobby or free time interest that you have. Imagine that you are teaching another person how to do it. Explain everything step by step. Describe any equipment or tools that are needed. Then pick another hobby and do it again.
6. **Read books, watch movies and TV.** Think about a book, film, or TV show that you really enjoy. In your mind, tell another person what it is about and why you like it. Think about a book, film, or TV show that you dislike. Explain why you don't like it.
7. **Read about the news.** When you read the newspaper or watch the news on TV, think about it in English. How could you explain it to another person in English? How could you explain your own opinions or feelings about particular news events?

What the Examiner Measures

Fluency and Coherence

When you answer the examiner's questions or talk about a topic, your speech must be fluent and cohesive. This means the words you use must fit the situation, and these words must come quickly. You must address the topic fully, and your ideas must be tied together.

It is important to speak for a least one full minute during Part 2. You can speak longer if you can. There is no penalty for speaking over one minute. The examiner will tell you to stop.

Accuracy

Accuracy is very important. An examiner will listen to your vocabulary, your grammar, and your pronunciation. She or he will want to make sure that you have a large enough vocabulary to express yourself easily and be understood completely.

The examiner will want to make sure that the grammar you use is varied and appropriate to what you want to say.

The examiner will, of course, be paying close attention to your pronunciation. Your speech must be comprehensible. You can have an accent, but the words must be intelligible.

SPEAKING SKILLS

Target 1—Describing Yourself

There are three ways you can talk about yourself—factual, physical, and emotional. Look at these model introductions.

Factual—My name is Jose Maria Menendez. My first name is spelled J-O-S-E and my last name ends in "Z" not "S". People often have trouble when spelling my name. My identity number is C-9870-667.
Physical—I am almost 6 feet tall. My hair color is brown, the same color as my eyes.
Emotional—I'm a serious student, but I like to laugh, too. I spend a lot of time studying, but on weekends, I like to go to out with my friends.

TEST TIP
When you say a string of numbers, use the single digit number. For example, for C-9870-667, don't say: C-ninety-eight seventy sixty-six seven. You'll be less likely to make a mistake by keeping it simple: C nine eight seven zero six six seven.

Useful Words

Factual	Physical	Emotional
first name	tall	serious
last name	feet/meters	lucky
surname	inches/centimeters	cheerful
ends with	curly	nervous
begins with	straight	calm
	brown/blue/green/red	excited
		worried
		confident

PRACTICE 1

Complete this form about yourself. This will help you organize your personal information.

Personal Information Form

Factual
First Name ____________
Middle Name ____________
Last Name[1] ____________
Age ________
Nationality ________
Native Language ____________
Occupation ____________

Physical
Height ____________
Weight ____________
Eye Color ____________
Hair:
Color ____________ (check one) long__ short__ medium length __
(check one) straight __ curly __ wavy __
Other characteristics (glasses? beard? etc.) ________________

Emotional
(circle all that apply)
optimistic pessimistic easygoing serious fun loving studious nervous calm
shy confident outgoing friendly hardworking talkative quiet cheerful

PRACTICE 2

Write three sentences about yourself. Use the examples as models. Then without looking at the form or sentences, describe yourself out loud. Record your description and listen to it. Record yourself speaking about the topic in different ways. Vary the vocabulary that you use and the order that you present the information. You only get one chance during the exam. This is your time to practice.

Factual

1. ________________________________

2. ________________________________

3. ________________________________

[1]BRITISH: surname

Physical

1. ______________________________

2. ______________________________

3. ______________________________

Emotional

1. ______________________________

2. ______________________________

3. ______________________________

Target 2—Describing Your Family

When talking about your family, it is simpler to talk about them factually.

EXAMPLE 1

I have a very small family. There is only my mother, father, and me. I'm an only child.

EXAMPLE 2

I have a very large family. I have three brothers and two sisters. I am the youngest. One of my brothers still lives with my parents; my other siblings have all married and moved to their own homes.

EXAMPLE 3

My father died when I was ten. I was brought up by my mother and grandparents. My mother and two sisters and I still live with my grandfather.

TEST TIP

You don't have to tell the examiner everything. She or he is not judging you. Just provide some basic information. If you don't want to talk about your family, talk about someone else's family.

Useful Words

parents	married	live with
relations	single	die/passed away
youngest/oldest	divorced	moved out
middle child	widowed	raised by
only child		

PRACTICE 1

Complete this form about your family. This will help you organize your personal information.

Family Information Form

	Relationship to You	Name	Age	Marital Status	Occupation	Other Information
Parents	mother					
	father					
Siblings						
Other Relatives						

PRACTICE 2

Write three sentences about your family. Use the above as a model. Then without looking at the form or sentences, describe your family out loud. Record your description and listen to it. Record it over and over until you are satisfied with your presentation.

1. ______________________________

2. ______________________________

3. ______________________________

Target 3—Describing Your Home or Hometown

You may be asked to talk about your home or your neighborhood. You can talk generally about either one, or you can talk more personally. Try to have a lot of specific details prepared. This will help your answers be more cohesive and fluent.

TEST TIP
If you don't understand the task, ask for clarification. This will give you time to think a bit.

These phrases will be helpful:
Do you mean the house I live in or my hometown?
Would you like me to describe the house generally or in great detail?

Home: General Description
We live in a flat[1] in the old section of the city. It was once a large home that was converted to several flats. Now, five families live in this home. We have two bedrooms: one for me and one for my parents. There is a large living room and a kitchen with a small balcony overlooking the street. The streets are very narrow, and there are no trees.

Neighborhood: General Description
I was born in Beijing. Even though it is a very large city and the capital, we live in a part that is like a small village. We know everyone here. On the corner of my street, there is a small grocery store. Across from that, there is a dry cleaner. Next to the dry cleaner is a big clothing store. On the corner opposite the grocery store, there is a bus stop so we can easily go anywhere in the city.

Home: Personal Description
My home is a small house in a new development. It was built by my father. The house has three bedrooms: a large one for my parents and two smaller bedrooms for my brother and me. In my bedroom, I have a bed, a desk, and a chair. I also have a lot of books in bookshelves along two walls. I have a window in my room that looks out over our garden. It's a small garden, but we can grow all our own vegetables.

Neighborhood: Personal Description
My mother and father live in my hometown, Burdur. In fact, my entire family—aunts, uncles, grandparents, everyone—lives in Burdur. We've lived there for over six generations. We know everyone in the area so when we sit outside, it is like being in our living room with our very large family. We live across the street from a park. My family spends a lot of time sitting in this park talking to neighbors and relatives.

[1] AMERICAN: apartment

Useful Words

Type	Relation	Description
balcony	across from	large/small
one-bedroom	along	spacious
kitchen	behind	airy
section/area	beside	narrow
grocery store	corner	old/new
park	end	lots
post office	facing	a lot of
department store	in back/front/middle of	big
taxi stand/rank	left-hand/right-hand side	
clothing store	near	
dry cleaner	next to	
park	overlooking	

PRACTICE 1

Complete these forms about your home and neighborhood. This will help you organize your personal information.

Home Information Form

Size __________
Age __________
Number of bedrooms __________
Other rooms __________
Garden/yard __________
Special features __________

My Bedroom:
Size
Furniture
Colors
Art
Other __________

Neighborhood[1] Information Form

Name
Style of houses __________
Shops/businesses
Schools
Religious buildings __________
Other buildings
Transportation
Parks/gardens __________
Special characteristics __________

[1]BRITISH: neighbourhood

PRACTICE 2

Write four sentences about your home. Use the above as models. Then without looking at the form or sentences, describe your home and hometown out loud. Record your description and listen to it. Record it over and over until you are satisfied with your presentation.

Home: General Description

1. ______________________________

2. ______________________________

3. ______________________________

4. ______________________________

Neighborhood: General Description

1. ______________________________

2. ______________________________

3. ______________________________

4. ______________________________

Home: Specific Description

1. ______________________________

2. ______________________________

3. ______________________________

4. ______________________________

Neighborhood: Specific Description

1. ______________________________

2. ______________________________

3. ______________________________

4. ______________________________

Target 4—Describing Your Occupation or School

You may be asked to discuss how you spend your day. Do you work or do you study? Be prepared with specific details about your occupation or your school life.

Occupation

I'm an engineer. I've worked for the same company for three years. My specific job is working with the senior engineer and helping her prepare presentations for contractors and their clients. I'd like to get an advanced[1] degree. That's why I'm applying to study at an engineering school in Australia.

School

I'm a third-year student at National University. I'm studying psychology. I'm in class most of the day, and when I'm not in class I have to spend a lot of time working on my assignments. My goal is to become a research psychologist, so I'll have to get a doctorate degree. I have a lot of years of studying ahead of me.

Useful Words

boss	duties	qualified
co-workers	assignments	goal
clients	position	advanced degree
classmates	schedule	master's degree
instructors	salary	doctorate degree

PRACTICE 1

Complete this form about your occupation or studies. This will help you organize your personal information.

Job Information Form

Company name ________________

Job title ________________

Length of time at this job ________________

Duties ________________

Training required for this job ________________

Skills required for this job ________________

Things I like about this job ________________

Things I don't like about this job ________________

Future career goals ________________

[1]BRITISH: higher degree

Education Information Form

Name of college/university ________________

Major/subject[1] ________________

Classes I am taking now ________________

Hours per week in class ________________

Years to complete degree/certificate ________________

Educational goals ________________

Future career goals ________________

PRACTICE 2

Write four sentences about your occupation or your studies. Use the above as models. Then without looking at the form or sentences, describe your job or school out loud. Record your discussion and listen to it. Record it over and over until you are satisfied with your presentation.

My occupation ____________ or My studies ____________

1. ____
2. ____
3. ____
4. ____

Target 5—Describing Your Hobbies or General Interests

The examiner may ask you how you spend your free time. Do you like to read, go to the cinema, play sports? Do you have any hobbies like collecting stamps, bird watching, photography?

Hobby *(EXAMPLE 1)*

I enjoy bird watching. I often go to a park near my house in the early morning to watch the birds. I also belong to a bird watching club. Several times a year we take trips to other places. We try to find birds that we've never seen before. You don't need much equipment for bird watching, just a pair of binoculars and a pair of strong legs for walking. I enjoy this hobby because I like to be outside, and I'm fascinated by the natural world.

Hobby *(EXAMPLE 2)*

I like to play the guitar. I took lessons when I was a child. Some friends and I had a rock band once, a long time ago. We played at parties. Now I mostly play on my own at home, and sometimes I get together with friends to play. I'm thinking about taking lessons again. I'd like to learn how to play jazz guitar. I have a large collection of jazz CDs.

[1]BRITISH: doing a degree in

Useful Words

interested in	club	equipment
enjoy	get together	collect/collection
join	learn how	passion
belong to	lessons	fascinate/fascinated by

PRACTICE 1

Complete this form about your hobbies or general interests. This will help you organize your personal information.

Hobby/Free-Time Activity Information Form

Hobby/Activity #1 ____________________
How often do you do this hobby or activity? ____________________
Do you do it on your own or with other people? ____________________
Do you belong to a club related to this hobby/activity? ____________________
How did you learn how to do this hobby/activity? ____________________
Do you need special equipment for it? ____________________
What do you like most about it? ____________________

Hobby/Activity #2 ____________________
How often do you do this hobby or activity? ____________________
Do you do it alone or with other people? ____________________
Do you belong to a club related to this hobby/activity? ____________________
How did you learn how to do this hobby/activity? ____________________
Do you need special equipment for it? ____________________
What do you like most about it? ____________________

PRACTICE 2

Write four sentences about how you spend your free time. Use the above as models. Then without looking at the form or sentences, describe your hobbies and general interests out loud. Record your description and listen to it. Record it over and over until you are satisfied with your presentation.

Hobby/Activity #1 ____________________

1. ____________________
2. ____________________
3. ____________________
4. ____________________

Hobby/Activity #2 ____________________

1. ____________________

2. ____________________

3. ____________________

4. ____________________

Target 6—Discussing a Topic

The examiner will give you a card. The card will have a topic and some questions to guide your discussion of the topic. You will have one minute to prepare your answer. The questions are very important. They will guide your organization. You can make notes on paper provided by the examiner. Your discussion will be more cohesive if you can provide a sequence of events or actions for your topic.

EXAMPLE

Describe a museum that you have visited.

You should say:
where it is located and what kind of museum it is
what specific things you can see there
when and why you last visited it

and discuss how it compares to other museums you have visited.

Notes:

- Greenport Ship Museum, in Greenport, a beach resort
- Parts of old ships and demonstrations of shipbuilding methods
- Last summer, took my niece and nephew to entertain them on a rainy day
- Not like a city museum: smaller, simpler exhibits, but friendlier staff

Useful Words for Establishing a Sequence

after	during	previously
as a teenager	earlier	prior to
at the same time as	in the 1990s	simultaneously
before	later	when

PRACTICE 1

Make notes about these topics. Give short answers to the question.

Topic 1

> Talk about a pet that you or someone you know once had.
>
> You should say:
> what kind of animal it was
> what kind of care it needed
> what you liked/didn't like about it
>
> and explain why this is or is not a popular type of pet to own.

Topic 2

> Describe a birthday celebration that you attended recently.
>
> You should say:
> whose birthday it was and that person's age
> who attended the party
> where the party took place
>
> and describe some activities that happened at the party.

Topic 3

Talk about a friend you had as a child or teenager. You should say: when and how you first met this friend what things you liked to do together what things you had in common and explain why this friendship was important to you.

Topic 4

Describe a trip you have taken recently. You should say: where you went who went with you why you went there and describe some things you saw and did on your trip.

Practice 2

Write a paragraph about each topic. Then without looking at your notes or your paragraph, discuss the topic out loud. Record your discussion and listen to it. Record it over and over until you are satisfied with your presentation.

Topic 1

Topic 2

Topic 3

Topic 4

Target 7—Responding to Follow-up Questions

The examiner will ask you specific questions about your discussion of a topic.

Follow-up questions for a topic on museums:

How often do you go to museums?
What kinds of museums do you generally prefer to visit? Why?
Is it important to take children to visit different kinds of museums?

Useful Words

According to my point of view	I believe	I'm in favor of ________ because________
As far as I'm concerned	I don't know if	It seems to me
I agree with/disagree with	I don't know whether	Personally I think
I'm certain/positive/sure that	I think it's a good idea because ________	The advantage of ________ is that
I assume	I'm against ________	The disadvantage of ______ is that

PRACTICE 1

Make notes to respond to these follow-up questions.

Topic 1

What are some advantages and disadvantages to owning pets?
Is it important for children to have pets? Why or why not?

1. ____________________

2. ____________________

Topic 2

How do you like to celebrate your birthday?
What other kinds of celebrations are important for you?

1. ____________________

2. ____________________

Topic 3

What are some things you like to do with your friends now?
Do you think it's better to have a lot of friends, or just a few good friends?

1. ______________________________

2. ______________________________

Topic 4

When you travel, what kinds of places do you usually visit?
Do you like to travel? Why or why not?

1. ______________________________

2. ______________________________

PRACTICE 2

Write an answer for each follow-up question. Then without looking at your notes or your sentences, respond to the question out loud. Record your answers and listen to them. Record them over and over until you are satisfied with your presentation.

Topic 1

1. ______________________________

2. ______________________________

Topic 2

1. ______________________________

2. ______________________________

Topic 3

1. ______________________________

2. ______________________________

Topic 4

1. ______________________________

2. ______________________________

Target 8—Discussing an Issue in Depth

In the last part of the Speaking section of the test, the examiner will ask you some more questions and give you an opportunity to discuss in depth some of the issues related to the topic in Part 2.

Issues from example topic asking for definition:

Why do people visit museums?
What role do museums play in a society?

Issues from example topic asking for comparison and contrast:

What do museums offer in terms of education that books or other sources don't?
How will museums be different in the future?

Useful Words for Definitions

characteristic	in explanation	to paraphrase
condition	in other words	
define	to explain	

Useful Words for Comparison

alike	in the same way	resemblance
almost the same as	just as	similar to
common characteristics	like	similarity
correspond to	likewise	to have in common

Useful Words for Contrast

although	however	nevertheless
different from	in contrast to	on the other hand
even so	less than	still
(larger) than	more / more than	unlike

PRACTICE 1

Make notes about these issues.

Issues from Topic 1

Definition:
Why do people have pets?
In your opinion, what kind of animal makes the best pet?

Comparison and contrast:
In what different ways have animals been useful to people throughout history?
How are people's attitudes toward animals different now than they were in the past?

Issues from Topic 2

Definition:
Are birthday celebrations important in your country? Why or why not?
How are older people treated in your culture?

Comparison and contrast:
Are birthday celebrations different now than they were in the past? How?
In your opinion, how will the role of older people in your culture change in the future?

Issues from Topic 3

Definition:
What are the qualities of a good friend?
What role do friends play in most people's lives?

Comparison and contrast:
What differences are there between men's and women's friendships?
Do you think the nature of friendship is changing?

Issues from Topic 4

Definition:
Why do people travel?
What are some transportation problems in your country?

Comparison and contrast:
How has plane travel changed the way people live?
What are some advantages and disadvantages that tourism can have for a specific place?

PRACTICE 2

Write a paragraph about each issue. Then without looking at your notes or your sentences discuss the issue out loud. Record your discussion and listen to it. Record them over and over until you are satisfied with your presentation.

Issues from Topic 1

Issues from Topic 2

Issues from Topic 3

Issues from Topic 4

8

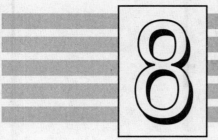

IELTS MODEL TESTS

ACADEMIC MODEL TEST 1

Model Test 1

Candidate Name ____

INTERNATIONAL ENGLISH LANGUAGE TESTING SYSTEM

LISTENING

TIME Approx. 30 minutes

INSTRUCTIONS TO CANDIDATES

Do not open this booklet until you are told to do so.

Write your name and candidate number in the space at the top of this page.

You should answer all questions.

All the recordings will be played ONCE only.

Write all your answers on the Question Paper.

At the end of the test, you will be given ten minutes to transfer your answers to an Answer Sheet.

Do not remove this booklet from the examination room.

INFORMATION FOR CANDIDATES

There are **40** questions on this question paper.

The test is divided as follows:

Section 1	Questions 1–10
Section 2	Questions 11–20
Section 3	Questions 21–30
Section 4	Questions 31–40

CD TRACK 22

SECTION 1 *QUESTIONS 1–10*

Question 1

Match the time with the event. Write the correct number next to the letter.

A _2_ Today
B ___ Next week
C ___ Next summer

1 Winston will go to Japan
2 Winston will register at the World Language Academy
3 Winston will study Japanese

Questions 2 and 3

Choose TWO *letters,* ***A–F***

2 What TWO classes are offered at the World Language Academy.

A Japanese for University Professors
B Japanese for Business Travelers
C Japanese for Tour Guides
D Japanese for Tourists
E Japanese for Language Teachers
F Japanese for Restaurant Workers

Choose TWO *letters,* ***A–F***

3 In Japan, Mark Winston says he will probably

A go shopping.
B climb mountains.
C attend a business meeting.
D try Japanese cuisine.
E take a university course.
F study with a tutor.

CD TRACK 23

Questions 4–8

Complete the schedule below.

Write NO MORE THAN TWO WORDS AND/OR A NUMBER *for each answer.*

Japanese Class Schedule

Morning	Days: Monday–Friday Time: **4** .... Level: Beginner
Afternoon	Days: Monday, Wednesday, Thursday Time: 1:00–3:00 Level: **5** ....
Evening	Days: Monday, Wednesday, Thursday Time: 5:30–7:30 Level: **6** .... Days: **7** .... Time: 7:30–9:30 Level: Advanced
8	Days: Saturday Time: 9:00–2:00 Level: Beginner

Questions 9 and 10

*Choose the correct letter, **A**, **B**, or **C***

9 Which class will Mark take?

A

B

C

10 How will he pay?

A

B

C

SECTION 2 *QUESTIONS 11–20*

Questions 11–13

Complete the notes below.

*Write **NO MORE THAN THREE WORDS** for each answer.*

There are **11** .... different kinds of parrots.

Parrots live all over the world.

12 .... is the most common color for parrots.

The smallest parrot is ten centimeters long.

The largest parrot is **13** .... long.

CD TRACK 25

Questions 14–17

Complete the table below.

*Write **NO MORE THAN THREE WORDS** for each answer.*

Cause	Effect
Parrots are **14** .... animals.	They are good pets. They need **15** ....
Parrots can feel **16**	They pull out their feathers.
Parrots can feel ignored.	They **17** .... all day.

Questions 18–20

Complete the information sheet below.

*Write **NO MORE THAN THREE WORDS** for each answer.*

Parrot Care Information Sheet
Parrots love to chew, so give them **18** .... Clean the cage daily because parrots **19** .... Feed your parrot **20** ...., fruit, and vegetables.

CD TRACK 26

SECTION 3 *QUESTIONS 21–30*

Questions 21–23

Complete the sentences below.

*Write **NO MORE THAN THREE WORDS** for each answer.*

21 There are high-speed trains in Japan and ....

22 The first high-speed train began operating in ....

23 High-speed trains can travel at speeds of .... kilometers an hour.

Questions 24–26

Complete the table below.

*Write **NO MORE THAN THREE WORDS** for each answer.*

Cause	Effect
We have better roads now than in the past.	**24** More people ....
Now we have plane service that is more **25**	More people use planes for long-distance travel.
There is a lot of **26**	We need to consider new forms of transportation.

CD ACK 27

Questions 27–30

*Choose **FOUR** letters, **A–G**.*

What are the advantages of trains over other types of transportation according to the people on the panel?

A Less expensive than car trips

B More relaxing than cars

C Less polluting than cars

D No traffic jams

E Better security systems than planes

F Larger capacity for passengers than planes

G More frequent service than planes

CD ACK 28

SECTION 4 *QUESTIONS 31–40*

Questions 31–40

Complete the timeline below.

*Write **NO MORE THAN THREE WORDS AND/OR ONE NUMBER** for each answer.*

1879	Einstein was born in **31** ______________
At age 12	Einstein began **32** ________________
33 _________	Einstein's family moved to Italy
34 _________	Einstein graduated from high school
35 _________	Einstein met Mileva Maric
1900	Einstein **36** ______________
1901	Einstein became **37** ____________
1902	Einstein began work at the Swiss Patent Office
	Einstein **38** _____________
39 _________	Einstein and Mileva Maric got married
40 _________	Einstein's first son was born

Model Test 1

Candidate Name ______________________________

INTERNATIONAL ENGLISH LANGUAGE TESTING SYSTEM

ACADEMIC READING

TIME 1 Hour

INSTRUCTIONS TO CANDIDATES

Do not open this booklet until you are told to do so.

Write your name and candidate number in the space at the top of this page.

Start at the beginning of the test and work through it.

You should answer all questions.

If you cannot do a particular question, leave it and go on to the next. You can return to it later.

All answers must be written on the Answer Sheet.

Do not remove this booklet from the examination room.

INFORMATION FOR CANDIDATES

There are **40** questions on this question paper.

The test is divided as follows:

Reading Passage 1	Questions 1–14
Reading Passage 2	Questions 15–27
Reading Passage 3	Questions 28–40

READING PASSAGE 1

*You should spend about 20 minutes on **Questions 1–14**, which are based on Reading Passage 1 below.*

The Value of a College Degree

The escalating cost of higher education is causing many to question the value of continuing education beyond high school. Many wonder whether the high cost of tuition, the opportunity cost of choosing college over full-time employment, and the accumulation of thousands of dollars of debt is, in the long run, worth the investment. The risk is especially large for low-income families who have a difficult time making ends meet without the additional burden of college tuition and fees.

In order to determine whether higher education is worth the investment, it is useful to examine what is known about the value of higher education and the rates of return on investment to both the individual and to society.

THE ECONOMIC VALUE OF HIGHER EDUCATION

There is considerable support for the notion that the rate of return on investment in higher education is high enough to warrant the financial burden associated with pursuing a college degree. Though the earnings differential between college and high school graduates varies over time, college graduates, on average, earn more than high school graduates. According to the Census Bureau, over an adult's working life, high school graduates earn an average of $1.2 million; associate's degree holders earn about $1.6 million; and bachelor's degree holders earn about $2.1 million (Day and Newburger, 2002).

These sizeable differences in lifetime earnings put the costs of college study in realistic perspective. Most students today—about 80 percent of all students—enroll either in public four-year colleges or in public two-year colleges. According to the U.S. Department of Education report, Think College Early, a full-time student at a public four-year college pays an average of $8,655 for in-state tuition, room, and board (U.S. Department of Education, 2002). A full-time student in a public two-year college pays an average of $1,359 per year in tuition (U.S. Department of Education, 2002).

These statistics support the contention that, though the cost of higher education is significant, given the earnings disparity that exists between those who earn a bachelor's degree and those who do not, the individual rate of return on investment in higher education is sufficiently high to warrant the cost.

OTHER BENEFITS OF HIGHER EDUCATION

College graduates also enjoy benefits beyond increased income. A 1998 report published by the Institute for Higher Education Policy reviews the individual benefits that college graduates enjoy, including higher levels of saving, increased personal/professional mobility, improved quality of life for their offspring, better consumer decision making, and more hobbies and leisure activities (Institute for Higher Education Policy, 1998). According to a report published by the Carnegie Foundation, nonmonetary individual benefits of higher education include the tendency for postsecondary students to become more open-minded, more cultured, more rational, more consistent, and less authoritarian; these benefits are also passed along to succeeding generations (Rowley and Hurtado, 2002). Additionally, college attendance has been shown to "decrease prejudice, enhance knowledge of world affairs and enhance social status" while increasing economic and job security for those who earn bachelor's degrees (Ibid.).

Research has also consistently shown a positive correlation between completion of higher education and good health, not only for oneself, but also for one's children. In fact, "parental schooling levels (after controlling for differences in earnings) are positively correlated with the health status of their children" and "increased schooling (and higher relative income) are correlated with lower mortality rates for given age brackets" (Cohn and Geske, 1992).

THE SOCIAL VALUE OF HIGHER EDUCATION

A number of studies have shown a high correlation between higher education and cultural and family values, and economic growth. According to Elchanan Cohn and Terry Geske (1992), there is the tendency for more highly educated women to spend more time with their children; these women tend to use this time to better prepare their children for the future. Cohn and Geske (1992) report that "college graduates appear to have a more optimistic view of their past and future personal progress."

Public benefits of attending college include increased tax revenues, greater workplace productivity, increased consumption, increased workforce flexibility, and decreased reliance on government financial support (Institute for Higher Education Policy, 1998). . . .

CONCLUSION

While it is clear that investment in a college degree, especially for those students in the lowest income brackets, is a financial burden, the long-term benefits to individuals as well as to society at large, appear to far outweigh the costs.

Questions 1–4

Do the following statements agree with the information in Reading Passage 1?

In boxes 1–4 on your Answer Sheet, write

TRUE	*if the statement is true according to the passage.*
FALSE	*if the statement contradicts the passage.*
NOT GIVEN	*if there is no information about this in the passage.*

1 The cost of a college education has remained steady for several years.

2 Some people have to borrow large amounts of money to pay for college.

3 About 80 percent of college students study at public colleges.

4 Public colleges cost less than private colleges.

Questions 5–9

Complete the fact sheet below.

*Choose **no more than three words** from the passage for each answer.*

Write your answers in boxes 5–9 on your Answer Sheet.

Financial Costs and Benefits of Higher Education

— The average high school graduate makes a little more than one million dollars in **5** ....

— The average person with an associate's degree earns **6** ....

— The average **7**................ makes over two million dollars.

— The average student at a four year college spends **8** $............... a year on classes, housing, and food.

— The average student at a two-year college spends $1,359 on **9** ....

Questions 10–13

The list below shows some benefits which college graduates may enjoy more of as compared to noncollege graduates.

Which four of these benefits are mentioned in the article?

*Write the appropriate letters **A–G** in boxes 10–13 on your Answer Sheet.*

A They own bigger houses.

B They are more optimistic about their lives.

C They save more money.

D They enjoy more recreational activities.

E They have healthier children.

F They travel more frequently.

G They make more purchases.

READING PASSAGE 2

*You should spend about 20 minutes on **Questions 14–26,** which are based on Reading Passage 2.*

Less Television, Less Violence and Aggression

Cutting back on television, videos, and video games reduces acts of aggression among schoolchildren, according to a study by Dr. Thomas Robinson and others from the Stanford University School of Medicine.

The study, published in the January 2001 issue of the *Archives of Pediatric and Adolescent Medicine*, found that third- and fourth-grade students who took part in a curriculum to reduce their TV, video, and video game use engaged in fewer acts of verbal and physical aggression than their peers.

The study took place in two similar San Jose, California, elementary schools. Students in one school underwent an 18-lesson, 6-month program designed to limit their media usage, while the others did not.

Both groups of students had similar reports of aggressive behavior at the beginning of the study. After the six-month program, however, the two groups had very real differences.

The students who cut back on their TV time engaged in six fewer acts of verbal aggression per hour and rated 2.4 percent fewer of their classmates as aggressive after the program.

Physical acts of violence, parental reports of aggressive behavior, and perceptions of a mean and scary world also decreased, but the authors suggest further study to solidify these results.

Although many studies have shown that children who watch a lot of TV are more likely to act violently, this report further verifies that television, videos, and video games actually cause the violent behavior, and it is among the first to evaluate a solution to the problem.

Teachers at the intervention school included the program in their existing curriculum. Early lessons encouraged students to keep track of and report on the time they spent watching TV or videos, or playing video games, to motivate them to limit those activities on their own.

The initial lessons were followed by TV-Turnoff, an organization that encourages less TV viewing. For ten days, students were challenged to go without television, videos, or video games. After that, teachers encouraged the students to stay within a media allowance of seven hours per week. Almost all students participated in the Turnoff, and most stayed under their budget for the following weeks.

Additional lessons encouraged children to use their time more selectively, and many of the final lessons had students themselves advocate reducing screen activities.

This study is by no means the first to find a link between television and violence. Virtually all of 3,500 research studies on the subject in the past 40 years have shown the same relationship, according to the American Academy of Pediatrics.

Among the most noteworthy studies is Dr. Leonard D. Eron's, which found that exposure to television violence in childhood is the strongest predictor of aggressive behavior later in life—stronger even than violent behavior as children.

The more violent television the subjects watched at age eight, the more serious was their aggressive behavior even 22 years later.

Another study by Dr. Brandon S. Centerwall found that murder rates climb after the introduction of television. In the United States and Canada, murder rates doubled 10 to 15 years after the introduction of television, after the first TV generation grew up.

Centerwall tested this pattern in South Africa, where television broadcasts were banned until 1975.

Murder rates in South Africa remained relatively steady from the mid-1940s through the mid-1970s. By 1987, however, the murder rate had increased 130 percent from its 1974 level. The murder rates in the United States and Canada had leveled[1] off in the meantime.

Centerwall's study implies that the medium of television, not just the content, promotes violence, and the current study by Dr. Robinson supports that conclusion.

The Turnoff did not specifically target violent television, nor did the following allowance period. Reducing television in general reduces aggressive behavior.

Even television that is not "violent" is more violent than real life and may lead viewers to believe that violence is funny, inconsequential, and a viable solution to problems. Also, watching television of any content robs us of the time to interact with real people.

Watching too much TV may inhibit the skills and patience we need to get along with others without resorting to aggression. TV, as a medium, promotes aggression and violence. The best solution is to turn it off.

Questions 14–20

Complete the summary using words from the box below.

Write your answers in boxes 14–20 on your Answer Sheet.

A study that was published in January 2001 found that when children **14**.......... less, they behaved less **15**.......... . Students in a California elementary school participated in the study, which lasted **16**.......... . By the end of the study, the children's behavior had changed. For example, the children's **17**.......... reported that the children were acting less violently than before. During the study, the children kept a record of the **18**.......... they watched TV. Then, for ten days, they **19**.......... . Near the end of the study, the students began to suggest watching **20**.......... .

parents	eighteen days
teachers	classmates
six months	nonviolent programs
violently	time of day
watched TV	number of hours
scared	avoided TV
less TV	favorite[2] programs

[1]BRITISH: levelled

[2]BRITISH: favourite

Questions 21–24

Do the following statements agree with the information in Reading Passage 2?

In boxes 21–24 write

TRUE	*if the statement is true according to the passage.*
FALSE	*if the statement contradicts the passage.*
NOT GIVEN	*if there is no information about this in the passage.*

21 Only one study has found a connection between TV and violent behavior.

22 There were more murders in Canada after people began watching TV.

23 The United States has more violence on TV than other countries.

24 TV was introduced in South Africa in the 1940s.

Questions 25 and 26

*For each question, choose the correct letter **A–D** and write it in boxes 25 and 26 on your Answer Sheet.*

25 According to the passage,
- **A** only children are affected by violence on TV.
- **B** only violent TV programs cause violent behavior.
- **C** children who watch too much TV get poor grades in school.
- **D** watching a lot of TV may keep us from learning important social skills.

26 The authors of this passage believe that
- **A** some violent TV programs are funny.
- **B** the best plan is to stop watching TV completely.
- **C** it's better to watch TV with other people than on your own.
- **D** seven hours a week of TV watching is acceptable.

READING PASSAGE 3

*You should spend about 20 minutes on **Questions 27–40**, which are based on Reading Passage 3 below.*

Questions 27–30

*Reading Passage 3 has four sections (**A–D**). Choose the most suitable heading for each section from the list of headings below.*

*Write the appropriate numbers (**i–vii**) in boxes 27–30 on your Answer Sheet. There are more headings than sections, so you will not use all of them.*

List of Headings

i Top Ocean Predators
ii Toxic Exposure
iii Declining Fish Populations
iv Pleasure Boating in the San Juan Islands
v Underwater Noise
vi Smog in Large Cities
vii Impact of Boat Traffic

27 Section A

28 Section B

29 Section C

30 Section D

Issues Affecting the Southern Resident Orcas

A

Orcas, also known as killer whales, are opportunistic feeders, which means they will take a variety of different prey species. J, K, and L pods (specific groups of orcas found in the region) are almost exclusively fish eaters. Some studies show that up to 90 percent of their diet is salmon, with chinook salmon being far and away their favorite. During the last 50 years, hundreds of wild runs of salmon have become extinct due to habitat loss and overfishing of wild stocks. Many of the extinct salmon stocks are the winter runs of chinook and coho. Although the surviving stocks have probably been sufficient to sustain the resident pods, many of the runs that have been lost were undoubtedly traditional resources favored by the resident orcas. This may be affecting the whales' nutrition in the winter and may require them to change their patterns of movement in order to search for food.

Other studies with tagged whales have shown that they regularly dive up to 800 feet in this area. Researchers tend to think that during these deep dives the whales may be feeding on bottomfish. Bottomfish species in this area would include halibut, rockfish, lingcod, and greenling. Scientists estimate that today's lingcod population in northern Puget Sound and the Strait of Georgia is only 2 percent of what it was in 1950. The average size of rockfish in the recreational catch has also declined by several inches since the 1970s, which is indicative of overfishing. In some locations, certain rockfish species have disappeared entirely. So even if bottomfish are not a major food resource for the whales, the present low numbers of available fish increases the pressure on orcas and all marine animals to find food. (For more information on bottomfish see the San Juan County Bottomfish Recovery Program.)

B

Toxic substances accumulate in higher concentrations as they move up the food chain. Because orcas are the top predator in the ocean and are at the top of several different food chains in the environment, they tend to be more affected by pollutants than other sea creatures. Examinations of stranded killer whales have shown some extremely high levels of lead, mercury, and polychlorinated hydrocarbons. Abandoned marine toxic waste dumps and present levels of industrial and human refuse pollution of the inland waters probably presents the most serious threat to the continued existence of this orca population. Unfortunately, the total remedy to this huge problem would be broad societal changes on many fronts. But because of the fact that orcas are so popular, they may be the best species to use as a focal point in bringing about the many changes that need to be made in order to protect the marine environment as a whole from further toxic poisoning.

C

The waters around the San Juan Islands are extremely busy due to international commercial shipping, fishing, whale watching, and pleasure boating. On a busy weekend day in the summer, it is not uncommon to see numerous boats in the vicinity of the whales as they travel through the area. The potential impacts from all this vessel traffic with regard to the whales and other marine animals in the area could be tremendous.

The surfacing and breathing space of marine birds and mammals is a critical aspect of their habitat, which the animals must consciously deal with on a moment-to-moment basis throughout their lifetimes. With all the boating activity in the vicinity, there are three ways in which surface impacts are most likely to affect marine animals: (a) collision, (b) collision avoidance, and (c) exhaust emissions in breathing pockets.

The first two impacts are very obvious and don't just apply to vessels with motors. Kayakers even present a problem here because they're so quiet. Marine animals, busy hunting and feeding under the surface of the water, may not be aware that there is a kayak above them and actually hit the bottom of it as they surface to breathe.

The third impact is one most people don't even think of. When there are numerous boats in the area, especially idling boats, there are a lot of exhaust fumes being spewed out on the surface of the water. When the whale comes up to take a nice big breath of "fresh" air, it instead gets a nice big breath of exhaust fumes. It's hard to say how greatly this affects the animals, but think how breathing polluted air affects us (i.e., smog in large cities like Los Angeles, breathing the foul air while sitting in traffic jams, etc).

D

Similar to surface impacts, a primary source of acoustic pollution for this population of orcas would also be derived from the cumulative underwater noise of vessel traffic. For cetaceans, the underwater sound environment is perhaps the most critical component of their sensory and behavioral lives. Orcas communicate with each other over short and long distances with a variety of clicks, chirps, squeaks, and whistles, along with using echolocation to locate prey and to navigate. They may also rely on passive listening as a primary sensory source. The long-term impacts from noise pollution would not likely show up as noticeable behavioral changes in habitat use, but rather as sensory damage or gradual reduction in population health. A new study at The Whale Museum called the SeaSound Remote Sensing Network has begun studying underwater acoustics and its relationship to orca communication.

Questions 31–32

For each question, choose the appropriate letter **A–D** and write it in boxes 31 and 32 on your Answer Sheet.

31 Killer whales (orcas) in the J, K, and L pods prefer to eat
- **A** halibut.
- **B** a type of salmon.
- **C** a variety of animals.
- **D** fish living at the bottom of the sea.

32 Some groups of salmon have become extinct because
- **A** they have lost places to live.
- **B** whales have eaten them.
- **C** they don't get good nutrition.
- **D** the winters in the area are too cold.

Questions 33–40

Complete the chart below.

Choose **NO MORE THAN THREE WORDS** *for each answer.*

Write your answers in boxes 33–40 on your Answer Sheet.

Cause	**Effect**
Scientists believe some whales feed **33**	These whales dive very deep.
Scientists believe that the area is being over fished.	Rockfish caught today is **34** .... than rockfish caught in the past.
Orcas are at the top of the ocean food chain.	**35** .... affects orcas more than it does other sea animals.
Orcas are a **36** .... species.	We can use orcas to make society aware of the problem of marine pollution.
People enjoy boating, fishing, and whale watching in the San Juan Islands.	On weekends there are **37** .... near the whales.
Kayaks are **38**	Marine animals hit them when they come up for air.
A lot of boats keep their motors running.	Whales breathe **39** ....
Boats are noisy.	Whales have difficulty **40** ....

Model Test 1

Candidate Name ____

INTERNATIONAL ENGLISH LANGUAGE TESTING SYSTEM

ACADEMIC WRITING

TIME 1 hour

INSTRUCTIONS TO CANDIDATES

Do not open this booklet until you are told to do so.

Write your name and candidate number in the space at the top of this page.

All answers must be written on the separate answer booklet provided.

Do not remove this booklet from the examination room.

INFORMATION FOR CANDIDATES

There are **2** tasks on this question paper.

You must do **both** tasks.

Underlength answers will be penalized.

WRITING TASK 1

You should spend about 20 minutes on this task.

The table below shows the sales at a small restaurant in a downtown business district.

Summarize the information by selecting and reporting the main features, and make comparisons where relevant.

Write at least 150 words.

Sales: week of October 7–13

	Mon.	Tues.	Wed.	Thurs.	Fri.	Sat.	Sun.
Lunch	$2,400	$2,450	$2,595	$2,375	$2,500	$1,950	$1,550
Dinner	$3,623	$3,850	$3,445	$3,800	$4,350	$2,900	$2,450

WRITING TASK 2

You should spend about 40 minutes on this task.

Write about the following topic:

As the world becomes technologically advanced, computers are replacing more and more jobs.

Describe some job positions that may be lost because of computers, and discuss at least one problem that may result.

Give reasons for your answer and include any relevant examples from your own knowledge or experience.

Write at least 250 words.

SPEAKING

Examiner questions:

Part 1

Let's talk about friendship.
Who is your best friend?
Why do you call this person your best friend?
What makes this friend closer than your other friends?
Do you think it's better to have a large group of friends or a few close friends?
Describe what you and your friends like to do.
Have you remained friends with people from your childhood? Why or why not.
How do people choose their friends?

Part 2

Describe a relative who you are like.

You should say:
who the relative is and how close you are to them
what makes you and your relative alike
why you think you and your relative have these shared qualities

You will have one to two minutes to talk about this topic.
You will have one minute to prepare what you are going to say.

Part 3

Do you enjoy spending time with relatives? Why or why not?
Which of your relatives do you spend the most time with?
Who do you spend the least amount of time with?
When do you and your extended family gather?
What types of traditions do you and your relatives have?
Do you think family members are more important than friends?
Is there anyone in your life who is not related but is considered part of the family anyway?

ACADEMIC MODEL TEST 2

Model Test 2

Candidate Name ________________________________

INTERNATIONAL ENGLISH LANGUAGE TESTING SYSTEM

LISTENING

TIME Approx. 30 minutes

INSTRUCTIONS TO CANDIDATES

Do not open this booklet until you are told to do so.

Write your name and candidate number in the space at the top of this page.

You should answer all questions.

All the recordings will be played ONCE only.

Write all your answers on the Question Paper.

At the end of the test you will be given ten minutes to transfer your answers to an Answer Sheet.

Do not remove this booklet from the examination room.

INFORMATION FOR CANDIDATES

There are **40** questions on this question paper.

The test is divided as follows:

Section 1	Questions 1–10
Section 2	Questions 11–20
Section 3	Questions 21–30
Section 4	Questions 31–40

SECTION 1 *QUESTIONS 1–10*

Questions 1–7

*Choose the correct letters, **A, B, or C.***

EXAMPLE

What is the man doing?
A Shopping at the mall[1]
(B) Asking shoppers questions
C Looking for a certain shop

1 The interviewer wants to find out about
A when the mall is open.
B people's shopping habits.
C the best stores[2] in the shopping center[1].

2 The interviewer wants to speak with
A married women.
B any shopper.
C children.

3 What is the respondent's age?
A 18–25
B 26–35
C 36–45

4 How often does the respondent shop at the mall?
A Less than once a month
B Once a week
C Two or more times a week

5 What does the respondent usually shop for?
A Clothes
B Books
C Groceries

6 How much time does the respondent usually spend at the mall?
A One hour or less
B Between one and two hours
C More than two hours

7 What method of transportation does the respondent use to get to the mall?
A Car
B Bus
C Subway

[1]BRITISH: shopping centre
[2]BRITISH: shops, shoppes

Questions 8–10

Write NO MORE THAN THREE WORDS for each answer.

8 Why does the respondent like the shoe store?

____

9 Why doesn't the respondent like the food court?

____

10 What improvement does the respondent suggest?

____

SECTION 2 *QUESTIONS 11–20*

Question 11

*Choose the correct letter, **A, B, or C.***

11 The tour of the health club is for
- **A** people who want to become members of the club
- **B** people who are already members of the club
- **C** people who work at the club

Questions 12–14

*Choose THREE letters, **A–F.***

What are three things that members can do at the club?
- **A** Learn to play tennis
- **B** Buy exercise equipment
- **C** Consult a nutrition expert
- **D** Exercise on a machine
- **E** Run on a track
- **F** Try out for the swim team

Questions 15–17

*Choose THREE letters, **A–F***

What three things should club members bring with them to the locker room?
- **A** Towels
- **B** Soap
- **C** Shampoo
- **D** Hair dryers
- **E** Rubber sandals
- **F** Locks

Questions 18–20

Complete the notice below.

Write **NO MORE THAN THREE WORDS** *for each answer.*

Swimming Pool Rules

— Children must be accompanied **18** ________________.

— No **19** ________________ near the pool.

— Please **20** ________________ before entering the pool.

SECTION 3 *QUESTIONS 21–30*

Questions 21–22

Write **NO MORE THAN THREE WORDS** *for each answer.*

21 How often will the students have to write essays?

____

22 What should be the word length of each essay?

____

Questions 23–26

Complete the chart below.

Write **NO MORE THAN THREE WORDS** *for each answer.*

Essay Type	**Sample Topic**
23 ________________	How to change the oil in a car
24 ________________	Three kinds of friends
25 ________________	Student cafeteria food and restaurant food
Argumentative	The necessity of **26** ________

Questions 27–30

*Choose the correct letters, **A, B,** or **C.***

27 How will the students get their essay topics?
- **A** The professor will assign them.
- **B** Students will choose them.
- **C** They will come from books.

28 When are the essays due?
- **A** Every Monday
- **B** Every Wednesday
- **C** Every Friday

29 The essays count for __________ percent of the final grade[1].
A 15
B 20
C 65

30 The professor wants the students to
A type their essays on a computer.
B write their essays by hand.
C photocopy their essays.

SECTION 4 *QUESTIONS 31–40*

Questions 31–32

Answer the questions.

Write **NO MORE THAN THREE WORDS** *for each answer.*

31 What is the name of the class? ______________________________

32 What day does the class meet? ______________________________

Questions 33–36

Complete the notes below.

Write **NO MORE THAN THREE WORDS** *for each answer.*

In hunter-gatherer societies, gathering is done by **33** ____________________

All humans lived in hunter-gatherer societies until **34** __________________ ago.

Today we can find hunter-gatherer societies in the Arctic, **35** ______________, and

36 ____________________.

Questions 37–40

The following are characteristics of which types of society?

Check column A if it is a characteristic of hunter-gatherer societies.
Check column B if it is a characteristic of farming societies.

Characteristic	**A**	**B**
37 They usually stay in one place.		
38 They are nomadic.		
39 They have a higher population density.		
40 They have a nonhierarchical social structure.		

[1]BRITISH: mark

Model Test 2

Candidate Name ______________________________

INTERNATIONAL ENGLISH LANGUAGE TESTING SYSTEM

ACADEMIC READING

TIME 1 Hour

INSTRUCTIONS TO CANDIDATES

Do not open this booklet until you are told to do so.

Write your name and candidate number in the space at the top of this page.

Start at the beginning of the test and work through it.

You should answer all questions.

If you cannot do a particular question, leave it and go on to the next. You can return to it later.

All answers must be written on the Answer Sheet.

Do not remove this booklet from the examination room.

INFORMATION FOR CANDIDATES

There are **40** questions on this question paper.

The test is divided as follows:

Reading Passage 1	Questions 1–14
Reading Passage 2	Questions 15–27
Reading Passage 3	Questions 28–40

READING PASSAGE 1

You should spend about 20 minutes on Questions 1–15, which are based on Passage 1 below.

Questions 1–5

Reading Passage 1 has five paragraphs, ***A–E.*** *Choose the most suitable heading for each paragraph from the list of headings below. Write the appropriate numbers (i–viii) on your Answer Sheet. There are more headings than paragraphs, so you will not use them all.*

1 Paragraph A

2 Paragraph B

3 Paragraph C

4 Paragraph D

5 Paragraph E

List of Headings

i Glacial Continents

ii Formation and Growth of Glaciers

iii Glacial Movement

iv Glaciers in the Last Ice Age

v Glaciers Through the Years

vi Types of Glaciers

vii Glacial Effects on Landscape

viii Glaciers in National Parks

Glaciers

A

Besides the earth's oceans, glacier ice is the largest source of water on earth. A glacier is a massive stream or sheet of ice that moves underneath itself under the influence of gravity. Some glaciers travel down mountains or valleys, while others spread across a large expanse of land. Heavily glaciated regions such as Greenland and Antarctica are called *continental glaciers.* These two ice sheets encompass more than 95 percent of the earth's glacial ice. The Greenland ice sheet is almost 10,000 feet thick in some areas, and the weight of this glacier is so heavy that much of the region has been depressed below sea level. Smaller glaciers that occur at higher elevations are called *alpine* or *valley glaciers.* Another way of classifying glaciers is in terms of their internal temperature. In *temperate glaciers,* the ice within the glacier is near its melting point. *Polar glaciers,* in contrast, always maintain temperatures far below melting.

B

The majority of the earth's glaciers are located near the poles, though glaciers exist on all continents, including Africa and Oceania. The reason glaciers are generally formed in high alpine regions is that they require cold temperatures throughout the year. In these areas where there is little opportunity for summer *ablation* (loss of mass), snow changes to compacted *firn* and then crystallized ice. During periods in which melting and evaporation exceed the amount of snowfall, glaciers will retreat rather than progress. While glaciers rely heavily on snowfall, other climactic conditions including freezing rain, avalanches, and wind, contribute to their growth. One year of below average precipitation can stunt the growth of a glacier tremendously. With the rare exception of *surging glaciers,* a common glacier flows about

10 inches per day in the summer and 5 inches per day in the winter. The fastest glacial surge on record occurred in 1953, when the Kutiah Glacier in Pakistan grew more than 12 kilometers in three months.

C

The weight and pressure of ice accumulation causes glacier movement. Glaciers move out from under themselves, via *plastic deformation* and *basal slippage*. First, the internal flow of ice crystals begins to spread outward and downward from the thickened snow pack also known as the *zone of accumulation*. Next, the ice along the ground surface begins to slip in the same direction. Seasonal thawing at the base of the glacier helps to facilitate this slippage. The middle of a glacier moves faster than the sides and bottom because there is no rock to cause friction. The upper part of a glacier rides on the ice below. As a glacier moves it carves out a U-shaped valley similar to a riverbed, but with much steeper walls and a flatter bottom.

D

Besides the extraordinary rivers of ice, glacial erosion creates other unique physical features in the landscape such as horns, fjords, hanging valleys, and cirques. Most of these landforms do not become visible until after a glacier has receded. Many are created by moraines, which occur at the sides and front of a glacier. Moraines are formed when material is picked up along the way and deposited in a new location. When many alpine glaciers occur on the same mountain, these moraines can create a *horn*. The Matterhorn, in the Swiss Alps is one of the most famous horns. *Fjords*, which are very common in Norway, are coastal valleys that fill with ocean water during a glacial retreat. *Hanging valleys* occur when two or more glacial valleys intersect at varying elevations. It is common for waterfalls to connect the higher and lower hanging valleys, such as in Yosemite National Park. A *cirque* is a large bowl-shaped valley that forms at the front of a glacier. Cirques often have a lip on their down slope that is deep enough to hold small lakes when the ice melts away.

E

Glacier movement and shape shifting typically occur over hundreds of years. While presently about 10 percent of the earth's land is covered with glaciers, it is believed that during the last Ice Age glaciers covered approximately 32 percent of the earth's surface. In the past century, most glaciers have been retreating rather than flowing forward. It is unknown whether this glacial activity is due to human impact or natural causes, but by studying glacier movement, and comparing climate and agricultural profiles over hundreds of years, glaciologists can begin to understand environmental issues such as global warming.

Questions 6–10

Do the following statements agree with the information in Passage 1? In boxes 6–10 on your Answer Sheet, write

TRUE *if the statement is true according to the passage.*
FALSE *if the statement contradicts the passage.*
NOT GIVEN *if there is no information about this in the passage.*

6 Glaciers exist only near the north and south poles.

7 Glaciers are formed by a combination of snow and other weather conditions.

8 Glaciers normally move at a rate of about 5 to 10 inches a day.

9 All parts of the glacier move at the same speed.

10 During the last Ice Age, average temperatures were much lower than they are now.

Questions 11–15

Match each definition below with the term it defines.

*Write the letter of the term, **A–H**, on your Answer Sheet. There are more terms than definitions, so you will not use them all.*

11 a glacier formed on a mountain

12 a glacier with temperatures well below freezing

13 a glacier that moves very quickly

14 a glacial valley formed near the ocean

15 a glacial valley that looks like a bowl

Terms

A fjord
B alpine glacier
C horn
D polar glacier
E temperate glacier
F hanging valley
G cirque
H surging glacier

READING PASSAGE 2

You should spend about 20 minutes on Questions 16–28, which are based on Passage 2 below.

Irish Potato Famine

A

In the ten years following the Irish potato famine of 1845, over 750,000 Irish people died, including many of those who attempted to immigrate to countries such as the United States and Canada. Prior to the potato blight, one of the main concerns in Ireland was overpopulation. In the early 1500s, the country's population was estimated at less than three million, but by 1840 this number had nearly tripled. The bountiful potato crop, which contains almost all of the nutrients that a person needs for survival, was largely to blame for the population growth. However, within five years of the failed crop of 1845, the population of Ireland was reduced by a quarter. A number of factors contributed to the plummet of the Irish population, namely the Irish dependency on the potato crop, the British tenure system, and the inadequate relief efforts of the English.

B

It is not known exactly how or when the potato was first introduced to Europe, however, the general assumption is that it arrived on a Spanish ship sometime in the 1600s. For more than one hundred years, Europeans believed that potatoes belonged to a botanical family of a poisonous breed. It was not until Marie Antoinette wore potato blossoms in her hair in the mid-eighteenth century that potatoes became a novelty. By the late 1700s, the dietary value of the potato had been discovered, and the monarchs of Europe ordered the vegetable to be widely planted.

C

By 1800, the vast majority of the Irish population had become dependent on the potato as its primary staple. It wasn't uncommon for an Irish potato farmer to consume more than six pounds of potatoes a day. Families stored potatoes for the winter and even fed potatoes to their livestock. Because of this dependency, the unexpected potato blight of 1845 devastated the Irish. Investigators at first suggested that the blight was caused by static energy, smoke from railroad trains, or vapors from underground volcanoes; however, the root cause was later discovered as an airborne fungus that traveled from Mexico. Not only did the disease destroy the potato crops, it also infected all of the potatoes in storage at the time. Their families were dying from famine, but weakened farmers had retained little of their agricultural skills to harvest other crops. Those who did manage to grow things such as oats, wheat, and barley relied on earnings from these exported crops to keep their rented homes.

D

While the potato blight generated mass starvation among the Irish, the people were held captive to their poverty by the British tenure system. Following the Napoleonic Wars of 1815, the English had turned their focus to their colonial land holdings. British landowners realized that the best way to profit from these holdings was to extract the resources and exports and charge expensive rents and taxes for people to live on the land. Under the tenure system, Protestant landlords owned 95 percent of the Irish land, which was divided up into five-acre plots for the people to live and farm on. As the population of Ireland grew, however, the plots were continuously subdivided into smaller parcels. Living conditions declined dramatically, and families were forced to move to less fertile land where almost nothing but the potato would grow.

E

During this same period of colonization, The Penal Laws were also instituted as a means of weakening the Irish spirit. Under the Penal Laws, Irish peasants were denied basic human rights, such as the right to speak their own native language, seek certain kinds of employment, practice their faith, receive education, and own land. Despite the famine that was devastating Ireland, the landlords had little compassion or sympathy for tenants unable to pay their rent. Approximately 500,000 Irish tenants were evicted by their landlords between 1845 and 1847. Many of these people also had their homes burned down and were put in jail for overdue rent.

F

The majority of the British officials in the 1840s adopted the laissez-faire philosophy, which supported a policy of nonintervention in the Irish plight. Prime Minister Sir Robert Peel was an exception. He showed compassion toward the Irish by making a move to repeal the Corn Laws, which had been put in place to protect British grain producers from the competition of foreign markets. For this hasty decision, Peel quickly lost the support of the British people and was forced to resign. The new Prime Minister, Lord John Russell, allowed assistant Charles Trevelyan to take complete control over all of the relief efforts in Ireland. Trevelyan believed that the Irish situation should be left to Providence. Claiming that it would be dangerous to let the Irish become dependent on other countries, he even took steps to close food depots that were selling corn and to redirect shipments of corn that were already on their way to Ireland. A few relief programs were eventually implemented, such as soup kitchens and workhouses; however, these were poorly run institutions that facilitated the spread of disease, tore apart families, and offered inadequate food supplies considering the extent of Ireland's shortages.

G

Many of the effects of the Irish potato famine are still evident today. Descendants of those who fled Ireland during the 1840s are dispersed all over the world. Some of the homes that were evacuated by absentee landlords still sit abandoned in the Irish hills. A number of Irish descendents still carry animosity toward the British for not putting people before politics. The potato blight itself still plagues the Irish people during certain growing seasons when weather conditions are favorable for the fungus to thrive.

Questions 16–20

*The passage has seven paragraphs, **A–G**.*

Which paragraph contains the following information?

Write the correct letter in boxes 16–20 on your Answer Sheet.

16 the position of the British government towards the potato famine

17 a description of the system of land ownership in Ireland

18 early European attitudes toward the potato

19 explanation of the lack of legal protection for Irish peasants

20 the importance of the potato in Irish society

Questions 21–28

*Complete each sentence with the correct ending, **A–L** from the box at the top of the next page.*

Write the correct letter in boxes 21–28 on your Answer Sheet. There are more endings than sentences, so you won't use them all.

21 At first Europeans didn't eat potatoes

22 European monarchs encouraged potato growing

23 The potato blight was devastating to the Irish

24 Farmers who grew oats, wheat, and barley didn't eat these crops

25 Many Irish farmers lived on infertile plots

26 Many Irish farmers were arrested

27 Sir Robert Peel lost his position as prime minister

28 Soup kitchens and workhouses didn't relieve the suffering

Sentence Endings

A because they couldn't pay the rent on their farms.
B because railroad trains caused air pollution.
C because potatoes were their main source of food.
D because Charles Trevelyan took over relief efforts.
E because they needed the profits to pay the rent.
F because they weren't well-managed.
G because there wasn't enough land for the increasing population.
H because his efforts to help the Irish were unpopular among the British.
I because they believed that potatoes were poisonous.
J because the British instituted penal laws.
K because it was discovered that potatoes are full of nutrients.
L because Marie Antoinette used potato blossoms as decoration.

READING PASSAGE 3

You should spend about 20 minutes on Questions 29–40, which are based on Reading Passage 3.

Anesthesiology

Since the beginning of time, man has sought natural remedies for pain. Between 40 and 60 A.D., Greek physician, Dioscorides traveled with the Roman armies, studying the medicinal properties of plants and minerals. His book, *De materia medica*, written in five volumes and translated into at least seven languages, was the primary reference source for physicians for over sixteen centuries. The field of anesthesiology[1], which was once nothing more than a list of medicinal plants and makeshift remedies, has grown into one of the most important fields in medicine.

Many of the early pain relievers were based on myth and did little to relieve the suffering of an ill or injured person. The mandragora (now known as the mandrake plant) was one of the first plants to be used as an anesthetic[1]. Due to the apparent screaming that the plant made as it was pulled from the ground, people in the Middle Ages believed that the person who removed the mandrake from the earth would either die or go insane. This superstition may have resulted because the split root of the mandrake resembled the human form. In order to pull the root from the ground, the plant collector would loosen it and tie the stem to an animal. It was believed that the safest time to uproot a mandrake was in the moonlight, and the best animal to use was a black dog. In his manual, Dioscorides suggested boiling the root with wine and having a man drink the potion to remove sensation before cutting his flesh or burning his skin. Opium and Indian hemp were later used to induce sleep before a painful procedure or to relieve the pain of an illness. Other remedies such as cocaine did more harm to the patient than good as people died from their addictions. President Ulysses S. Grant became addicted to cocaine before he died of throat cancer in 1885.

[1]BRITISH: anaesthesiology/an anesthetic

The modern field of anesthetics dates to the incident when nitrous oxide (more commonly known as laughing gas) was accidentally discovered. Humphrey Davy, the inventor of the miner's lamp, discovered that inhaling the toxic compound caused a strange euphoria, followed by fits of laughter, tears, and sometimes unconsciousness. U.S. dentist, Horace Wells, was the first on record to experiment with laughing gas, which he used in 1844 to relieve pain during a tooth extraction. Two years later, Dr. William Morton created the first anesthetic machine. This apparatus was a simple glass globe containing an ether-soaked sponge. Morton considered ether a good alternative to nitrous oxide because the numbing effect lasted considerably longer. His apparatus allowed the patient to inhale vapors[1] whenever the pain became unbearable. In 1846, during a trial experiment in Boston, a tumor[2] was successfully removed from a man's jaw area while he was anesthetized with Morton's machine.

The first use of anesthesia in the obstetric field occurred in Scotland by Dr. James Simpson. Instead of ether, which he considered irritating to the eyes, Simpson administered chloroform to reduce the pain of childbirth. Simpson sprinkled chloroform on a handkerchief and allowed laboring[3] women to inhale the fumes at their own discretion. In 1853, Queen Victoria agreed to use chloroform during the birth of her eighth child. Soon the use of chloroform during childbirth was both acceptable and fashionable. However, as chloroform became a more popular anesthetic, knowledge of its toxicity surfaced, and it was soon obsolete.

After World War II, numerous developments were made in the field of anesthetics. Surgical procedures that had been unthinkable were being performed with little or no pain felt by the patient. Rather than physicians or nurses who administered pain relief as part of their profession, anesthesiologists became specialists in suppressing consciousness and alleviating pain. Anesthesiologists today are classified as perioperative physicians, meaning they take care of a patient before, during, and after surgical procedures. It takes over eight years of schooling and four years of residency until an anesthesiologist is prepared to practice in the United States. These experts are trained to administer three different types of anesthetics: general, local, and regional. General anesthetic is used to put a patient into a temporary state of unconsciousness. Local anesthetic is used only at the affected site and causes a loss of sensation. Regional anesthetic is used to block the sensation and possibly the movement of a larger portion of the body. As well as controlling the levels of pain for the patient before and throughout an operation, anesthesiologists are responsible for monitoring and controlling the patient's vital functions during the procedure and assessing the medical needs in the post-operative room.

The number of anesthesiologists in the United States has more than doubled since the 1970s, as has the improvement and success of operative care. In addition, complications from anesthesiology have declined dramatically. Over 40 million anesthetics are administered in the United States each year, with only 1 in 250,000 causing death.

[1]BRITISH: vapours

[2]BRITISH: tumour

[3]BRITISH: labouring

Questions 29–34

Do the following statements agree with the information in Passage 3? In boxes 29–34 on your Answer Sheet, write

TRUE	*if the statement is true according to the passage.*
FALSE	*if the statement contradicts the passage.*
NOT GIVEN	*if there is no information about this in the passage.*

29 Dioscorides' book, *De materia medica*, fell out of use after 60 A.D.

30 Mandragora was used as an anesthetic during the Middle Ages.

31 Nitrous oxide can cause the user to both laugh and cry.

32 During the second half of the 19th century, most dentists used anesthesia.

33 Anesthesiologists in the United States are required to have 12 years of education and training.

34 There are fewer anesthesiologists in the United States now than in the past.

Questions 35–40

Match each fact about anesthesia with the type of anesthetic that it refers to. There are more types of anesthetics listed than facts, so you won't use them all. Write the correct letter, **A–H** in boxes 35–40 on your Answer Sheet.

35 used by sprinkling on a handkerchief

36 used on only one specific part of the body

37 used by boiling with wine

38 used first during a dental procedure

39 used to stop feeling over a larger area of the body

40 used in the first anesthetic machine

Types of Anesthetic

A	general anesthetic
B	local anesthetic
C	regional anesthetic
D	chloroform
E	ether
F	nitrous oxide
G	opium
H	mandrake

Model Test 2

Candidate Name ____

INTERNATIONAL ENGLISH LANGUAGE TESTING SYSTEM

ACADEMIC WRITING

TIME 1 hour

INSTRUCTIONS TO CANDIDATES

Do not open this booklet until you are told to do so.

Write your name and candidate number in the space at the top of this page.

All answers must be written on the separate answer booklet provided.

Do not remove this booklet from the examination room.

INFORMATION FOR CANDIDATES

There are **2** tasks on this question paper.

You must do **both** tasks.

Underlength answers will be penalized.

WRITING TASK 1

You should spend no more than 20 minutes on this task.

The flowchart below shows the process involved in completing the work experience requirement for university students.

Summarize the information by selecting and reporting the main features, and make comparisons where relevant.

You should write at least 150 words.

Fulfilling the Work Experience Requirement
Credits will be awarded when the final report is submitted.

Application

Choose potential workplaces from approved list and arrange interviews. Submit applications to places of interest.

↓

Approval

When acceptance letter is received, submit it to professor for approval.

↓

Schedule

Arrange schedule to work a minimum of 10 hours/ week over 20 weeks.

↓

Reports

Complete weekly Report Form and submit to professor every Friday.

↓

Evaluation

During final work week, participate in evaluation meeting with work supervisor. Supervisor submits Evaluation Form.

↓

Final Report

Submit Final Report before last week of spring term.

WRITING TASK 2

You should spend no more than 40 minutes on this task.

Write about the following topic:

> ***Families who do not send their children to government-financed schools should not be required to pay taxes that support universal education.***

To what extent do you agree or disagree with this statement? Give reasons for your answer, and include any relevant examples from your own knowledge or experience.

You should write at least 250 words.

SPEAKING

Examiner Questions:

Part 1

Let's talk about work.
Do you have a job? Do you like it? Why or why not?
Why did you choose this job?
What kind of education or training did you need to get this job?
If you don't have a job, what kind of job would you like to have?
Why would you like this kind of job?
How can you prepare yourself to get this kind of job?
How do people choose jobs?

Part 2

Describe a holiday[1] that you have celebrated recently.

You should say:
what the purpose of the holiday is
who you celebrated with
why this holiday is important to you

and describe some activities that you did as part of the celebration

You will have one to two minutes to talk about this topic.
You will have one minute to prepare what you are going to say.

Part 3

What are some important holidays in your country?
Why do people celebrate holidays?
Do you think holiday celebrations have changed over the years? Why or why not?
Do you think the importance of holiday celebrations has changed over the years? Why or why not?
How will holidays be different in the future?

[1]AMERICAN and BRITISH: A special day commemorating a religious, historical, social or political event.

ACADEMIC MODEL TEST 3

Model Test 3

Candidate Name ____

INTERNATIONAL ENGLISH LANGUAGE TESTING SYSTEM

LISTENING

TIME Approx. 30 minutes

INSTRUCTIONS TO CANDIDATES

Do not open this booklet until you are told to do so.

Write your name and candidate number in the space at the top of this page.

You should answer all questions.

All the recordings will be played ONCE only.

Write all your answers on the Question Paper.

At the end of the test, you will be given ten minutes to transfer your answers to an Answer Sheet.

Do not remove this booklet from the examination room.

INFORMATION FOR CANDIDATES

There are **40** questions on this question paper.

The test is divided as follows:

Section 1	Questions 1–10
Section 2	Questions 11–20
Section 3	Questions 21–30
Section 4	Questions 31–40

SECTION 1 *QUESTIONS 1–10*

Questions 1–4

Complete the form below. Write NO MORE THAN ONE WORD AND/OR A NUMBER *for each answer.*

Lost Item Report

Day item was lost:
Example *Monday*

Reported by:

Last Name Brown	First name **1** ______________	Phones: Home (not given)
Address **2** __________	High Street, **3** ______________ #5	Office (not given)
City Riverdale		**4** ________ 305–5938

Questions 5–10

Choose the correct letter, ***A, B,*** *or* ***C.***

5 What do the woman's glasses look like?

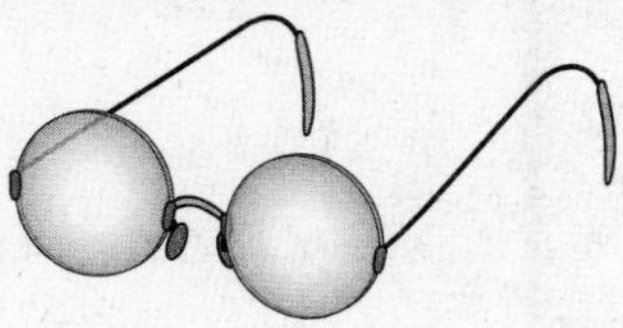

A

B

C

6 Where was the woman sitting when she lost her glasses?
A By the window
B Next to the door
C In the train station

7 What was the woman reading?
A A book
B A newspaper
C A magazine

8 Where was the woman going on the train?
A Home
B To work
C To visit her aunt

9 What time did the train arrive?
A 5:00
B 10:00
C 10:30

10 Where did the woman find her glasses?

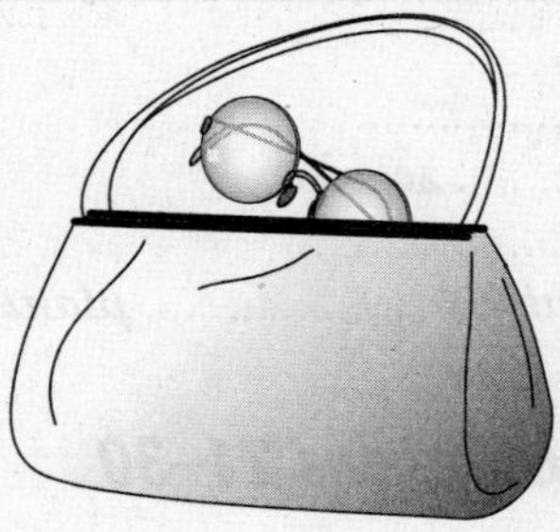

A

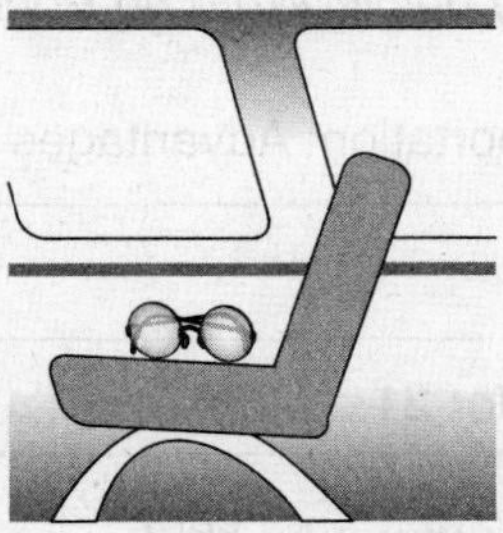

B

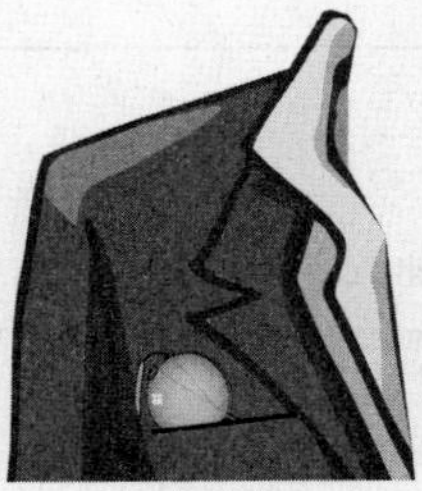

C

SECTION 2 *QUESTIONS 11–20*

Complete the notes. Write **NO MORE THAN THREE WORDS** *for each answer.*

Places to look for housing

Not recommended:

Near university *too expensive*

Downtown[1] 11 ....

12 .... *from the university*

Recommended:

Uptown[2] 13 ....

a lot of buses go there

Greenfield Park *closer to the university*

you need 14 ....

Places to look for ads[3]

15 ....

University newspaper

16 ....

Internet

Available at the Student Counseling Center[4]

city maps

17 *city* ....

18 .... *service*

list of 19 ....

information about 20 .... *plans*

SECTION 3 *QUESTIONS 21–30*

Questions 21–25

Complete the table below. Write **NO MORE THAN THREE WORDS** *for each answer.*

Bicycles as Transportation: Advantages and Disadvantages

Advantages	**Disadvantages**
They are good for **21**	You can't ride in **24** ....
They are **22** .... cars	You can't ride if you have bad health
They don't cause **23**	You can't ride if your trip is **25** ....

[1]BRITISH: city centre

[2]BRITISH: area north of city centre

[3]BRITISH: advertisements/adverts

[4]BRITISH: centre

Questions 26–30

*Complete the notes below. Write **NO MORE THAN THREE WORDS** for each answer.*

<u>Encouraging Bicycle Riding</u>

Cities can:

26 .... on roads

make places to **27** .... at subway stations

provide **28** ....

<u>Bicycling Equipment</u>

Safety: wear a **29** ....

reflective tape

Comfort: light clothes

30 ....

SECTION 4 *QUESTIONS 31–40*

Questions 31–40

*Complete the outline. Write **NO MORE THAN THREE WORDS** for each answer.*

Writing a Research Paper

I. Choose a topic

A Look at **31** ....

B Make topic more specific

C Get **32** ....

II. **33** ....

A. Library

1. Reference and other types of books

2. Journals, **34** ....

3. Atlases and other similar sources

B. Internet

1. Online journals and newspapers

2. Online **35** ....

III. **36** ....

IV. Write an outline

A. Introduction

B. **37** ....

C. **38** ....

V. **39** ....

VI. Write first draft

VII. **40** ....

VIII. Type final draft

Model Test 3

Candidate Name ____

INTERNATIONAL ENGLISH LANGUAGE TESTING SYSTEM

ACADEMIC READING

TIME 1 Hour

INSTRUCTIONS TO CANDIDATES

Do not open this booklet until you are told to do so.

Write your name and candidate number in the space at the top of this page.

Start at the beginning of the test and work through it.

You should answer all questions.

If you cannot do a particular question, leave it and go on to the next. You can return to it later.

All answers must be written on the Answer Sheet.

Do not remove this booklet from the examination room.

INFORMATION FOR CANDIDATES

There are **40** questions on this question paper.

The test is divided as follows:

Reading Passage 1	Questions 1–14
Reading Passage 2	Questions 15–27
Reading Passage 3	Questions 28–40

READING PASSAGE 1

You should spend about 20 minutes on Questions 1–14, which are based on Reading Passage 1 below.

Allergy Testing

Allergic reactions are triggered by the contact, inhalation, or ingestion of a number of different allergens. Some of the most common allergens are made up of proteins found in plants, mold, food, venom, animal skin, and medication. Symptoms of allergic reactions range from mild irritation such as itching, wheezing, and coughing to life-threatening conditions related to the respiratory and gastrointestinal organs. Serious allergic reactions are more likely to result from food, drugs, and stinging insects. A person does not become allergic to a particular substance until after the first exposure. However, in some cases, even trace amounts of a substance, such as peanuts or seafood in a mother's breast milk, can cause an allergic reaction in a subsequent exposure.

A variety of allergy tests are available for determining specific substances that trigger allergic reactions in individuals. Allergists, also known as immunologists, are trained in selecting the types of tests that are both safe and appropriate, depending on the suspected allergies. By using allergen extracts, tiny amounts of commonly bothersome allergens (usually in the form of purified liquid drops), immunologists are often able to isolate which substances cause reactions in allergy sufferers.

One of the most common types of environmental allergy tests is the skin-prick test. This technique involves placing small drops of potential allergen onto the skin of the forearm about one to two inches apart. After the drops are placed on the arm, a needle is used to puncture the skin at the site of each drop. (Though the procedure is virtually painless, this test is often done on the upper back of children to prevent them from seeing the needle.) If an allergy is present, an allergic antibody called *immunoglobulin* E (IgE) will activate a special cell called a *mast* cell. Mast cells release chemicals (also known as *mediators*) that cause itching and swelling. The most common mediator is *histamine*. Histamine is what causes the controlled hive known as a *wheal and flare*. The white wheal is the small raised surface, while the flare is the redness that spreads out from it. In an uncontrolled allergic reaction, wheals and flares can get much bigger and spread all over a person's body. Results from a skin test can usually be obtained within 20 to 30 minutes, while the reaction usually fades within a few hours.

Another test that is very similar to the skin-prick test is the intradermal allergy test. This involves placing the allergen sample under the skin with a syringe. The intradermal test involves more risk and is usually saved for use if the allergy persists even after a skin-prick test comes back negative. People who have experienced serious allergic reactions called anaphylactic reactions are not advised to have these types of tests. These allergy sufferers may be hypersensitive to even trace amount of the allergens when they are introduced into the blood. Anaphylaxis is an allergic reaction that affects the whole body and is potentially life threatening. Hives on the lips and throat can become severe enough to block air passage. Anaphylactic shock occurs when enough histamine is released to cause the blood vessels to dilate and release fluid into the tissues. This lowers blood volume and can result in heart failure.

A blood test can be performed to safely isolate over 400 different allergies, including dangerous food and environmental allergens. The Radio Allergo Sorbant Test (RAST) measures specific IgE antibodies using a blood sample. IgE is normally found in very small amounts in the blood; it is created as a defense[1] mechanism when it senses an intruder. Separate tests are done for each potential allergen, and IgE results are graded from 0 to 6. For example, canine serum IgE will be high if a person has an allergy to dogs. The RAST is used if patients have pre-existing skin conditions or if patients cannot stop taking certain medications such as antidepressants or antihistamines for even a short period of time. (People must stop taking antihistamines several days prior to taking a skin allergy test because the medication can interfere with the results.) The RAST is a more expensive test that does not provide immediate results.

A number of other allergy tests are available, though many are considered unreliable according to *The Academy of Allergy, Asthma, and Immunology*. Applied kinesiology is a test that analyses the loss of muscle strength in the presence of potential allergens. Provocation and neutralization[2] testing involves injecting food allergens into the skin in different quantities, with the goal of determining the smallest dose needed to neutralize the symptoms. Sublingual provocation and neutralization is a similar test, except that the allergens are injected underneath the tongue. Cytotoxity testing involves watching for the reaction of blood cells after placing allergens on a slide next to a person's blood samples.

After using a reliable testing method, the cause of an allergic reaction is often identified, and a physician is able to help a patient develop a treatment plan with the goal of controlling or eliminating the allergic symptoms. Those who are allergic to furry pets, pollen, and plants are prescribed mild medication or taught how to control their reactions with simple lifestyle changes, while those with food allergies learn to safely remove certain foods from their diets. Allergy sufferers who are prone to anaphylactic reactions are educated about life-saving techniques such as carrying the drug epinephrine and wearing medical alert bracelets. As soon as people understand their allergies, they can begin to experience an improved quality of life.

Questions 1–7

The passage describes three different types of allergy tests. Which of the characteristics below belongs to which type of test? In boxes 1–7 on your Answer Sheet, write

A if it is a characteristic of the skin-prick test.
B if it is a characteristic of the intradermal test.
C if it is a characteristic of the blood test.

1 A substance is inserted beneath the skin with a needle.

2 It is often done on a patient's back.

3 It is advisable for patients who have skin problems.

4 It is not advisable for patients who have had serious allergic reactions in the past.

5 It shows results within half an hour.

6 It can cause red and white bumps on the patient's skin.

7 It has a higher cost than other tests.

[1] BRITISH: defence
[2] BRITISH: neutralisation/neutralise

Questions 8–14

Complete the summary of the reading passage below. Choose your answers from the box below, and write them in boxes 8–14 on your Answer Sheet. There are more words than spaces so you will not use them all.

Allergic reactions result from touching, breathing, or **8** .... certain substances called **9** .... Coughing or itching are two possible **10** .... of an allergic reaction. More serious allergic reactions may result from certain insect bites, foods, or **11** .... A severe allergic reaction is known as **12** .... It can result in loss of blood volume and heart failure. Doctors can use a variety of tests to **13** .... the source of an allergy. Treatment may include taking medication or **14** .... the substances that cause the allergic reaction.

mold	medicines	causes
avoiding	anaphylaxis	allergens
antihistamine	identify	treat
smelling	eating	signs

READING PASSAGE 2

You should spend about 20 minutes on Questions 15–27, which are based on Reading Passage 2 below.

The Sacred Pipe

The sacred pipe was one of the most important artifacts of the indigenous people of North America. In almost every culture, the sacred pipe was considered a gift from The Great Spirit. The Cree believed that the pipe, the tobacco, and the fire were given as parting gifts from the Creator, while the Iowa Black Bear clan believed that the pipe bowl and later the pipe stem emerged from the earth as gifts to the earth's first bears. In most cases, the sacred pipe was considered a medium through which humans could pray to The Great Spirit, asking for guidance, health, and the necessities of life. In order for the prayers to reach the Great Spirit, they had to travel in the plumes of smoke from the sacred pipe. Because of its connection to the spiritual world, the pipe was treated with more respect than any human being, especially when the pipe bowl was joined to the stem.

Unlike the common pipe, which was used by average tribesmen for casual smoking purposes, the sacred pipe was built with precise craftsmanship. Before a pipe was carved, the Catlinite (pipestone) was blessed and prayed over. The bowl of the traditional sacred pipe was made of Red Pipestone to represent the Earth. The wooden stem represented all that grew upon the Earth. In the Lakota Society, as in many Native American tribes, the people believed that the pipe bowl also represented a woman while the pipe stem represented a man. Joined together, the pipe symbolized the circle of love between a man and woman. The sacred pipe was the only object that was built by both genders; men carved the bowl and stem while women decorated the pipe with porcupine quills. In many tribes the man and woman held onto the sacred pipe during the marriage ceremony.

Cultivating the tobacco was the responsibility of certain members of the tribe. Generally, tobacco was mixed with herbs, bark, and roots, such as bayberry, mugwort, and wild cherry bark. These mixtures varied depending on the plants that were indigenous to the tribal area. Ceremonial tobacco was much stronger than the type that was used for everyday smoking. Rather than being inhaled, the smoke from the sacred pipe was puffed out the mouth in four directions.

In a typical pipe ceremony, the pipe holder stood up and held the pipe bowl in his left hand, with the stem held toward the East in his right hand. Before adding the first pinch of tobacco to the pipe bowl, he sprinkled some on the ground as an offering to both Mother Earth and The East. The East was acknowledged as the place where the morning star rose. Tribes believed that peace would evolve from wisdom if they prayed to the morning star.

Before offering a prayer to the South, the pipe holder again offered Mother Earth a sprinkling of tobacco and added another pinch into the bowl. The South was believed to bring strength, growth, and healing. While facing west the pipe holder acknowledged Mother Earth and prepared to thank the area where the sun sets. West was where the tribe believed the Spirit Helpers lived. At this time, they prayed for guidance from the spiritual world. The ceremony then proceeded to the North, which was thanked for blanketing Mother Earth with white snow, and for providing health and endurance.

After these four prayers, the pipe holder held the stem to the ground again and the tribe promised to respect and protect Mother Earth. Next, the stem was held up at an angle so that Father Sky could be thanked for the energy and heat he gave to the human body. Finally, the stem was held straight up and the tribe acknowledged The Great Spirit, thanking him for being the creator of Mother Earth, Father Sky, and the four directions.

After the pipe holder had worked his way around the four directions, he lit the pipe and passed it around the sacred circle in the same direction as the ceremonial prayers, starting from the East. Each member took a puff of smoke and offered another prayer. When the pipe had made a full circle, it was capped with bark, and the stem was removed. It was important for the stem and bowl to be stored in separate pockets in a pipe pouch. These pieces were not allowed to touch each other, except during a sacred pipe ceremony.

Pipestone, Minnesota, is considered hallowed ground for North American tribes. Regardless of their conflicts, tribes put their weapons down and gathered in peace in these quarries. According to the Dakota tribe, The Great Spirit once called all Indian nations to this location. Here the Spirit stood on the red pipestone and broke a piece away from the rock to make a giant pipe. He told his people that the red stone was their flesh and that it should be used to make a sacred pipe. He also said that the pipestone belonged to all native tribesmen and that the quarries must be considered a sacred place. Thus, people who had sacred pipes in their possession were considered caretakers, not owners.

Questions 15–19

Choose the correct letters, **A–C**, and write them in boxes 15–19 on your Answer Sheet.

15 The sacred pipe was important in native American cultures because
- **A** it was part of their spiritual practice.
- **B** it was used in gift exchanges between tribes.
- **C** it represented traditional handicrafts.

16 The pipe was made of
A stone and wood.
B bark and roots.
C red clay from the Earth.

17 The pipe was sometimes used at
A funerals.
B births.
C weddings.

18 During the pipe ceremony, tribe members smoked
A plain tobacco.
B a combination of plants.
C only bark.

19 Pipestone, Minnesota, is an important place because it is
A the site of a major battle.
B the origin of the Dakota tribe.
C source of stone for pipes.

Questions 20–27

Complete the flowchart about the pipe ceremony. Write **NO MORE THAN THREE WORDS** *for each answer.*

The pipe holder takes the **20** .... in his left hand and the **21** .... in his other hand.

↓

The pipe holder offers tobacco to Mother Earth and **22** .... , the place where the morning star rises, and then puts some in the pipe.

↓

The pipe holder prays to **23** .... to bring strength, growth, and healing and then prays to the remaining directions.

↓

The pipe holder points the pipe stem down and then up and prays to The Great Spirit, in appreciation for **24** ...., the sky, and **25** ....

↓

The pipe holder passes the pipe around the sacred circle, and all members of the circle **26** .... and pray.

↓

The bowl and stem are **27** .... because they can only touch each other during the ceremony.

READING PASSAGE 3

You should spend about 20 minutes on Questions 28–40, which are based on Reading Passage 3 below.

Bathymetry

The ocean floor is often considered the last frontier on earth, as it is a domain that remains greatly unexplored. Bathymetry, also known as seafloor topography, involves measuring and mapping the depths of the underwater world. Today much of the ocean floor still remains unmapped because collecting bathymetry data in waters of great depth is a time consuming and complex endeavor[1].

Two hundred years ago most people assumed that the ocean floor was similar to the beaches and coastlines. During the nineteenth century attempts to produce maps of the seafloor involved lowering weighted lines from a boat, and waiting for the tension of the line to change. When the hand line hit the ocean floor, the depth of the water was determined by measuring the amount of slack. Each of these measurements was called a sounding, and thousands of soundings had to be done just to get a rough measurement of a small portion of the ocean floor. Besides estimating the depth, these surveys helped in identifying large shipping hazards, especially near the shoreline. A naval officer published the first evidence of underwater mountains in a bathymetric chart in 1855.

During World War I, scientists developed the technology for measuring sound waves in the ocean. Anti-Submarine Detection Investigation Committee (ASDICs) was the original name for these underwater sound projectors, but by World War II the term *sonar* was adopted in the United States and many other nations. Sonar, which stands for Sound, Navigation, and Ranging, was first used to detect submarines and icebergs. By calculating the amount of time it took for a sound signal to reflect back to its original source, sonar could measure the depth of the ocean as well as the depth of any objects found within it. The first sonar devices were passive systems that could only receive sound waves. By the 1930s, single-beam sonar was being used to transmit sound waves in a vertical line from a ship to the seafloor. The sound waves were recorded as they returned from the surface to the ship. However, this type of sonar was more useful in detecting submerged objects than mapping the seafloor. Throughout World War II, technology improved, and active sonar systems that both received and produced sound waves were being used. It was the invention of the acoustic transducer and the acoustic projector that made way for this modern sonar. The newer systems made it possible to identify certain material, such as rock or mud. Since mud absorbed a good portion of a sound signal, it provided a much weaker echo than rocks, which reflected much of the sound wave.

The multibeam sonar, which could be attached to a ship's hull, was developed in the 1960s. With this type of sonar, multiple beams could be adjusted to a number of different positions, and a larger area of the ocean could be surveyed. Maps created with the aid of multibeam sonar helped to explain the formation of ridges and trenches, including the Ring of Fire and the Mid-Ocean Ridge. The Ring of Fire is a zone that circles the Pacific Ocean and is famous for its seismic activity. This area, which extends from the coast of New Zealand to the coast of North and South America, also accounts for more than 75 percent of the world's active and dormant volcanoes. The Mid-Ocean Ridge is a section of undersea mountains that extends over 12,000 feet high and 1,200 miles wide. These mountains, which zigzag around the continents, are generally considered the most outstanding topographical features on earth.

[1]BRITISH: endeavour

The invention of the side scan sonar was another modern breakthrough for the field of bathymetry. This type of sonar is towed on cables, making it possible to send and receive sound waves over a broad section of the seafloor at much lower angles than the multibeam sonar. The benefit of the side scan sonar system is that it can detect very specific features over a large area. The most modern form of bathymetry, which is also the least accurate, is done with data collected by satellite altimetry. This method began to be used in the 1970s. This type of mapping relies on radar altimeters that receive echoes from the sea surface. These signals measure the distance between the satellite and the ocean floor. Unfortunately, due to water vapor[1] and ionization, electromagnetic waves are often decelerated as they move through the atmosphere; therefore, the satellite receives inaccurate measurements. The benefit of using satellites to map the ocean is that it can take pictures of the entire globe, including areas that have not yet been measured by sonar. At this time, satellite altimetry is mainly used to locate areas where detailed sonar measurements need to be conducted.

Due to a constant flux of plate activity, the topography of the seafloor is ever changing. Scientists expect bathymetry to become one of the most important sciences as humans search for new energy sources and seek alternate routes for telecommunication. Preserving the ocean's biosphere for the future will also rely on an accurate mapping of the seafloor.

Questions 28–33

Complete the table below. Write **NO MORE THAN THREE WORDS** *for each answer. Write your answers in boxes 28–33 on your Answer Sheet.*

Mapping the Ocean Floor

Method	First Used . . .	Used for . . .	How It Works
weighted line	**28**......................	measuring **29**......................	drop a line until it hits the bottom
30....................	1930s	detecting objects underwater	send **31**.................. to ocean floor
multibeam sonar	**32**...................... ocean floor	mapping larger areas of the different directions	send multiple sound waves in
satellite altimetry	1970s	taking pictures of **33**......................	send signals from satellite

[1]BRITISH: vapour

Questions 34–37

Match each description below with the ocean region that it describes.

In boxes 34–37 on your Answer Sheet, write

A if it describes the Ring of Fire
B if it describes the Mid-Ocean Ridge

34 It is known for the earthquakes that occur there.

35 It is over one thousand miles wide.

36 It is a mountain range.

37 It contains the majority of the earth's volcanoes.

Questions 38–40

The list below gives some possible reasons for mapping the ocean floor.

Which three of these reasons are mentioned in the reading passage?

*Write the appropriate Roman numerals **i–iv** in boxes 38–40 on your Answer Sheet.*

i Predicting earthquakes
ii Finding new fuel resources
iii Protecting ocean life
iv Understanding weather patterns
v Improving communications systems
vi Improving the fishing industry

Model Test 3

Candidate Name ______________________________

INTERNATIONAL ENGLISH LANGUAGE TESTING SYSTEM

ACADEMIC WRITING

TIME 1 hour

INSTRUCTIONS TO CANDIDATES

Do not open this booklet until you are told to do so.

Write your name and candidate number in the space at the top of this page.

All answers must be written on the separate answer booklet provided.

Do not remove this booklet from the examination room.

INFORMATION FOR CANDIDATES

There are **2** tasks on this question paper.

You must do **both** tasks.

Underlength answers will be penalized.

WRITING TASK 1

You should spend no more than 20 minutes on this task.

The charts below show the percentage of their food budget the average family spent on restaurant meals in different years. The graph shows the number of meals eaten in fast food restaurants and sit-down restaurants.

Summarize[1] the information by selecting and reporting the main features, and make comparisons where relevant.

You should write at least 150 words.

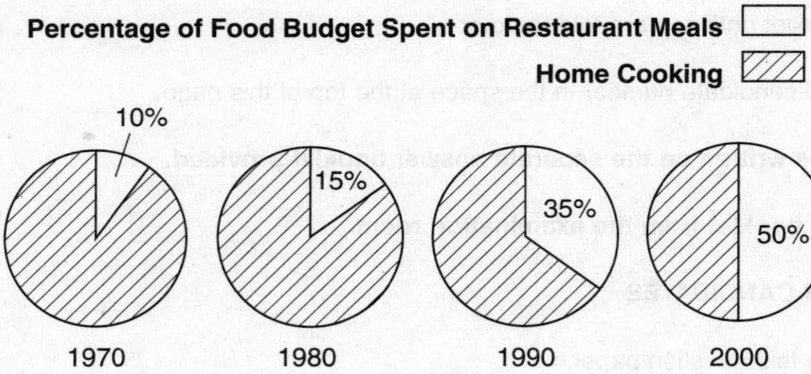

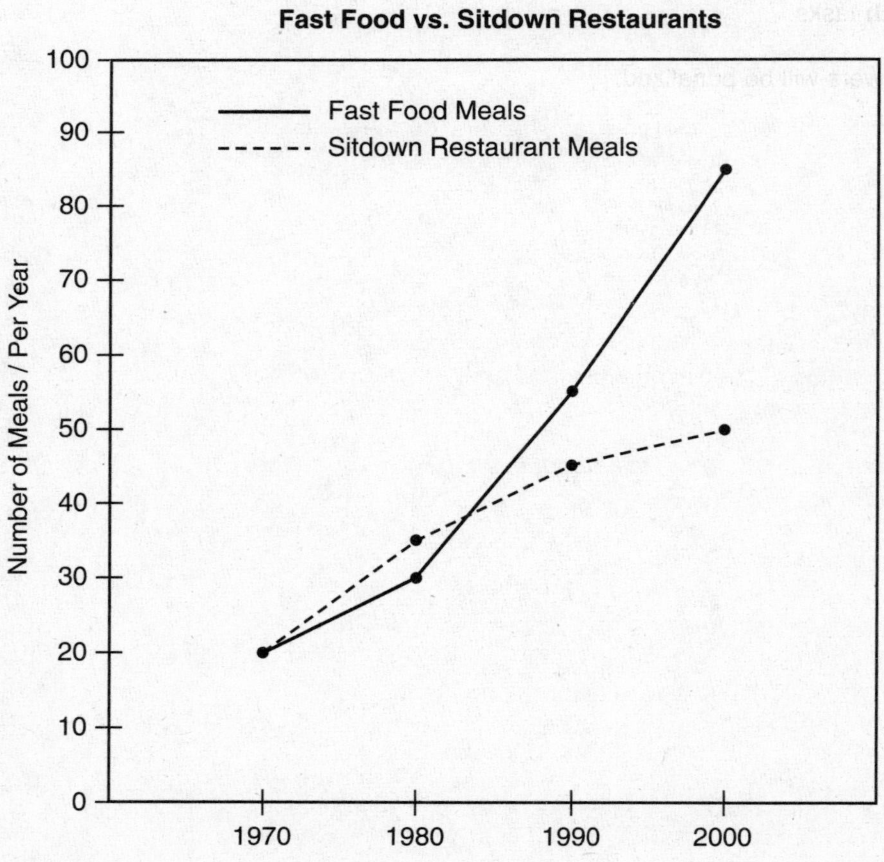

[1]BRITISH: summarise

WRITING TASK 2

You should spend no more than 40 minutes on this task.

Write about the following topic.

> ***By punishing murderers with the death penalty, society is also guilty of committing murder. Therefore, life in prison is a better punishment for murderers.***

To what extent do you agree or disagree with this statement?

Give reasons for your answer and include any relevant examples from your own knowledge or experience.

You should write at least 250 words.

SPEAKING

Examiner Questions:

Part 1

Let's talk about food.
What kind of food do you enjoy eating?
What are some kinds of food you never eat? Why?
Do you generally prefer to eat at home or at a restaurant? Why?
What are some reasons that people eat at restaurants?
Describe a popular food in your country. Why do people like this food?

Part 2

Describe a teacher from your past that you remember.

You should say:
what class the teacher taught you and how old you were
what the teacher's special qualities and characteristics were
why you remember this teacher

You will have one to two minutes to talk about this topic.
You will have one minute to prepare what you are going to say.

Part 3

What kind of person makes a good teacher?
Why do people choose to become teachers?
Do you think education will change in the future? How?
How does technology affect education?

ACADEMIC MODEL TEST 4

Model Test 4

Candidate Name ______________________________

INTERNATIONAL ENGLISH LANGUAGE TESTING SYSTEM

LISTENING

TIME Approx. 30 minutes

INSTRUCTIONS TO CANDIDATES

Do not open this booklet until you are told to do so.

Write your name and candidate number in the space at the top of this page.

You should answer all questions.

All the recordings will be played ONCE only.

Write all your answers on the Question Paper.

At the end of the test, you will be given ten minutes to transfer your answers to an Answer Sheet.

Do not remove this booklet from the examination room.

INFORMATION FOR CANDIDATES

There are **40** questions on this question paper.

The test is divided as follows:

Section 1	Questions 1–10
Section 2	Questions 11–20
Section 3	Questions 21–30
Section 4	Questions 31–40

SECTION 1 *QUESTIONS 1–10*

Questions 1–2

Choose the correct letter, ***A, B,*** *or* ***C.***

EXAMPLE

Where will the man get the information he needs?

A The information desk
B The ticket office
Ⓒ The Special Events Department

1 What does the man want to do?
A Look at art
B Hear a lecture
C Listen to music

2 What day will he get tickets for?
A Thursday
B Saturday
C Sunday

Questions 3–5

Complete the form.

Ticket Order Form

Customer name: Steven **3** ....
Credit card number: **4** ....
Number of tickets: 2
Amount due: **5** £...............................

Questions 6–10

Label the map below. Write the correct place names in boxes 6–10 on your Answer Sheet.

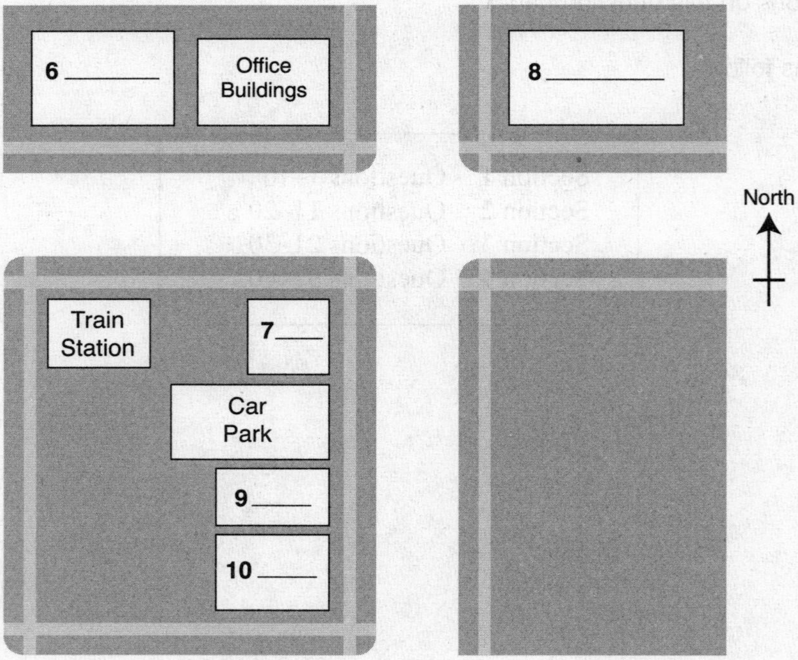

[1]AMERICAN: parking garage

SECTION 2 *QUESTIONS 11–20*

Questions 11–17

Complete the table comparing the two towns. Write NO MORE THAN THREE WORDS for each answer.

	Ravensburg	Blackstone Beach
Population	**11** ____________	12,000
Summer climate	average temp: **12** ________ weather: sunny	average temp: **13** ________ weather: **14** ________
Advantage	**15** ____________	good seafood
Disadvantage	crowded in summer	**16** ____________
Distance from airport	25 kilometers	**17** ____________

Questions 18–20

Which three of the following do tourists usually shop for on Raven Island?

*Write the correct letters, **A–F,** in boxes 18–20 on your Answer Sheet.*

A native handicrafts
B native music
C perfume
D jewelry[1]
E fish
F fishing gear[2]

SECTION 3 *QUESTIONS 21–30*

Questions 21–23

Write NO MORE THAN THREE WORDS for each answer.

21 When is the research project due?

22 What percentage of the final grade[3] does it count for?

23 What topic did Janet choose?

[1]BRITISH: jewellery
[2]BRITISH: tackle
[3]BRITISH: mark

Questions 24–30

Complete the chart showing the steps Janet took to complete her research project.

Write **NO MORE THAN THREE WORDS** *for each answer.*

A. Choose topic

B. Do **24** ________________

C. Choose **25** ________________

D. Submit research **26** ________________

E. Choose subjects

F. **27** ________________

G. Send out **28** ________________

H. **29** ________________ and graphs

I. Write a **30** ________________

SECTION 4 *QUESTIONS 31–40*

Questions 31–34

According to the talk, in which parts of the world do crows live? Choose four places and write the correct letters, ***A–F*** *in boxes 31–34 on your Answer Sheet.*

A North America
B South America
C Antarctica
D Hawaii
E Europe
F Asia

Questions 35–40

Complete the table with information about the American crow.

Write **NO MORE THAN THREE WORDS AND/OR A NUMBER** *for each answer.*

Length	**35** ________ centimeters
Color	**36** ________
Favorite food	corn
Nest material	**37** ________
Nesting place	**38** ________
Number of eggs	**39** ________
Days to hatch	18
Days to fly	**40** ________

Model Test 4

Candidate Name ____

INTERNATIONAL ENGLISH LANGUAGE TESTING SYSTEM

ACADEMIC READING

TIME 1 Hour

INSTRUCTIONS TO CANDIDATES

Do not open this booklet until you are told to do so.

Write your name and candidate number in the space at the top of this page.

Start at the beginning of the test and work through it.

You should answer all questions.

If you cannot do a particular question, leave it and go on to the next. You can return to it later.

All answers must be written on the Answer Sheet.

Do not remove this booklet from the examination room.

INFORMATION FOR CANDIDATES

There are **40** questions on this question paper.

The test is divided as follows:

Reading Passage 1	Questions 1–14
Reading Passage 2	Questions 15–27
Reading Passage 3	Questions 28–40

READING PASSAGE 1

You should spend about 20 minutes on Questions 1–13, which are based on Reading Passage 1.

One Hundred Days of Reform

Since the early 1800s, the term *One Hundred Days* has represented a political phrase, referring to a short period of concentrated political reform. In most cases, this period comes immediately after a new leader takes over a nation. The original Hundred Days took place between March and June of 1815, when Napoleon escaped from Elba, and King Louis XVIII reclaimed his throne. This was one of the results of the Battle of Waterloo. The Hundred Days of Reform in China (also known as the Wuxu Reform) was inspired by a similar event. After losing the Sino-Japanese war, the Emperor Guwangxu found his country to be in a major crisis. Desperate for change, the emperor hired the help of a young political activist named K'ang Yu-wei. At the age of only 27, K'ang had graduated with the highest degree (chin-shih), written two books on reform, and initiated several of his own political reform movements. K'ang impressed the court and convinced the emperor that China, like Japan, should form a constitutional government and do away with its monarchy.

On June 11, 1898, Emperor Guwangxu entrusted the reform movement to K'ang and put the progressive scholar-reformer in control of the government. Immediately, K'ang, with the help of a few other reformers, began work on changing China into a more modern society. Within days, the imperial court issued a number of statutes related to the social and political structure of the nation. First, K'ang planned to reform China's education system. The edicts called for a universal school system with an emphasis on practical and Western studies rather than Neo-Confucian orthodoxy. The new government also wanted to modernize[1] the country's examination systems, and send more students abroad to gain firsthand knowledge of how technology was developing in other countries. K'ang also called for the establishment of a national parliamentary government, including popularly elected members and ministries. Military reform and the establishment of a new defense[2] system as well as the modernization of agriculture and medicine were also on the agenda.

These edicts were threatening to Chinese ideologies and institutions, especially, the army, which at the time was controlled by a few governor-generals. There was intense opposition to the reform at all levels of society, and only one in fifteen provinces made attempts to implement the edicts. The Manchus, who considered the reform a radical and unrealistic idea, suggested that more gradual changes needed to be made. Just three months after the reform had begun, a coup d'etat was organized by Yuan Shikai and Empress Dowager Cixi to force Guangxu and the young reformers out of power and into seclusion. A few of the reformer's chief advocates who refused to leave were executed. After September 21st, the new edicts were abolished, and the conservatives regained their power.

Many Chinese civilians felt that the aftermath of the One Hundred Days of Reform was more detrimental to China than the short-lived failed attempt at reform. Immediately following the conservative takeover, anti-foreign and anti-Christian secret societies tore through northern China targeting foreign concessions and missionary facilities. The violence of these "Boxer bands" provoked retaliation from the offended nations, and the government was forced to declare war on the invaders. By August, an Allied force made up of armies from nine European nations as well as the United States and Japan entered Peking. With little effort,

[1]BRITISH: modernise
[2]BRITISH: defence

north China was occupied, and foreign troops had stationed themselves inside the border. The court was ordered to either execute or punish many of its high officials under the Protocol of 1901. Rather than dividing up the occupied territory among the powers, the Allies settled on an "open door" trade policy. Within a decade, the court ordered many of the original reform measures, including the modernization of the education and military system.

The traditional view of the One Hundred Days of Reform depicted Emperor Guwangxu and K'ang Yu-wei as heroes and Empress Dowager Cixi as the villain who refused to reform even though the change was inevitable. However, since the *One Hundred Days* has turned into a cliché related to political failures, historians in the 20th century often portray the Wuxu Reform as an irrational dream. The fact that the reforms were implemented in a matter of decades, rather than months, suggests that the conservative elites may have been more opposed to the immediacy of the proposed edicts rather than the changes themselves.

Questions 1–4

What were some of the reforms planned during the One Hundred Days of Reform in China? Choose four answers from the list below, and write the correct letters, ***A–F*** *in boxes 1–4 on your Answer Sheet.*

A Modernization of the school system
B Establishment of a parliament
C Focus on the study of Confucianism
D Reorganization of the military
E Abolition of elections
F Improvement of farming
G Initiation of foreign trade

Questions 5–13

Complete the sentences about the reading passage below.

Choose your answers from the box below, and write them in boxes 5–13 on your Answer Sheet. There are more choices than spaces so you will not use them all.

5 China ______________ with Japan.

6 Emperor Guwangxu put K'ang Yu-wei ______________.

7 After June 11, 1898, the reforms ______________.

8 People throughout China ______________.

9 Yuan Shikai and Empress Dowager Cixi ______________.

10 The reforms ______________ after September 21st.

11 Secret societies attacked ______________.

12 European, U.S., and Japanese troops ______________.

13 Eventually, the reforms ______________.

A overthrew the government
B in charge of the reform movement
C were voted in
D in prison
E were abolished
F lost a war
G began trade
H foreigners in China
I were executed
J reform supporters
K occupied China
L were initiated
M opposed the reforms
N were reestablished

READING PASSAGE 2

You should spend about 20 minutes on Questions 14–27, which are based on Reading Passage 2.

Sleep Apnea

Sleep apnea is a common sleeping disorder. It affects a number of adults comparable to the percentage of the population that suffers from diabetes. The term *apnea* is of Greek origin and means "without breath." Sufferers of sleep apnea stop breathing repeatedly while they sleep. This can happen hundreds of times during the night, each gasp lasting from 10 to 30 seconds. In extreme cases, people stop breathing for more than a minute at a time.

There are three different types of sleep apnea, with obstructive sleep apnea being the most common. Obstructive sleep apnea (OSA), which affects 90 percent of sleep apnea sufferers, occurs because of an upper airway obstruction. A person's breathing stops when air is somehow prevented from entering the trachea. The most common sites for air to get trapped include the nasal passage, the tongue, the tonsils, and the uvula. Fatty tissue or tightened muscles at the back of a throat can also cause the obstruction. Central sleep apnea has a different root cause, though the consequences are the same. In central sleep apnea, the brain forgets to send the signal that tells the muscles that it's time to breathe. The term *central* is used because this type of apnea is related to the central nervous system rather than the blocked airflow. The third type of sleep apnea, known as mixed apnea, is a combination of the two and is the most rare form. Fortunately, in all types of apnea, the brain eventually signals for a person to wake up so that breathing can resume. However, this continuous pattern of interrupted sleep is hard on the body and results in very little rest.

Sleep apnea is associated with a number of risk factors, including being overweight, male, and over the age of forty. However, like many disorders, sleep apnea can affect children and in many cases is found to be the result of a person's genetic makeup. Despite being so widespread, this disorder often goes undiagnosed. Many people experience symptoms for their whole lives without realizing they have a serious sleep disorder. Often times, it is not the person suffering from sleep apnea who notices the repetitive episodes of sleep interruption, but a partner or family member sleeping nearby. The air cessation is generally accompanied by heavy snoring, loud enough to rouse others from sleep. Those who live alone are less likely to receive early diagnosis, though other symptoms such as headaches, dizziness, irritability, and exhaustion may cause a person to seek medical advice. If left untreated, sleep apnea, which is a progressive disorder, can cause cardiovascular problems, increasing the risk of heart disease and stroke. Sleep apnea is also blamed for many cases of impaired driving and poor job performance.

In order to diagnose sleep apnea, patients are generally sent to a sleep center for a polysomnography test. This test monitors brain waves, muscle tension, breathing, eye movement, and oxygen in the blood. Audio monitoring for snoring, gasping, and episodic waking is also done during a polysomnogram. Nonintrusive solutions for treating sleep apnea involve simple lifestyle changes. In many cases, symptoms of sleep apnea can be eliminated when patients try losing weight or abstaining from alcohol. People who sleep on their backs or stomachs often find that their symptoms disappear if they try sleeping on their sides. Sleep specialists also claim that sleeping pills interfere with the natural performance of the throat and mouth muscles and suggest patients do away with all sleep medication for a trial period. When these treatments prove unsuccessful, sleep apnea sufferers can be fitted with a CPAP mask, which is worn at night over the mouth and nose, similar to an oxygen mask. CPAP stands for Continuous Positive Airway Pressure.

In extreme cases, especially when facial deformities are the cause of the sleep apnea, surgery is needed to make a clear passage for the air. Many different types of surgeries are available. The most common form of surgery used to combat sleep apnea is uvulo-palato-pharyngoplasty (UPPP). This procedure involves removing the uvula and the excess tissue around it. UPPP helps about 50 percent of patients who undergo the procedure, while the other half continue to rely on the CPAP machine even after the surgery. Another type of surgery called mandibular myotomy involves removing a piece of the jaw, and adjusting the tongue. By reattaching[1] the tongue to a position about ten millimeters forward, air is able to flow more freely during sleep. This delicate procedure is performed only by surgeons with expertise in facial surgery and is almost always successful in eliminating the air obstruction. The latest surgical procedures use radio frequencies to shrink the tissue around the tongue, throat, and soft palate.

Questions 14–18

The passage describes three different types of sleep apnea. Which of the characteristics below belongs to which type of sleep apnea? In boxes 14–18 on your Answer Sheet, write

A if it is a characteristic of obstructive sleep apnea.
B if it is a characteristic of central sleep apnea.
C if it is a characteristic of mixed apnea.

14 Its root cause is a blockage at the trachea.

15 It is connected exclusively with the nervous system.

16 It involves blocked airflow and a brain malfunction.

17 It is the most unusual type of sleep apnea.

18 It is the most common form of sleep apnea.

Questions 19–23

Do the following statements agree with the information in Reading Passage 2?

In boxes 19–23 on your Answer Sheet, write

TRUE *if the statement is true according to the passage.*
FALSE *if the statement contradicts the passage.*
NOT GIVEN *if there is no information about this in the passage.*

19 Sleep apnea only affects men over 40.

20 Most people with sleep apnea have the problem diagnosed.

[1]BRITISH: re-attaching

21 Often a relative of the sleep apnea sufferer is the first to notice the problem.

22 Sleep apnea is more common in Greece than in other countries.

23 Sleep apnea can cause problems at work.

Questions 24–27

Which treatments for sleep apnea are mentioned in the passage?

*Choose four answers from the list below, and write the correct letters, **A–G,** in boxes 1–4 on your Answer Sheet.*

A getting surgery
B wearing a mask
C taking sleeping pills
D reducing one's weight
E massaging the throat muscles
F sleeping on one's side
G drinking moderate amounts of alcohol

READING PASSAGE 3

You should spend about 20 minutes on Questions 28–40, which are based on Reading Passage 3.

Adult Intelligence

Over 90 years ago, Binet and Simon delineated two different methods of assessing intelligence. These were the psychological method (which concentrates mostly on intellectual processes, such as memory and abstract reasoning) and the pedagogical method (which concentrates on assessing what an individual knows). The main concern of Binet and Simon was to predict elementary school performance independently from the social and economic background of the individual student. As a result, they settled on the psychological method, and they spawned an intelligence assessment paradigm which has been substantially unchanged from their original tests.

With few exceptions, the development of adult intelligence assessment instruments proceeded along the same lines of the Binet-Simon tests. Nevertheless, the difficulty of items was increased for older examinees. Thus, extant adult intelligence tests were created as little more than upward extensions of the original Binet-Simon scales. The Binet-Simon tests are quite effective in predicting school success in both primary and secondary educational environments. However, they have been found to be much less predictive of success in post-secondary academic and occupational domains. Such a discrepancy provokes fundamental questions about intelligence. One highly debated question asks whether college success is actually dependent on currently used forms of measured intelligence, or if present measures of intelligence are inadequately sampling the wider domain of adult intellect. One possible answer to this question lies in questioning the preference of the psychological method over the pedagogical method for assessing adult intellect. Recent research across the fields of education, cognitive science, and adult development suggests that much of adult intellect is indeed not adequately sampled by extant intelligence measures and might be better assessed through the pedagogical method (Ackerman, 1996; Gregory, 1994).

Several lines of research have also converged on a redefinition of adult intellect that places a greater emphasis on content (knowledge) over process. Substantial strides have been made in delineating knowledge aspects of intellectual performance which are divergent from traditional measures of intelligence (e.g., Wagner, 1987) and in demonstrating that adult performance is greatly influenced by prior topic and domain knowledge (e.g., Alexander et al., 1994). Even some older testing literature seems to indicate that the knowledge measured by the Graduate Records Examination (GRE) is a comparable or better indicator of future graduate school success and post-graduate performance than traditional aptitude measures (Willingham, 1974).

Knowledge and Intelligence

When an adult is presented with a completely novel problem (e.g., memorizing a random set of numbers or letters), the basic intellectual processes are typically implicated in predicting which individuals will be successful in solving problems. The dilemma for adult intellectual assessment is that the adult is rarely presented with a completely novel problem in the real world of academic or occupational endeavors[1]. Rather, the problems that an adult is asked to solve almost inevitably draw greatly on his/her accumulated knowledge and skills—one does not build a house by only memorizing physics formulae. For an adult, intellect is better conceptualized by the tasks that the person can accomplish and the skills that he/she has developed rather than the number of digits that can be stored in working memory or the number of syllogistic reasoning items that can be correctly evaluated. Thus, the content of the intellect is at least as important as the processes of intellect in determining an adult's real-world problem solving efficacy.

From the artificial intelligence field, researchers have discarded the idea of a useful General Problem Solver in favor[2] of knowledge-based expert systems. This is because no amount of processing power can achieve real-world problem solving proficiency without an extensive set of domain-relevant knowledge structures. Gregory (1994) describes the difference between such concepts as "potential intelligence" (knowledge) and "kinetic intelligence" (process). Similarly, Schank and Birnbaum (1994) say that "what makes someone intelligent is what he [/she] knows."

One line of relevant educational research is from the examination of expert-novice differences which indicates that the typical expert is found to mainly differ from the novice in terms of experience and the knowledge structures that are developed through that experience rather than in terms of intellectual processes (e.g., Glaser, 1991). Additional research from developmental and gerontological perspectives has also shown that various aspects of adult intellectual functioning are greatly determined by knowledge structures and less influenced by the kinds of process measures which have been shown to decline with age over adult development (e.g., Schooler, 1987; Willis & Tosti-Vasey, 1990).

Shifting Paradigms

By bringing together a variety of sources of research evidence, it is clear that our current methods of assessing adult intellect are insufficient. When we are confronted with situations in which the intellectual performance of adults must be predicted (e.g., continuing education or adult learning programs), we must begin to take account of what they know in addition to the traditional assessment of intellectual processes. Because adults are quite diverse in their

[1]BRITISH: endeavours

[2]BRITISH: favour

knowledge structures (e.g., a physicist may know many different things than a carpenter), the challenge for educational assessment researchers in the future will be to develop batteries of tests that can be used to assess different sources of intellectual knowledge for different individuals. When adult knowledge structures are broadly examined with tests such as the Advanced Placement [AP] and College Level Exam Program [CLEP], it may be possible to improve such things as the prediction of adult performance in specific educational endeavors, the placement of individuals, and adult educational counseling.

Questions 28–34

Complete the sentences about the reading passage below.

Choose your answers from the box below, and write them in boxes 28–34 on your Answer Sheet. There are more choices than sentences so you will not use them all.

28 The psychological method of intelligence assessment measures ____________.

29 Binet and Simon wanted to develop an assessment method that was not influenced by the child's ____________.

30 The Binet-Simon tests have been successfully used to predict ____________.

31 The Binet-Simon tests are not good predictors of ____________.

32 According to ____________, the pedagogical method is the best way to assess adult intelligence.

33 The pedagogical method is a better measure of adult intelligence because most problems that adults encounter in real life are not completely ____________.

34 In the area of artificial intelligence, ____________ systems are preferred.

A tests	**H** thought processes
B psychological issues	**I** Ackerman and Gregory
C new	**J** social class
D potential for achievement in school	**K** recent research
E knowledge-based	**L** future job performance
F knowledge	**M** problem solving
G Binet and Simon	

Questions 35–39

Do the following statements agree with the information in Reading Passage 3?

In boxes 35–39 on your Answer Sheet, write

TRUE	*if the statement is true according to the passage.*
FALSE	*if the statement contradicts the passage.*
NOT GIVEN	*if there is no information about this in the passage.*

35 The Binet-Simon tests have not changed significantly over the years.

36 Success in elementary school is a predictor of success in college.

37 Research suggests that experts generally have more developed intellectual processes than novices.

38 Knowledge structures in adults decrease with age.

39 Better methods of measuring adult intelligence need to be developed.

Question 40

Choose the correct letter, ***A–C****, and write it in box 40 on your Answer Sheet.*

40 The Advanced Placement and College Level Exam Program tests measure

A thought processes.
B job skills.
C knowledge.

Model Test 4

Candidate Name ____

INTERNATIONAL ENGLISH LANGUAGE TESTING SYSTEM

ACADEMIC WRITING

TIME 1 hour

INSTRUCTIONS TO CANDIDATES

Do not open this booklet until you are told to do so.

Write your name and candidate number in the space at the top of this page.

All answers must be written on the separate answer booklet provided.

Do not remove this booklet from the examination room.

INFORMATION FOR CANDIDATES

There are **2** tasks on this question paper.

You must do **both** tasks.

Underlength answers will be penalized.

WRITING TASK 1

You should spend about 20 minutes on this task.

Write about the following topic:

The table below shows the sales made by a coffee shop in an office building on a typical weekday.

Summarize the information by selecting and reporting the main features, and make comparisons where relevant.

You should write at least 150 words.

	Coffee	Tea	Pastries	Sandwiches
7:30–10:30	265	110	275	50
10:30–2:30	185	50	95	200
2:30–5:30	145	35	150	40
5:30–8:30	200	75	80	110

WRITING TASK 2

You should spend no more than 40 minutes on this task.

Write about the following topic.

More and more people are relying on the private car as their major means of transportation.

Describe some of the problems overreliance on cars can cause, and suggest at least one possible solution.

Give reasons for your answer and include any relevant examples from your own knowledge or experience.

You should write at lest 250 words.

SPEAKING

Examiner Questions:

Part 1

Let's talk about housing.
Where do you live now?
Who do you live with?
What kind of place do you live in (a house or an apartment)?
Do you think it's better to live in a house or an apartment? Why?
Describe your neighborhood.
Do you like it? Why or why not?
How do people choose their place to live?

Part 2

Describe a gift you have received that was important to you.

You should say:
- who gave it to you and for what occasion
- what it looks like and how you use it
- why it is important to you

You will have one to two minutes to talk about this topic.
You will have one minute to prepare what you are going to say.

Part 3

Do you enjoy giving and receiving gifts? Why or why not?
Who usually gives you gifts?
Who do you give gifts to?
In your country when do people usually give gifts?
What kinds of gifts do they give?
Do you think gift-giving customs are different now than they were in the past? How?
Do you think they will change in the future? How?

IELTS MODEL TESTS

GENERAL TRAINING
READING
WRITING
MODEL TEST 1

General Training Model Test 1

Candidate Name ______________________________

INTERNATIONAL ENGLISH LANGUAGE TESTING SYSTEM

GENERAL TRAINING READING

TIME 1 Hour

INSTRUCTIONS TO CANDIDATES

Do not open this booklet until you are told to do so.

Write your name and candidate number in the space at the top of this page.

Start at the beginning of the test and work through it.

You should answer all questions.

If you cannot do a particular question, leave it and go on to the next. You can return to it later.

All answers must be written on the answer sheet.

Do not remove this booklet from the examination room.

INFORMATION FOR CANDIDATES

There are **40** questions on this question paper.

The test is divided as follows:

Section 1	Questions 1–14
Section 2	Questions 15–27
Section 3	Questions 28–40

SECTION 1 *QUESTIONS 1–14*

You are advised to spend 20 minutes on questions 1–14.

Questions 1–7

*Look at the five apartment advertisements **A–E**.*

Write the letters of the appropriate advertisements in boxes 1–7 on your answer sheet. You may use any letter more than once.

Which apartment is appropriate for a person who

1 owns a car?

2 is a university student?

3 has children?

4 likes to swim?

5 usually uses public transportation?

6 wants to rent for two months only?

7 often entertains large groups of people?

A Sunny 1 bedroom, central location, washer/dryer in building. Storage space, parking included in rent. One year lease required. Call 837–9986 before 6 P.M.

B Cozy one bedroom with study available in elevator building[1]. Near City Park. Amenities include exercise room, pool, and party room. Other apartments also available. One- and two-year leases. Call 592–8261.

C Small one-bedroom, reasonable rent, near shopping, bus routes, university. References required. No pets. Call Mr. Watkins 876–9852.

D Don't miss this unique opportunity. Large two-bedroom plus study, which could be third bedroom. Quiet neighborhood. Walk to elementary and high school, park, shops. Small pets allowed.

E Furnished flats[2], convenient to central business district. Studios, one-, and two-bedrooms. Weekly and monthly rentals available. Call our office 376–0923 9–5 M–F.

[1]BRITISH: Building with lift

[2]AMERICAN: apartments

Questions 8–14

Thank you for buying a Blau Automatic Coffeemaker. If you use and maintain your Blau product correctly, you will enjoy it for years to come.

A Preparing Coffee with Your Blau Coffeemaker
Your coffeemaker is guaranteed to make a perfect cup of coffee every time. First, fill the reusable coffee basket with coffee grounds, adding two tablespoons of grounds per cup. Next, fill the reservoir with eight ounces of water for each cup of coffee. Place the coffee pot under the coffee basket, making sure that it is directly underneath the drip spout. Press the "on" button located on the coffeemaker's base.

B Built-in Convenience
Your Blau Coffeemaker is equipped with a built-in timer. You can set the timer so that your coffee is ready when you get up in the morning, when you return from work in the evening, or at any other time you choose. Just follow the directions above for preparing your coffee. Then set the timer by pushing the button underneath the clock at the front of the coffeemaker. Push twice to put the clock in timer mode. The minutes will flash. Push the button until the minutes are set. Push twice again and the hours will flash. Push the button until the hours are set. Push twice to return the timer to clock mode.

C Maintaining Your Coffeemaker
Monthly cleaning will keep your coffeemaker functioning properly and your coffee tasting fresh. Just follow these easy steps. Fill the reservoir with a small bottle of vinegar. Turn your coffeemaker on and let the vinegar run through it, filling the coffeepot. Then fill the reservoir with fresh water and let it run through the coffeemaker. Do this twice to make sure all traces of vinegar are removed.

D Really Fresh Coffee
If your Blau Coffeemaker came equipped with a coffee grinder, then you can enjoy extra fresh coffee every day. Simply add whole beans to the grinder compartment, being careful not to pass the "full" line below the rim. Make sure the lid is securely in place, then press the "grind" button.

E Our Guarantee
Your Blau Coffeemaker has a lifetime guarantee. If your coffeemaker suffers any type of malfunction, just call our toll-free customer service line at 888–936–8721, 24 hours a day. If we are unable to help you over the phone, you may have to mail the coffee grinder to us for service.

Questions 8–11

Match each picture below with the appropriate section in the instructions.

Write the correct letter, ***A–E*** *in boxes 8–11 on your Answer Sheet.*

8

9

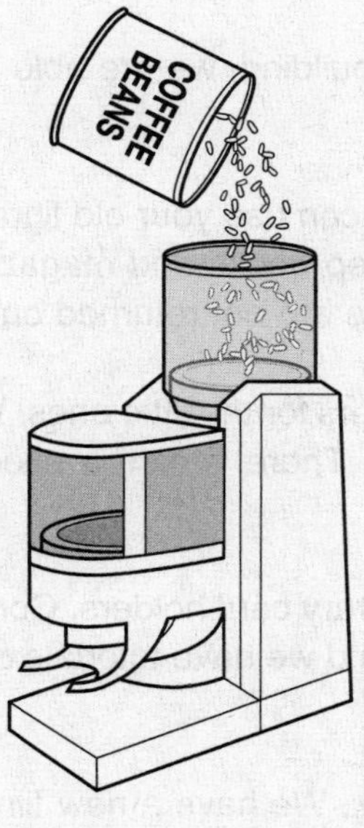

10

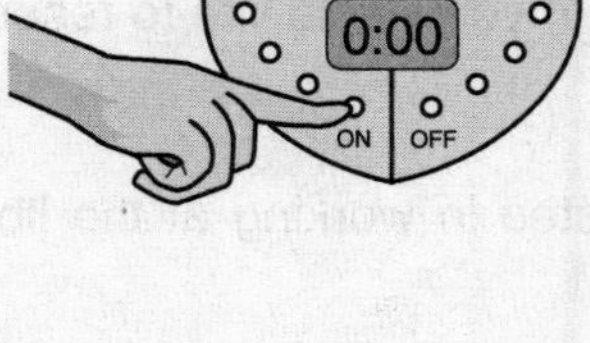

11

Questions 12–14

Answer the questions using **NO MORE THAN THREE WORDS** *for each answer. Write your answers in boxes 12–14 on your Answer Sheet.*

12 How much water should you use to make one cup of coffee?

13 How often should you clean the coffeemaker?

14 When can you call the company for assistance?

SECTION 2 *QUESTIONS 15–27*

You are advised to spend 20 minutes on questions 15–27.

Questions 15–20

Look at the information about the library.

*There are six paragraphs **A–F**.*

Choose the most suitable heading for each paragraph from the list below.

*Write the appropriate numbers (**i–vii**) in boxes 15–20 on your Answer Sheet. There are more headings than paragraphs, so you won't need to use them all.*

15 Paragraph A

16 Paragraph B

17 Paragraph C

18 Paragraph D

19 Paragraph E

20 Paragraph F

List of Headings

i	Places for Meetings
ii	Services for Children
iii	New Authors
iv	Borrowing Library Materials
v	Employment Opportunities
vi	Getting Online
vii	Cultural Events
viii	Using Library Computers

Windsor Library
Welcome to the new Windsor Library. Now that we have moved into our new building, we are able to bring you expanded services and new opportunities.

A We have added many new titles to our book and periodical collection. You can use your old library card at the new facility, and the check-out rules remain the same. You may keep books and magazines for four weeks, and videos and CDs for one week. You will be fined if materials are not returned on time.

B We are always adding to our collection of picture books and beginning readers for the little ones. We now have a story hour twice a week, on Monday and Wednesday afternoons. There is also a special film series for ages 5–8 on the first Saturday of every month.

C We continue to have free Internet access available to all Windsor Public Library card holders. Computers are also available to library patrons for word processing and other needs, and we have tutorials on using the world wide web, basic word processing, and beginning keyboarding.

D Don't forget to pick up your monthly events brochure at the check-out desk. We have a new film series as well as book signings by local authors and occasional concerts by both visiting and local musicians.

E The new library has several conference rooms available to library patrons. If you would like to reserve a room for your group or club, please inquire at the check-out desk.

F There are a number of library staff positions available. If you are interested in working at the library, please ask for a job application at the Human Resources office.

Questions 21–27

Read the text below about a language school.

New World Language Center

As a student at the New World Language Center, you are entitled to use the school's facilities and participate in extracurricular activities.

Building Guide

All classrooms are located on the first and second floors of the building. The language lab is located in room 243 on the second floor and is open from 9 to 5 Monday through Friday and 9 to 12 on Saturday. Use of the language lab is included in your class tuition. Students enrolled in classes are also entitled to free use of the school's multilingual DVD collection. This is located in room 245 right next to the language lab. You may borrow DVDs to take home for a week at a time.

The International Café is located on the third floor, room 306, next to the counselor's[1] office. The hours are Monday–Friday from 11 to 8, and Saturdays from 10 to 2. There is no fee for counseling services. If you need help choosing classes, please drop by the office to make an appointment. The school bookstore is located on the first floor, next to the main entrance. All required texts for our classes are available there. You can also buy New World Language Center T-shirts, shopping bags, and classroom supplies.

Activities

The school organizes[2] weekly trips to museums, embassies, film festivals, and other locations of cultural interest. You can sign up for these trips in the counselor's office. There is a nominal fee for trip participation. The monthly International Banquet is open to all students. You can buy tickets from your teacher or in the counselor's office.

Questions 21–24

On which floor of the school building can you do each of the following activities.

Complete the chart below. Write a floor number for each answer.

Write your answers in boxes 21–24 on your Answer Sheet.

Floor	Activity
(example) *second*	use the language lab
21	borrow a DVD
22	have a snack
23	buy a shirt
24	sign up for a trip

[1]BRITISH: counsellor's/counselling

[2]BRITISH: organises

Questions 25–27

*Choose the correct answer. Write the correct letter, **A–C**, in boxes 25–27 on your Answer Sheet.*

25 Which day is the language lab closed?
A Monday
B Saturday
C Sunday

26 Which of the following is free for students?
A School T-shirts
B Trips to museums
C Advice from counselors

27 What happens once a month?
A There are new classes.
B There is a special dinner.
C There is a film festival.

SECTION 3 *QUESTIONS 28–40*

You should spend 20 minutes on Questions 28–40, which are based on the reading passage below.

Questions 28–33

Reading Passage 3 has six sections, **A–F**.

*Choose the correct heading for sections **A–F** from the list of headings below.*

*Write the correct number **i–ix** in boxes 28–33 on your Answer Sheet.*

28 Section **A**

29 Section **B**

30 Section **C**

31 Section **D**

32 Section **E**

33 Section **F**

List of Headings

i	Newer Subway[1] Systems
ii	Early Subways in the Americas
iii	Asian Subway Systems
iv	A New Device
v	The Longest Subway
vi	Subway Art
vii	Europe's First Subways
viii	The World's Largest Subways
ix	The Moscow Metro

A

People have been traveling by subway for well over a hundred years. The first subway systems began operating in Europe in the second half of the nineteenth century. London's subway system, known as "The Underground" or "The Tube," opened in early 1863. In 1896, subways began running in both Budapest, Hungary and Glasgow, Scotland. The Budapest subway ran from the center of the city to City Park and was just under four kilometers long.

[1]BRITISH: underground

The city of Paris, France began operating its subway system in 1900. Its famous name, Metro, is short for *Chemin de Fer Metropolitan* or Metropolitan Railway. Many other cities have since adopted the name Metro for their own subways.

B

The city of Boston, Massachusetts boasts the oldest subway system in the United States, beginning operations in 1897. It had only two stations when it first opened. The New York City Subway, now one of the largest subway systems in the world, began running in 1904. The original line was 14.5 kilometers long and ran from City Hall in downtown Manhattan to 145th Street. The city of Philadelphia opened its first subway line in 1907. The oldest subway in Latin America began operations in Buenos Aires, Argentina in 1913. It is called the *subte*, short for *subterraneo* or underground.

C

The second half of the twentieth century saw new subway systems constructed in cities around the world. Many Korean cities have modern subway systems, the largest one in the capital city of Seoul, with 287 kilometers of track. The first subway in Brazil opened in the city of Sao Paulo in 1974. Since then subways have been built in a number of other Brazilian cities, including Rio de Janeiro and the capital, Brasilia. Washington, DC began running the Washington Metro in 1976. Hong Kong opened its subway in 1979. This system includes four lines that run under Victoria Harbour. In 2000, a 17-mile long subway system was completed in Los Angeles, a city infamous for its traffic problems and resulting smog. Construction of this system took fourteen years to complete.

D

With a total of 468 stations and 656 miles of passenger service track, the New York City Subway is among the largest subway systems in the world. If the tracks in train yards, shops, and storage areas are added in, the total track length of the New York Subway comes to 842 miles. Measured by number of riders, the Moscow Metro is the world's largest system, with 3.2 billion riders annually. Other cities with busy subways include Tokyo, with 2.6 billion riders a year, and Seoul and Mexico City, both carrying 1.4 billion riders annually.

E

In some cities, the subway stations are famous for their architecture and artwork. The stations of the Moscow Metro are well-known for their beautiful examples of socialist-realist art. The Baker Street station in London honors the fictional detective, Sherlock Holmes, who supposedly lived on Baker Street. Decorative tiles in the station's interior depict the character, and a Sherlock Holmes statue sits outside one of the station exits. Each of the stations of the new Los Angeles subway system contains murals, sculptures, or other examples of decorative artwork.

F

A new feature now often included in the construction of new subway stations is the Platform Screen Door (PSD). The Singapore subway was the first to be built with the inclusion of PSDs. The original purpose was to reduce high air-conditioning costs in underground stations. Since then, there has been more and more focus on the safety aspects of this device, as it can prevent people from accidentally falling or being pushed onto the track. PSDs also keep the station platforms quieter and cleaner and allow trains to enter stations at higher rates of speed. The subway system in Hong Kong was the first to have PSDs added to an already existing system. They are becoming more common in subway systems around the world. Tokyo, Seoul, Bangkok, London, and Copenhagen are just some of the cities that have PSDs in at least some of their subway stations. PSDs are also often used with other forms of transportation, such as monorails, light rail systems, and airport transportation systems.

Questions 34–40

Look at the following descriptions (Questions 33–40) of some of the subway systems mentioned in Reading Passage 3.

*Match the cities (**A–L**) listed below with the descriptions of their subway systems.*

*Write the appropriate letters **A–L** in boxes 33–40 on your Answer Sheet.*

33 has a station celebrating a storybook character

34 is the busiest subway system in the world

35 has lent its name to subway systems around the world

36 has several lines running under water

37 was the first subway system constructed with PSDs

38 has a total length of 287 kilometers

39 was the first subway built in Latin America

40 opened in 1976

A Hong Kong
B Paris
C Washington
D Sao Paulo
E London
F Tokyo
G Seoul
H Buenos Aires
I Singapore
J Budapest
K Moscow
L New York

GENERAL TRAINING Model Test 1

Candidate Name ______________________________

INTERNATIONAL ENGLISH LANGUAGE TESTING SYSTEM

GENERAL TRAINING WRITING

TIME 1 hour

INSTRUCTIONS TO CANDIDATES

Do not open this booklet until you are told to do so.

Write your name and candidate number in the space at the top of this page.

All answers must be written on the separate answer booklet provided.

Do not remove this booklet from the examination room.

INFORMATION FOR CANDIDATES

There are **2** tasks on this question paper.

You must do **both** tasks.

Underlength answers will be penalized[1].

[1]BRITISH: penalised

WRITING TASK 1

You should spend about 20 minutes on this task.

> ***You are going to spend your vacation in a city in a foreign country. You have never been there before. Your cousin has a friend who lives there. Write a letter to the friend.***
> ***In your letter***
> ***- introduce yourself***
> ***- say why you are making this trip***
> ***- ask some questions about the city (e.g. places to see, things to do, things to bring)***

Write at least 150 words.

You do NOT need to write any addresses.

Begin your letter as follows:

Dear John,

WRITING TASK 2

You should spend about 40 minutes on this task.

Write about the following topic:

> ***Modern technology, such as personal computers and the Internet, have made it possible for many people to do their work from home at least part of the time instead of going to an office everyday. What are some of the advantages and disadvantages of this situation?***

Give reasons for your answer and include any relevant examples from your own knowledge or experience.

Write at least 250 words.

IELTS MODEL TESTS

GENERAL TRAINING
READING
WRITING
MODEL TEST 2

General Training Model Test 2

Candidate Name ______________________________

INTERNATIONAL ENGLISH LANGUAGE TESTING SYSTEM

GENERAL TRAINING READING

TIME 1 Hour

INSTRUCTIONS TO CANDIDATES

Do not open this booklet until you are told to do so.

Write your name and candidate number in the space at the top of this page.

Start at the beginning of the test and work through it.

You should answer all questions.

If you cannot do a particular question, leave it and go on to the next. You can return to it later.

All answers must be written on the answer sheet.

Do not remove this booklet from the examination room.

INFORMATION FOR CANDIDATES

There are **40** questions on this question paper.

The test is divided as follows:

Section 1	Questions 1–14
Section 2	Questions 15–27
Section 3	Questions 28–40

SECTION 1 *QUESTIONS 1–13*

You are advised to spend 20 minutes on Questions 1–13.

Questions 1–7

Read the notice below. Answer the questions below using NO MORE THAN THREE WORDS for each answer. Write your answers in boxes 1–6 on your Answer Sheet.

To all tenants of Parkside Towers:
Please be advised of the building painting schedule.

Dec. 1–4: Main foyer. Please don't use the main entrance at this time. Use the parking garage entrance to access the building.

Dec. 5–8: Garage stairway and elevator[1]. Please stay away from these areas at this time. If you park in the garage, you will have to walk outside to the front of the building to gain access through the main entrance.

Dec. 9–13: East stairway and elevators. If your apartment is in the East Wing, please use the West Wing elevators or stairway at this time.

Dec. 14–21: West and north stairways and elevators. If your apartment is in these areas of the building, please use the east stairway or elevator at this time.

Dec. 22–27: Parking garage. The garage will not be available to tenants at this time. In order to avoid illegal on-street parking, spaces in the parking lot[2] across the street will be made available to all tenants.

We are sorry for the inconvenience. If you have any questions or complaints, please contact the building manager.

If you would like to schedule painting for your apartment[3], please fill out a painting request form, available in the main lobby.

1 It's December 3rd. Which part of the building is being painted?

2 It's December 7th. How can you enter the building?

3 It's December 12th. How can you reach a tenth floor apartment in the East Wing?

4 You live on the sixth floor in the North Wing. How can you reach your apartment on December 15th?

5 Where should you park your car on December 24th?

6 What should you do if you are unhappy about the painting schedule?

7 What should you do if you want to have your apartment painted?

[1]BRITISH: lift
[2]BRITISH: car park
[3]BRITISH: flat

Questions 8–13

Read the bill from the electric company and answer the questions.

Write **NO MORE THAN THREE WORDS** *for each answer.*

Write your answers in boxes 8–14 on your Answer Sheet.

EnviroElectric Company

Date: 2 August

Customer name:
Oswald Robertson
15A Peacock Lane
Mayfield

For: 1 July–31 July—Total charges:		£35
	Previous bill:	£29
	Payment:	–£29
	Total due:	£35

We must receive your payment in full by 21 August or a late fee of $2.50 will be assessed. Please make out your check to EnviroElectric Company and mail it to:
EnviroElectric Company
PO Box 30682
East Bradfield

Or, pay by credit card:
Number: ______________________ Expiration date: __________
Signature: ______________________

Cash payments may be made by visiting any branch of the Bradfield Bank.

Account questions? Call (01 223) 385–9387
For repair service, call (01 223) 385–9856

8 How much did Mr. Robertson pay on his electric bill in June?

9 When is his July bill due?

10 What is the total amount Mr. Robertson will owe if he makes a late payment on his July bill?

11 Where is the EnviroElectric Company located?

12 If Mr. Robertson wants to pay cash, what should he do?

13 If Mr. Robinson thinks the company has charged him too much, what should he do?

SECTION 2 *QUESTIONS 14–27*

You are advised to spend 20 minutes on Questions 14–27.

Questions 14–20

Read the information about the city for international students.

International Student House
Guide for New Arrivals

Welcome to the International Student House. The purpose of this guide is to inform you of services and opportunities available in the area.

The International Student House is located close to public transportation. Across the street is a bus stop that serves several major bus routes. Two blocks away is a subway station with trains going to the city center as well as to the University District. Bus schedules and bus and subway maps are available at the City Office of Transport, located on State Street. Also close to the International Student House is Evergreen Books, the city's largest bookstore, located close to Nelson Boulevard.

The city's entertainment district is located in the city center and is easily reachable by subway. There you will find theaters, clubs, and some of the city's finest restaurants. The Festival of International Films is held every summer at the State Street Theater.

The University District is also easy to reach by subway. There are many popular coffeehouses in the vicinity as well as the famous Jim's Ice Cream Shop. Close to the university you will find the main branch of the public library. Just show your International Student House card, and you will be able to get a library card free of charge.

Across the street from the library is the University Sport and Health Club, equipped with exercise rooms, tennis courts, and an Olympic-sized pool. International Student House residents are entitled to a discount on club membership fees.

The Pleasant Gardens neighborhood, reachable by bus route 44, is the home of the City Art Museum and the Museum of History. Also located in that neighborhood is City Symphony Hall.

Questions 14–20

The passage mentions four different neighborhoods.

Which neighborhood would you visit if you wanted to do the following activities?

In boxes 14–20 on your Answer Sheet, write

A if you would visit the neighborhood of the International Student House.
B if you would visit the city center.
C if you would visit the University District.
D if you would visit Pleasant Gardens.

You may use any neighborhood more than once.

14 You want to buy a book.

15 You want information about bus routes.

16 You want to see a film.

17 You want to have a nice dinner.

18 You want to get a quick snack.

19 You want to go swimming.

20 You want to view some art.

Questions 21–27

Read the information about registering for college classes.

Hickory Ridge College
Registration information for summer session students

Dates

Summer session classes begin 2 June. Registration dates for the summer session are 19 May–1 June. Students may register after classes have started on a space-available basis. A late registration fee of £50 will be charged.

Tuition and Fees

Tuition for summer session classes is £150 per class for city residents and £250 per class for non-residents. There is also a nonrefundable £35 registration fee per class. All books and classroom supplies are extra.

Refunds

Students withdrawing from a class before classes begin will get a complete refund minus the registration fee. Students withdrawing from a class during the first week of classes will receive a 50 percent refund minus the registration fee. There will be no refunds after June 6.

Use of Facilities

Anybody registered for at least one class during the summer session is entitled to use the college library free of charge. The college pool and tennis courts are also available to summer session students at no cost.

Questions 21–27

Do the following statements agree with the information in the reading passage?

In boxes 21–27 on your Answer Sheet, write

TRUE	*if the statement is true according to the passage.*
FALSE	*if the statement contradicts the passage.*
NOT GIVEN	*if there is no information about this in the passage.*

21 Students can register for summer classes in May.

22 Students who live in the city pay a lower tuition than students who live outside the city.

23 A student who withdraws from classes before 2 June will receive all her money back.

24 A student who withdraws from class on 5 June will get half his tuition back.

25 The price of textbooks is included in the tuition.

26 Students may not register for more than three classes during the summer.

27 A student must enroll in more than one class in order to use the pool for free.

SECTION 3 *QUESTIONS 28–40*

You should spend 20 minutes on Questions 28–40, which are based on the reading passage below.

Stonehenge

Approximately two miles west of Amesbury, Wiltshire, in southern England stands Stonehenge, one of the world's most famous megalithic monuments. The remains of Stonehenge consist of a series of stone structures arranged in layers of circular and horseshoe-like patterns. Theories and myths concerning this mysterious monument have flourished for thousands of years. The Danes, Egyptians, and Druids are just a few of the groups who have been credited with building Stonehenge. Some people have even made attempts to prove that aliens erected Stonehenge. Early historians believed that the monument was constructed as a memorial to nobles killed in combat, while other later theorists described Stonehenge as a place for sacrificial ceremonies. Regardless of who built the monument and why, all of the legends surrounding these megaliths are based on speculation. With the exception of archeological evidence, very little of what we understand about Stonehenge today can actually be called fact.

Stonehenge was constructed in three phases during the Neolithic and Bronze Age periods. Stonehenge period 1, also commonly referred to as Phase 1, is believed to have occurred sometime around 3000 B.C., during the middle Neolithic period. In this first step of the construction, picks made of deer antlers were used to dig a series of 56 pits. These pits were later named "Aubrey Holes" after an English scholar. Outside of the holes was dug a large circular henge (a ditch with an earthen wall). During this phase, a break, or entranceway was also dug on the northeast corner of the henge. Archeologists[1] today refer to this break as the Avenue. Two stones were set in the Avenue. The "Slaughter Stone" was placed just inside

[1]BRITISH: archaeologists

the circle, while the "Heel Stone" was placed 27 meters down the Avenue. The Heel Stone weighs about 35 tons and is made of natural sandstone, believed to have originated from Marlborough Downs, an area 20 miles north of the monument. The 35-foot-wide Avenue is set so that, from the center of Stonehenge, a person would be able to see the sunrise to the left of the heel stone. Just inside the henge, four other "Station Stones" were placed in a rectangular formation.

There is great debate over how long the first phase of Stonehenge was used and when the original alterations were made; however, the second phase is generally placed between 2900 B.C. and 2400 B.C. and accredited to the Beaker people. It is thought that many wooden posts were added to the monument during this phase. One of the problems archeologists have had with Phase 2 is that unlike stone or holes in the earth, wood does not hold up over thousands of years. The numerous stake holes in the earth tell the story of where these posts were positioned. Besides the ones in the center of the henge, six rows of posts were placed near the entrance. These may have been used to mark astronomical measurements, or to guide people to the center. The original Aubrey holes were filled in either with earth or cremation remains. Many archeologists believed that the Beaker people were sun worshipers[1], and that they may have purposely changed the main axis of the monument and widened the entrance during this phase in order to show their appreciation for the sun.

The final phase of Stonehenge is usually described in terms of three subphases, each one involving a setting of large stones. The first stones that arrived were bluestones, brought all the way from the Preseli Hills in Pembrokeshire, Wales. A horseshoe of paired bluestones was placed in the center of the henge, with a tall Altar Stone marking the end of the formation. In the next subphase, a 30-meter ring of sandstones called the Sarsen Circle was built around the bluestones. Only 17 of the original 30 stones remain. These sarasen stones were connected with lintel blocks, each precisely carved in order to fit end-to-end and form perfectly with the stone circle. Approximately 60 more bluestones were then added inside the original horseshoe.

How these enormous stones were transported and raised in Phase 3 remains a mystery. The fact that these monoliths were built before the wheel means an incredible amount of manual labor was used. It is believed that a pulley system using rollers still would have required at least one hundred men to operate. Raising the lintels and fitting them into one another would have been another major struggle without the use of machines. Stonehenge remains one of the world's greatest mysteries and one of England's most important icons.

[1]BRITISH: worshippers

Questions 28–31

Complete the labels on the diagram of Stonehenge below.

Choose your answers from the box below the diagram, and write them in boxes 28–31 on your Answer Sheet. There are more words than spaces, so you will not use them all.

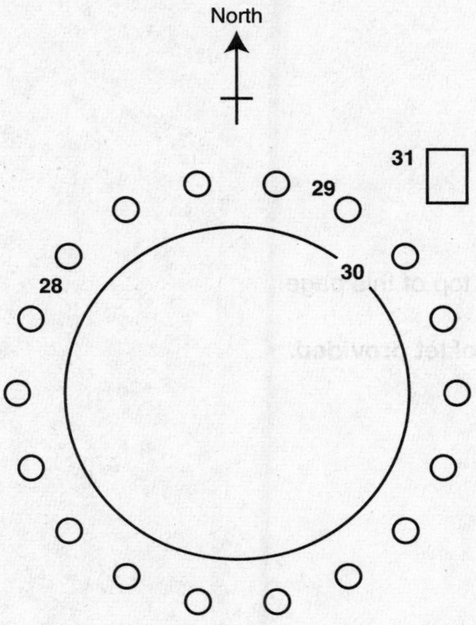

Stonehedge Phase 1

- Aubrey Holes
- Heel Stone
- Marlborough Downs
- Avenue
- Henge
- Station Stones

Questions 32–40

Stonehenge was built in three phases. During which phase did the following things occur? In boxes 32–40 on your Answer Sheet, write

A if it occurred during Phase 1.
B if it occurred during Phase 2.
C if it occurred during Phase 3.

32 The entrance was made wider.

33 The Slaughter Stone was erected.

34 Stones were placed in a horseshoe formation.

35 Wooden posts were set near the entrance.

36 Deer antlers were used to dig holes.

37 Bluestones were brought from a distant location.

38 A ring of sandstones was constructed.

39 Holes were filled with dirt.

40 The Altar Stone was erected.

GENERAL TRAINING Model Test 2

Candidate Name ____

INTERNATIONAL ENGLISH LANGUAGE TESTING SYSTEM

GENERAL TRAINING WRITING

TIME 1 hour

INSTRUCTIONS TO CANDIDATES

Do not open this booklet until you are told to do so.

Write your name and candidate number in the space at the top of this page.

All answers must be written on the separate answer booklet provided.

Do not remove this booklet from the examination room.

INFORMATION FOR CANDIDATES

There are **2** tasks on this question paper.

You must do **both** tasks.

Underlength answers will be penalized.

WRITING TASK 1

You should spend about 20 minutes on this task.

> ***You stayed at a hotel last week. After you got home you realized that you had left your watch behind. Write a letter to the hotel manager, and explain what happened. Describe the watch, and ask them to help you find it.***

Write at least 150 words.

You do NOT need to write any addresses.

Begin your letter as follows:

Dear Sir or Madam,

WRITING TASK 2

You should spend about 40 minutes on this task.

Write about the following topic:

> ***Children today spend more time watching television than they did in the past. Describe some of the advantages and disadvantages of television for children.***

Give reasons for your answer and include any relevant examples from your own knowledge or experience.

Write at least 250 words.

9

ANSWER KEYS FOR THE MODULE ACTIVITIES

LISTENING MODULE

Completing the Blanks

Number of Words and Spelling

2. *the subway station*. The word *to* is unnecessary after near. The word *station* is misspelled[1].
3. *pay a fine* The other words are unnecessary and exceed the three-word limit.
4. *the weather* or *the bad weather* The expression *because of* must be followed by a noun, not by a clause. The words *very bad* are unnecessary.
5. *rose garden* The word *rose* must be singular because it serves as an adjective to describe *garden.* The words *beautiful, sunny* are not necessary and make the answer exceed the three-word limit.
6. *can choose* The word *usually* is not necessary. The word *can* is always followed by the base form of the verb, not the infinitive form.
7. *About ten thousand* Use *about* instead of *more or less* to stay within the three-word limit. The word *thousand* is misspelled. An exact number is not followed by *of.*
8. *ask the professor* The phrase *have to* cannot correctly follow *should* or any other modal.
9. *going to Alaska* or *traveling to Alaska* It is not necessary to repeat the word *about.* Using *going to* or *traveling to* instead of *his trip to* keeps the answer within the three-word limit. (BRITISH: travelling)
10. *spend the winter* The word *long* is not necessary and makes the answer exceed the three-word limit. The word *winter* is misspelled.

Gender and Number

1. *build their nests* The word *their* is misspelled and *nests* must be plural because it refers to many nests belonging to many ducks.
2. *business travelers* The word *business* is misspelled. The word *travelers* should be plural because *among* implies that there are many. (BRITISH: travellers)
3. *tropical climates* It isn't necessary to repeat the word *in.* The word *a* is incorrect before a plural noun. The word *tropical* is misspelled.
4. *costs more* The word *fruit* is a non-count noun and takes a singular verb. The word *more* is misspelled.
5. *her old clothes* The feminine possessive adjective *her* agrees with the feminine subject Mrs. Smith. The word *clothes* is misspelled.
6. *take two exams* Don't use *must* after *have to*—they have the same meaning. The word *exams* must be plural because there are *two.*
7. *a new house* The singular noun *house* must be preceded by an article.
8. *took their vacation* The plural adjective *their* agrees with the plural subject. The word *vacation* is singular. (BRITISH: took their holiday)
9. *has a garden* The verb *has* agrees with the singular subject *Every house.*
10. *lays her eggs* or *lays its eggs* The words *like to* are unnecessary and make the answer exceed the three-word limit. The possessive adjective must agree with the subject *female dragonfly*—*her* because the subject is female, or *its* because the subject is an animal.

[1]BRITISH: mis-spelt

Listening Skills

Target 1—Making Assumptions

Section 1

1. Kingston
2. State
3. 7
4. 721-1127
5. December
6. C
7. D
8. F
9. month
10. 50 percent

Section 2

11. 15
12. 11
13. Tuesday
14. Modern art
15. City Gallery
16. Portraits
17. East Room
18. art reproductions
19. repairs
20. Second floor

Target 2—Understanding Numbers

Example: 33

1. 8677532148
2. C
3. 575-3174
4. B
5. XY 538
6. 6370550
7. 2651811
8. 2876216
9. 4553021
10. 3058480

Target 3—Understanding the Alphabet

Example: Lynne

1. Tomas
2. Maine
3. Patti
4. Roberts
5. Springvale
6. Dixson
7. A. Miranda
   B. 7043218
8. A. Bijou
   B. 232–5488
9. A. Janson
   B. 335
10. A. String
    B. 15 B
11. A. Willard
    B. 70
12. A. 1705
    B. Landover

Target 4—Listening for Descriptions

Example

A. It's a house with a flat roof. It's two floors high. On the first floor there is a large window and a door. On the second floor there is a row of windows.
B. It's a small house that's only one floor high. It has a door with a window on each side of it.
C. It's a single-story house for two families. It has two doors and one small window.

1. A. He's a short man with short hair and a mustache[1]. He's neither fat nor thin.
   B. He's a tall, thin man. He has long hair.
   C. He's a fat, bald man with a beard. He's neither short nor tall.
2. A. She's a young woman with long hair. She's very thin, and she's wearing earrings.
   B. She's a middle-aged woman with long grey hair. She's wearing earrings.
   C. She's a young woman with short, curly hair. She's wearing a necklace.
3. C
4. A

Target 5—Listening for Time

Example: A

TIME	DATE	DAY	YEAR	SEASON
1. B	1. 15	1. Monday	1. 1803	1. winter
2. A	2. December	2. Thursday	2. 1851	2. summer
3. C	3. September	3. Thursday	3. B	3. C
4. C	4. 7	4. Friday	4. C	4. B
5. 12:15	5. C	5. B	5. 1985	5. fall
6. 4:00	6. A	6. B	6. 1988	6. winter

Target 6—Listening for Frequency

Example: B

1. sometimes
2. seldom
3. always
4. never
5. often
6. always
7. daily
8. once a month
9. twice a week
10. from time to time
11. once a month
12. every other week

Target 7—Listening for Similar Meanings

Example 1: college graduates
Example 2: C
Example 3: A

1. party
2. checks
3. rate
4. vegetation
5. available
6. occupation

Target 8—Listening for Emotions

Example: A

1. C
2. A
3. B
4. C
5. A
6. C

[1]BRITISH: moustache

Target 9—Listening for an Explanation

Example

1. A
2. E
3. C
4. D
5. F
6. B
7. the electrical outlet/socket
8. the cord
9. the appliance
10. wires
11. hot
12. orange
13. turns brown
14. toast

Questions 1–12

1. cacao tree
2. cacao fruit
3. seeds/cocoa beans
4. vat for fermenting
5. drying trays
6. chocolate factory
7. is harvested
8. are removed
9. about a week
10. dry/are dried
11. are shipped/sent to
12. delicious chocolate treats

Target 10—Listening for Classifications

Example

Course Offerings

1 Academic Program	2 Business Program
Introduction to Art Basic Chemistry Beginning Spanish	Organizational Behavior/Behaviour Commercial Law Compensation and Benefits
History of Africa	Project Management
Literature of the 21st Century	The Art of Negotiating
International Relations	Creativity in the Workplace
Introduction to Philosophy	Labor/Labour Negotiations

Questions 1–5

1. A, C, E
2. (A) Horror, (B) Romantic
3. (A) Butterflies, (B) Moths
4. C, D
5. (A) Ornamental, (B) Shade, (C) Evergreen

Target 11—Listening for Comparisons and Contrasts

Example

A. Different
B. Alike
C. Different
D. Alike
E. Alike
F. Different
G. Alike
H. Different

1. A. Different
   B. Different
   C. Alike
   D. Different
   E. Alike

2. A. Alike
   B. Different
   C. Different
   D. Different
   E. Alike

3. A. Different
   B. Alike
   C. Alike
   D. Different
   E. Different

4. A. Alike
   B. Different
   C. Different
   D. Different
   E. Alike

Target 12—Listening for Negative Meanings

Example: B

1. A
2. A
3. B
4. A
5. A
6. B
7. B
8. A
9. C
10. A
11. C
12. A

Target 13—Listening for Chronology

Example

1. Orientation session
2. Do research
3. Final exam

Questions 1–5

1. 1,3,2,5,4,6
2. 1,2,3,5,4
3. 2,3,1,5,4
4. 2,1,4,3,5
5. 2,1,3,5,4

READING MODULE

Reading Skills

Target 1—Using the First Paragraph to Make Predictions

PRACTICE 1

1. **Topic Sentence.** The spread of wildfire is a natural phenomenon that occurs throughout the world and is especially common in forested areas of North America, Australia, and Europe.

   Definition of Topic. Locations that receive plenty of rainfall but also experience periods of intense heat or drought are particularly susceptible to wildfires.

   Author's Opinion. None given.

   Organizational Clues. Author may discuss
   - How wildfires start
   - How to control wildfires
   - Wildfires as a global problem

2. **Topic Sentence.** In reality, birds may actually be a great deal more intelligent than humans have given them credit for.

   Definition of Topic. For a long time, scientists considered birds to be of lesser intelligence because the cerebral cortex, the part of the brain that humans and other animals use for intelligence, is relatively small in size.

   Author's Opinion. None given.

Organizational Clues. Author may discuss
- Misunderstandings about the intelligence of birds
- The anatomy of a bird's brain
- Evidence of avian intelligence

3. **Topic Sentence.** She would grow up to become one of the richest women in the world.

Definition of Topic. Her name was Hetty Green, but she was known to many as the Witch of Wall Street.

Author's Opinion. None given.

Organizational Clues. Author may discuss
- Hetty Green's early years
- How Hetty Green got rich
- Why Hetty Green had a nickname

Target 2—Using the Topic Sentence to Make Predictions

Practice 2

1. **Topic Sentence.** To combat excessive thoughts and impulses, most OCD sufferers perform certain repetitive rituals that they believe will relieve their anxiety.

Questions to Ask Yourself
What types of rituals do they perform?
How does this help them?

2. **Topic Sentence.** A child's upbringing does not seem to be part of the cause of the disorder, though stress can make the symptoms stronger.

Questions to Ask Yourself
Is the disorder present at birth?
Are there outside factors involved?
What leads parents to seek treatment?

3. **Topic Sentence.** Research on OCD sufferers has found certain physiological trends.

Questions to Ask Yourself
What part of the body does it affect?
What are some common trends?
What can parents look for?

Target 3—Looking for Specific Details

Practice 3

1. **Supporting Details**
Compulsions can be mental or physical
Examples include: checking, hand washing, disturbing images
Compulsions and obsessions may or may not be related

2. **Supporting Details**
Most cases are genetic
Stress can add to the problem
Many members of the family may have OCD

3. **Supporting Details**
Over activity of blood in the brain
Less serotonin
Linked to other disorders such as Tourette Syndrome and ADHD

Target 4—Analyzing the Questions and Answers

Practice 4

Key Words in Statements 9–16: (Answers may vary.) child, stress, serotonin, age 17, psychotherapy, medication, treat, secret, antibiotics

1. *unreasonable*. Paragraph 1 states that, "OCD sufferers understand that their obsessions are unrealistic."
2. *control*. Paragraph 1 states that "they find it stressful to put these intrusive thoughts out of their minds."
3. *reduce*. The first sentence of paragraph 3 states: "To combat excessive thoughts and impulses, most OCD sufferers perform certain repetitive rituals that they believe will relieve their anxiety."
4. *obsession*. Paragraph 2 states that "Fear of dirt and contamination are very common obsessive thoughts."
5. *checking*. Paragraph 3 states that "Common rituals include excessive checking."
6. *throw away*. The last sentence in paragraph 3 states that, "Holding onto objects that would normally be discarded, such as newspapers and containers, is another common compulsion."
7. *inherited*. Paragraph 4 states that "a number of different genetic factors" have been found as underlying causes of the disease.
8. *cause*. Paragraph 5 gives an example of an illness (strep throat) that is thought to be the cause behind some OCD cases.
9. False. Paragraph 4 states: "A child's upbringing does not seem to be part of the cause of the disorder, though stress can make the symptoms stronger. The underlying causes of OCD have been researched greatly, and point to a number of different genetic factors."
10. True. Paragraph 4 states: "A child's upbringing does not seem to be part of the cause of the disorder, though stress can make the symptoms stronger."
11. True. Paragraph 5 states: "Studies have also shown that OCD sufferers have less serotonin than the average person."
12. False. Paragraph 4 states: "OCD symptoms generally begin between the age of 10 and 24 and continue indefinitely until a person seeks treatment."
13. Not Given. Paragraph 6 mentions both psychotherapy and medication but does not discuss which one patients prefer.
14. False. Paragraph 6 discusses different treatment options, and states that, "early diagnosis and proper medication can lessen many of the symptoms and allow people to live fairly normal lives."
15. True. Paragraph 6 begins with this sentence: "Because OCD sufferers tend to be so secretive about their symptoms, they often put off treatment for many years."
16. True. The final sentence in Paragraph 6 indicates that antibiotics can be used in special cases of OCD: "For cases when OCD is linked to streptococcal infection, antibiotic therapy is sometimes all that is needed."

Target 5—Identifying the Tasks

Practice 5

Topic Sentence. The South African province of KwaZulu-Natal, more commonly referred to as the Zulu Kingdom, is named after the Zulu people who have inhabited the area since the late 1400s.

Questions to Ask Yourself

Who are the Zulu people?
What is the history behind this clan?
What are they known for?

Supporting Details
Large South African ethnic group
Region explored by Europeans
Zulu wear traditional jewelry/jewellry and clothing
Beadwork is important to the culture

Analyzing the Questions
1. Where?
2. Where?
3. Who?
4. Where?
5. When?
6. How many?
7. Who? Where? **Key Words:** British
8. What? **Key Words:** Henry Frances Flynn
9. What? **Key Words:** precious stones
10. What? Why? **Key Words:** daily lives
11. What? Why? **Key Words:** gourds

PASSAGE 1

1. (E) Paragraph 1 states: "KwaZulu translates to mean 'Place of Heaven."
2. (B) Paragraph 1 states: "'Natal' was the name the Portuguese explorers gave this region when they arrived in 1497."
3. (C) Paragraph 1 states: "By the late 1700s, the AmaZulu clan, meaning 'People of Heaven,' constituted a significant nation."
4. *South Africa*. The first sentence of Paragraph 1 states that KwaZulu-Natal is a South African province.
5. *1497*. Paragraph 1 states: "Portuguese explorers . . . arrived in 1497."
6. *11 million*. Midway through paragraph 1 the passage states: "Today the Zulu clan represents the largest ethnic group in South Africa, with at least 11 million people in the kingdom."
7. *False*. Paragraph 2 talks about how the Egyptians were the first to bring beads to the area, though the British later facilitated the trade.
8. *Not Given*. Paragraph 2 states that Henry Frances Flynn brought glass beads to the region, but it doesn't state anywhere that he earned a lot of money doing this.
9. *False*. Paragraph 3 states: "The Zulu people were not fooled into believing that glass beads were precious stones but, rather, used the beads to establish certain codes and rituals in their society."
10. *True*. Paragraphs 3 discusses how beads are used for adornment, education, recreation, and communication.
11. *True*. Paragraph 3 discusses how bead-covered gourds are carried around by women who are having fertility problems. "Fertility problems" means *difficulty becoming and staying pregnant*.
12. *unmarried man*. Paragraph 4 states: "A triangle with the apex pointing downward signifies an unmarried man."
13. *married man*. Paragraph 4 states that "married men signify their marital status with two triangles that form an hourglass shape."
14. *married woman*. Paragraph 4 states: "Married women wear items with two triangles that form a diamond shape."
15. *unmarried woman*. Paragraph 4 states that a triangle "with the tip pointing upward is worn by an unmarried woman."

PASSAGE 2

Note: Alternative spellings: colour blindness, colour, colourful

1. iii. What is Colorblindness? Paragraph A discusses what people think color blindness is, and what it really is. In the middle of the paragraph it states, "The fact is that in most cases of colorblindness, there are only certain shades that a person cannot distinguish between. These people are said to be dichromatic."
2. viii. Colorblindness and the Sexes. Paragraph B discusses the fact that men are more prone to colorblindness than women, and states the genetic reasons why this is the case.
3. vii. Developing the Ability to See Color. Paragraph C discusses the fact that babies are all born colorblind and that they do not develop the ability to see colors until they are a few months old. This paragraph also discusses the possibility that infants may require a colorful environment in order to develop proper color vision.
4. ii. Diagnosing Colorblindness. Paragraph D discusses the reasons why colorblindness is difficult to diagnose. It also discusses the Ishihara Test, which distinguishes those who are colorblind from those who have normal color vision.
5. v. Unsolved Myths. Paragraph E mentions two beliefs about colorblindness that haven't been proven as myths: that colorblindness can aid military soldiers and that everyone is colorblind in an emergency.
6. (C) The second to the last sentence of Paragraph A states that: "People with trichromatic vision have all three cones in working order."
7. (B) The second sentence in Paragraph C states that: "A baby's cones do not begin to differentiate between many different colors until he is approximately four months old."
8. (C) Paragraph D states the main downfall of the Ishihara Test: "The Ishihara Test is the most common, though it is highly criticized because it requires that children have the ability to recognize numerals."
9. *myth*. Paragraph B introduces the idea that although color vision deficiency is predominant in males, it is still possible for females to be colorblind.
10. *a little less*. Paragraph B states: "In an average population, 8% of males exhibit some form of colorblindness."
11. *X chromosomes*. Paragraph B states: "Females have two X chromosomes."
12. *less likely*. Paragraph B explains that it is less likely for women to be colorblind, because if one of their X chromosomes "carries the defective gene, the other one naturally compensates."

"Compensate" means *to make up for another's weakness*.

PASSAGE 3

1. (A) Paragraph 2 discusses how Antarctic penguins "huddle in communities" to keep warm.
2. (A) The first sentence of Paragraph 3 states: "Antarctic penguins spend about 75 percent of their lives in the water."
3. (B) Paragraph 3 discusses the unique feathers of Antarctic penguins that that work similarly to a waterproof diving suit: "Tufts of down trap a layer of air within the feathers, preventing the water from penetrating the penguin's skin."
4. (A) Paragraph 4 states: "Temperate species have certain physical features such as fewer feathers and less blubber to keep them cool on a hot day."
5. (B) Paragraph 4 discusses the bald patches of a temperate species called African penguins.
6. rocks. Paragraph 2 states: "When it's time to create a nest, most penguins build up a pile of rocks on top of the ice to place their eggs."
7. feed/eat. Paragraph 2 discusses the Emperor penguin's gender roles: "The female Emperor lays just one egg and gives it to the male to protect while she goes off for weeks to feed."
8. brood patch. Paragraph 2 explains how the male Emperor penguin takes care of the egg: "The male balances the egg on top of his feet, covering it with a small fold of skin called a brood patch."

9. heels and tails. Toward the end of paragraph 2 the text states: "In order to reduce the cold of the ice, penguins often put their weight on their heels and tails."
10. (A) Paragraph 3 states that penguins have to keep moving to stay warm. Their swimming is compared to flight.
11. (D) The last sentence in Paragraph 3 describes the penguin's circulatory system: "Penguins also have an amazing circulatory system, which in extremely cold waters diverts blood from the flippers and legs to the heart."
12. (E) Paragraph 3 describes "porpoising" which penguins do in order to be able to breathe without having to stop swimming.
13. (H) Paragraph 3 describes how feathers keep Antarctic penguins dry: "Tufts of down trap a layer of air within the feathers, preventing the water from penetrating the penguin's skin."
Choice (B), (C), and (F) are incorrect because these are all of examples of how penguins stay cool.

WRITING MODULE

Target 1—Writing for a Specific Audience

A high school student	N
An experienced teacher	Y
A native speaker of English	P
A kindly grandmother	P
A strict grammarian	P
A famous author	P
A fair grader	Y

Target 2—Completing the Task

Practice

	Time	Words
Task 1	20 minutes	150
Task 2	40 minutes	250

Target 4—Developing a Thesis Statement

Practice

Topic 1

Task

(B) Support your opinion. You are asked your opinion about the amount and type of control that is needed. This answer must be related to the content of television programs.[1]

[1]British: programmes

Thesis Statement

(A) There are many types of programs[1] on television, and each person is free to choose which programs he or she wants to watch.

Topic 2

Task

(B) Support your opinion. You are asked for your opinion regarding home computers. You must talk about their advantages and disadvantages for children. You should also discuss whether or not parents should restrict the amount of time their children spend using the computer.

Thesis Statement

(B) Computers can contribute a lot to a child's education, but they can be overused.

Topic 3

Task

(A) Give a description. You are asked to describe the information shown in the table, reporting on the main features and making comparisons.

Thesis Statement

(C) Over the past century, the population in the Northwest Region has been shifting from largely rural to mostly suburban and urban.

Topic 4

Task

(C) Explain a problem, and ask for a solution. You are asked to write about a problem. The problem is that you have lost your friend's watch. Then explain the solution, what you want to do about the loss.

Thesis Statement

(C) An unfortunate thing happened last night while I was wearing your beautiful gold watch. (C) is the best choice because the writer is clearly leading into explaining a problem. Some students might also select (B). With (B), the letter could talk about the problem. On the other hand, it might not. For this reason, (C) is the correct answer.

Target 5—Organizing Your Writing

Practice 1

4. **Add general ideas.** The top circle shows the idea from paragraph 1, the introduction. The bottom three circles contain the ideas in the body paragraphs. The second body paragraph mentions "Modern technology."
   1. Technology
   2. for adults
   3. News

5. **Add supporting details.** These lines show the supporting details for each paragraph. Each line matches one of the body paragraphs. There are three body paragraphs in this essay. The answer "for adults" is expressed in the line, "Adults can also use this technology to avoid seeing programs/programmes that they don't want to see." The answer "news" is found in the statement: "There are news programs for serious people."
   1. Schedules, different channels
   2. Channel blocker for children (for adults)
   3. News

Practice 2

4. **Add general ideas.** The top circle expresses the idea from the thesis statement. Each of the three bottom circles represents a major idea from one of the three body paragraphs. In body paragraph 2, the writer mentions "a new four-lane highway/dual carriage way."
   1. four-land road/highway/dual carriage way.

5. **Add supporting details**. The years are found at the beginning of each paragraph.
   2. 1950
   3. 1978
   4. 2000

PRACTICE 3

Topic 1

Task: Support your opinion.

Thesis Statement: Physical education classes are so important that schools must require them.

Concept Map:

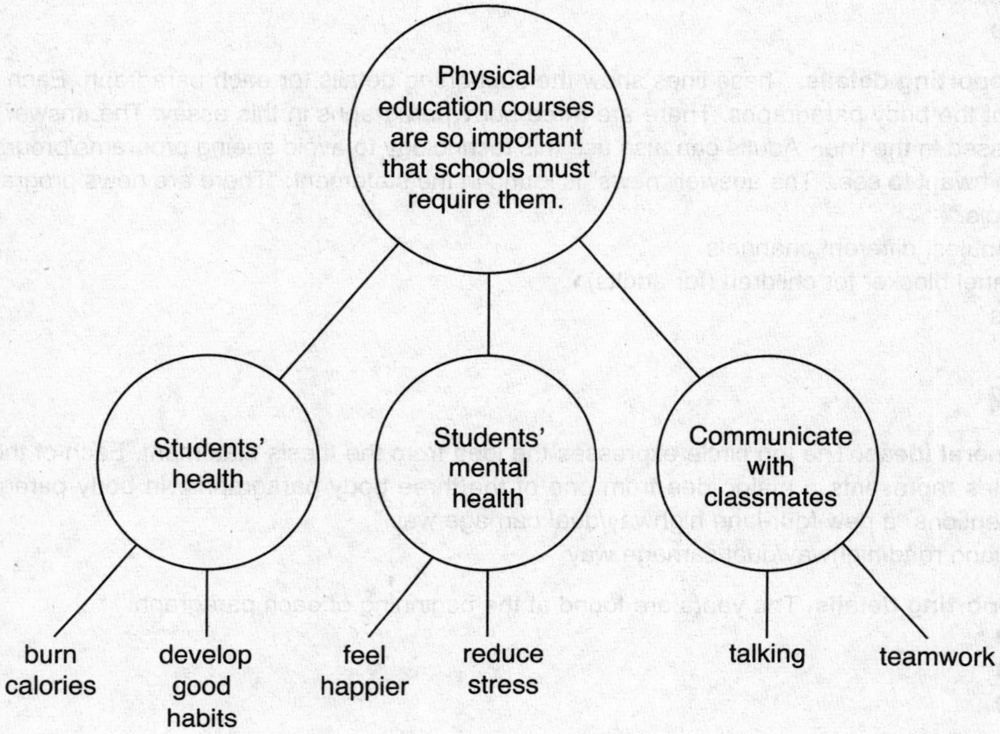

Some students hate exercising. They'd rather play computer games or talk to their friends. They would never take physical education classes if they had a choice. Physical education classes are so important that schools must require them.

These classes improve students' health, now and in the future. They burn calories, and this helps them to maintain a healthy weight. The classes' regular exercise develops good habits for the present and the future. People who exercise as children are more likely to continue exercising when they're adults. This reduces the risk of heart disease, diabetes, and other serious illnesses.

Physical education also improves students' mental health. It can be difficult to sit in class all day. Students can exercise and then relax after their physical activity. This helps them to feel happier and more comfortable at school. The classes also include activities that help with stress reduction. Walking, stretching, and yoga are just a few of the exercises that reduce stress.

The students' favorite part of physical education classes may be the opportunity to communicate with their classmates. They enjoy talking to their friends while they play games. The students also learn how to work in teams. Teamwork is an important skill that they will use when playing sports or even at their jobs in the future.

We know that some students really don't like physical education. We also know that there are many advantages to taking physical education classes. There are so many benefits that schools must require students to take these classes.

Topic 2

Task: Explain a problem and ask for a solution.

Thesis Statement: My bill for this month contained an incorrect late payment charge.

Concept Map:

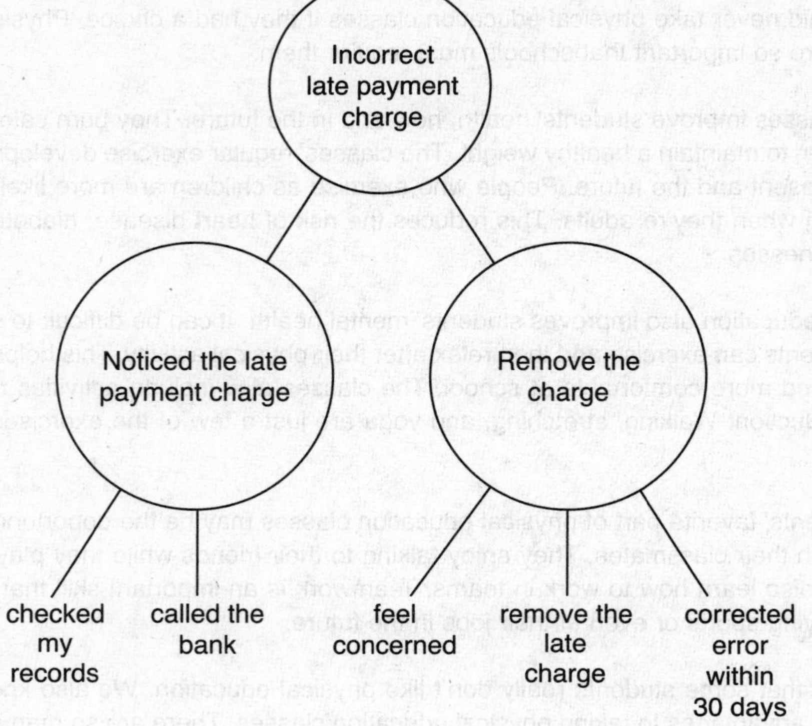

Dear National Credit Card Company,

My bill for this month contained an incorrect late payment charge. I was surprised to read this. My last payment was definitely made on time. To be sure, I checked my records. They show that I wrote and mailed a check to you fifteen days before it was due. Next I called my bank and they checked their records. They say that your company cashed the check five days before the payment was due.

I am very concerned about this mistake. Please remove this late charge from my credit card. I would like to have your mistake corrected as soon as possible and within the next 30 days. I always make my payments on time, so seeing this charge upsets me.

Please contact me immediately if you have any questions about this letter. I want to be sure that my credit record with your company continues to be excellent.

Sincerely,

Michel Danel

Topic 3

Task: Describe something.

Thesis Statement: Over the past century, the population in the Northwest Region has been shifting from largely rural to mostly suburban and urban.

Concept Map:

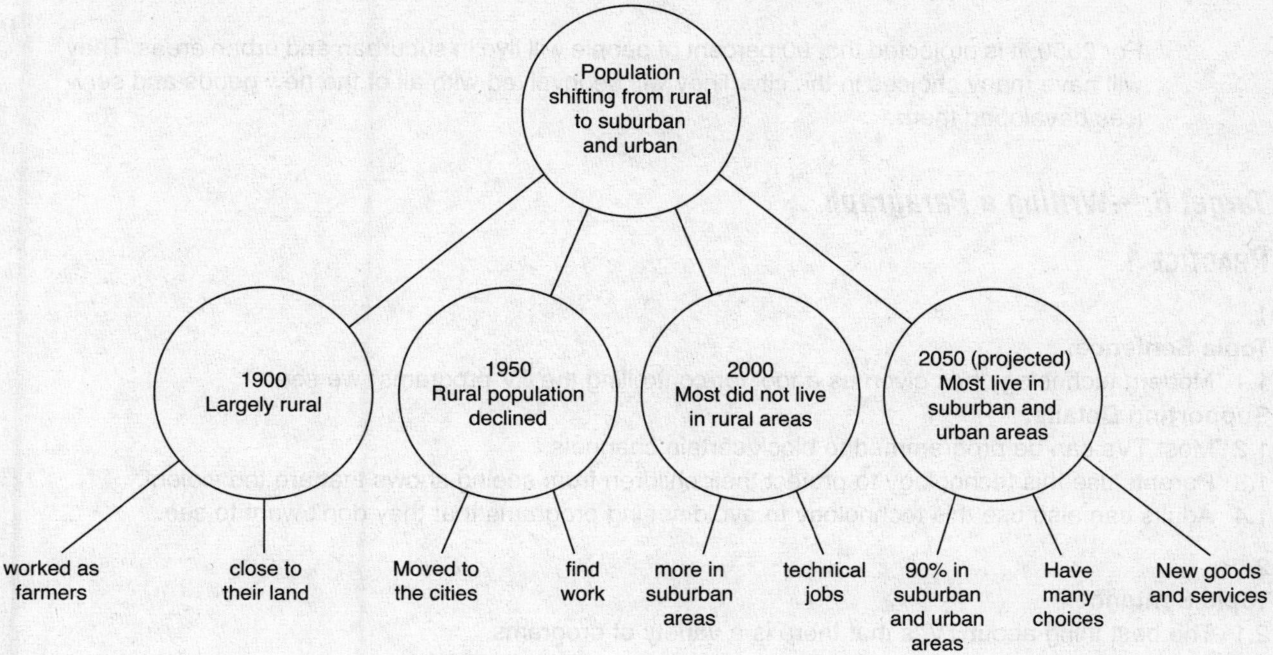

Over the past century, the population in the Northwest Region has been shifting from largely rural to mostly suburban and urban.

In 1900, the Northwest Region's population was largely rural. Many people worked as farmers. They needed to be close to their land. So, most people lived and worked at the same place, at their farm in the countryside.

By 1950, the rural population declined. Some people moved to the cities to be closer to them. They wanted to find work. More job opportunities were available outside of the rural regions.

By 2000, most people lived in suburban and urban areas. They worked in the city's technical jobs. Even fewer people worked as farmers.

For 2050, it is projected that 90 percent of people will live in suburban and urban areas. They will have many choices in the city. They will be involved with all of the new goods and services developed there.

Target 6:—Writing a Paragraph

PRACTICE 1

1.

Topic Sentence:

1.1 Modern technology has given us a tool for controlling the TV programs[1] we see.

Supporting Details:

1.2 Most TVs can be programmed to block certain channels.

1.3 Parents use this technology to protect their children from seeing shows that are too violent.

1.4 Adults can also use this technology to avoid seeing programs that they don't want to see.

2.

Topic Sentence:

2.1 The best thing about TV is that there is a variety of programs.

Supporting Details:

2.2 There are news programs for serious people.

2.3 There are movies and cartoons for people who want to be entertained.

2.4 The variety of TV programs needs to be protected, even if that means allowing some of them to show violence.

3.

Topic Sentence:

3.1 Physical education classes teach children important skills that they need in life.

Supporting Details:

3.2 They teach children how to work together on a team.

3.3 They teach children how to set a goal and work to achieve it.

3.4 They teach children about the importance of taking care of their health.

Target 7—Writing the Introduction

PRACTICE 1

Topic 1

Task: Make an argument and support an opinion.

Thesis Statement: "Learning by doing" is a better way to learn a language.

[1]BRITISH: programmes

Concept Map:

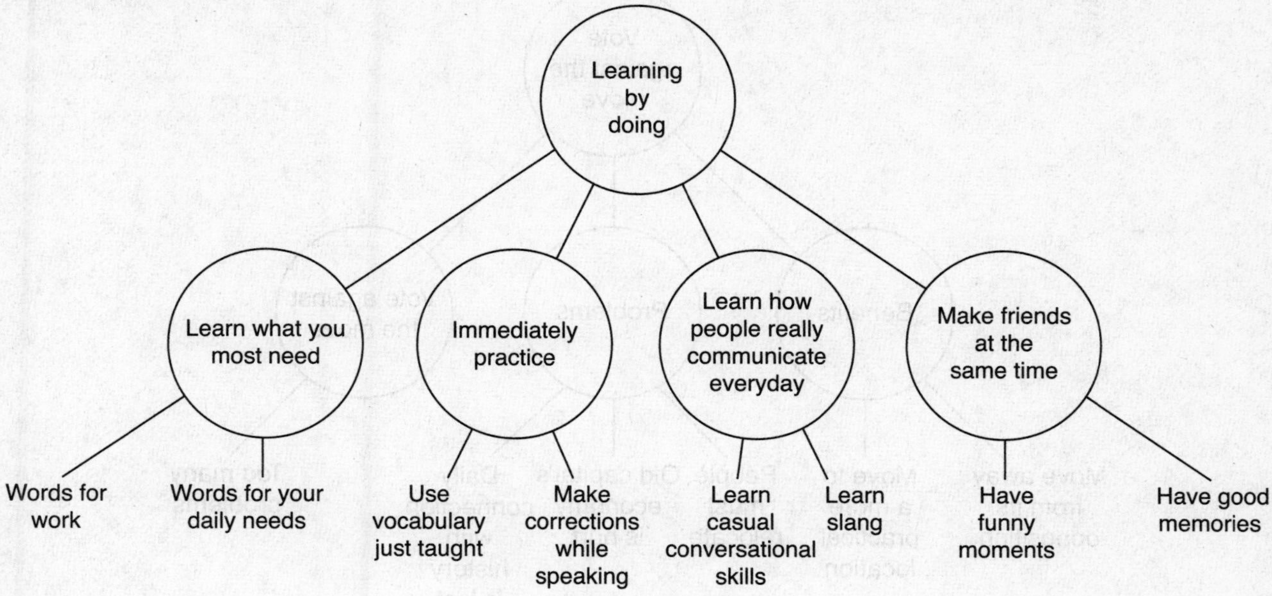

Topic Sentences:

1.1 You learn the most important words, the ones that you most need in order to communicate.
1.2 You immediately practice what you have learned.
1.3 You learn how people really communicate everyday, instead of formal language that may only be used at school.
1.4 You make friends and learn a language at the same time.

Introduction: People often discuss what the best way is to learn languages: "learning by doing" or from books and teachers. In "learning by doing," you learn the most important words that you need. You immediately practice what you have learned. You learn how people really communicate every day, instead of formal language that may only be used at school. You make friends and learn a language at the same time. "Learning by doing" is a better way to learn language.

Topic 2

Task: Make an argument and support your position.

Thesis Statement: Because of the tremendous challenges caused by this change, I would vote against moving my capital.

Concept Map:

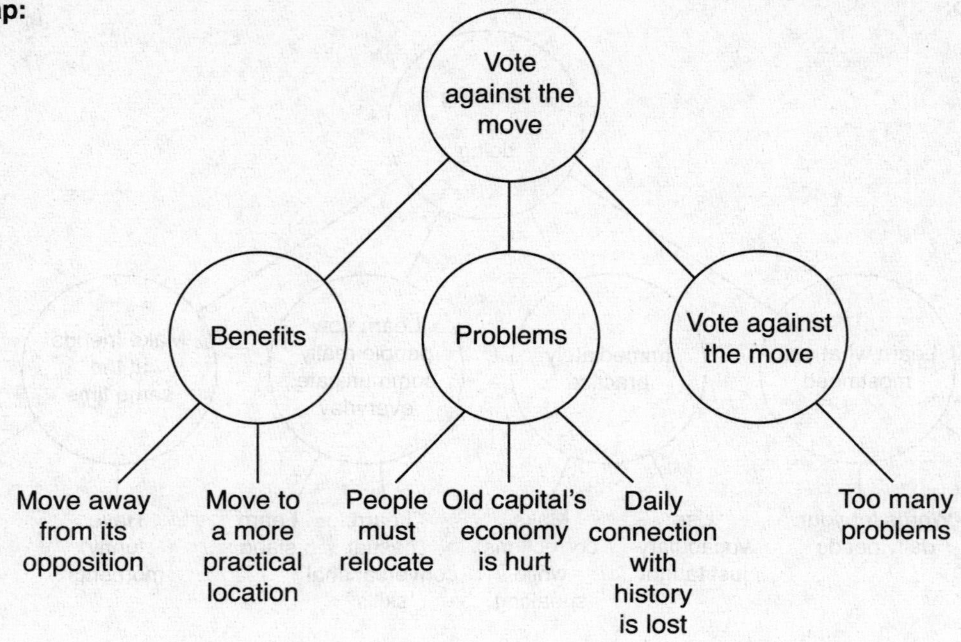

Topic Sentences:

2.1 A government may move its capital because of the benefits.
2.2 However, there are also some problems to consider.
2.3 If I were asked to move my capital, I would definitely vote against it.

Introduction: Perhaps you have never thought about moving your government's capital. However, it has happened worldwide and for hundreds of years. A government may move its capital because of the benefits. However, there are also some problems to consider. Because of the tremendous challenges caused by this change, I would vote against moving my capital.

Target 8—Writing with Variety

Chronological Order

Practice 1

1. Before the audience left the concert hall, the orchestra played the last note.
2. After looking at the menu, you can order your meal.
   While looking at the menu, you can order your meal.
3. After the lights went out, we lit a candle.
   Before the lights went out, we lit a candle.
4. While we were waiting for you in the coffee shop, you were waiting for us at the bookstore.
5. Before they filled/filled up the car with gas/petrol, the car ran out of gas/petrol.

Practice 2

1. 7
2. 3
3. 1
4. 5
5. 6
6. 2
7. 4

Practice 3

In the early 1900s, Winston on Hudson was just a small town on the Hudson River. Nothing happened in the town until after the start of the First World War when a munitions factory opened. Once the factory opened, river traffic increased bringing raw materials to the factories and taking munitions downstream to the major river port at the mouth of the river. Within ten years, cargo boats were followed by passenger boats bringing weekend sightseers. Soon Winston on Hudson became a tourist destination. Today, the town's munitions factory has been turned into artist studios. In the future, the town hopes to build an art museum next to the old factory.

Practice 4

Answers will vary. Here is one example:

On December 22, 1982, I was born. I am my parents' first child. I started school when I was six years old, in 1988. Later, my parents had another baby, my brother. He was born in 1990. I was going to school then and enjoyed taking science classes. I won an award in 1995, "Best Science Student of the Year." That inspired me to study science seriously. In 2003, I decided to earn a chemistry degree at a university in an English-speaking country. Now I am studying English to prepare for my studies and my future career.

Spatial Order

Practice 5

1. between
2. next to/beside
3. north
4. behind
5 in front of
6. west
7. south and west
8. behind/next to/beside
9. beside/next to
10. around/beside/next to

CLASSIFICATION

PRACTICE 6

Word List	Things That Are Not Alive	Things That Are Alive
table	table	boy
boy	car	frog
frog	chair	butterfly
car	pencil	teacher
chair		
butterfly		
pencil		
teacher		

Word List	People	Things
doctor	doctor	hospital
nurse	nurse	building plans
contractor	contractor	
hospital	plumber	
building plans	patient	
plumber	architect	
patient		
architect		

PRACTICE 7

Positive Values	Negative Values
B. charity	A. anger
F. hope	C. envy
G. humility	D. gluttony
H. justice	E. greed
I. kindness	J. laziness
K. patience	L. pride

1. L
2. I
3. C
4. D
5. K
6. A
7. E
8. G
9. F
10. J
11. H
12. B

Answers will vary. Here is one example:

People who say, "Tomorrow is another day," have hope. This is a positive virtue. Hope is good because it motivates us. After a bad day, it can be difficult thinking about the next day to come. Sometimes we want everything to stop. People with hope believe that tomorrow might be better. So, they continue because they believe in positive change. Sometimes we just need to survive a bad day and look ahead to tomorrow. Hope gives us the strength we need during the difficult times.

Definition

Practice 8

Words	Concrete	Abstract
printer	printer	success
success	sidewalk/pavement/curb	loyalty
loyalty	black	freedom
sidewalk	swimming	love
freedom		
love		
black		
swimming		

Practice 9

Loyalty to me is defined as my family and knowing that they will always love me.

A sidewalk is a place to walk along the side of a street. It is usually paved, so the walkway is smooth and hard.

Freedom to me is defined as being able to choose what I want to do, such as my type of job.

Love to me is defined as the strong feelings of caring that I have for my parents.

Black is a very dark color.

Swimming is to move through the water by moving your arms and legs or if you're a fish, by moving your fins and tail.

Comparison and Contrast

Practice 10

1. CON
2. CON
3. COMP
4. CON
5. COMP
6. COMP
7. CON
8. COMP

PRACTICE 11

A
1. difference
2. while
3. however
4. In contrast to

B
5. similar to
6. alike
7. both
8. just as
9. both

PRACTICE 12

Dogs and cats are alike because both of these animals make wonderful pets. Both dogs and cats show a great deal of affection for their owners. Dogs may jump on their owners and lick them. Cats may rub against their owners' legs and purr. While their ways of expressing affection are different, both dogs and cats love the people who care for them.

PRACTICE 13

1. In all three areas—urban, suburban, and rural—the housing costs increased from 1990 to 2000. However, the amount of the increase differed. The urban housing costs doubled. Similarly, the suburban costs increased a great deal. They more than doubled. In contrast to those soaring prices, the rural cost increase was smaller. Like the other areas, it increased, but not as much.
2. When comparing the costs at each restaurant, lunch is less expensive than dinner served at the same place. The meals' costs at these restaurants varies; however, they all have something in common. Customers take more time eating at the places where the food is more expensive. For example, a 20-minute dinner at a fast food restaurant is only $5.00. This differs from a 60-minute dinner at a sit-down restaurant. That costs $17.00, so it is more than three times more expensive. People who are looking for the cheapest option should eat lunch at the fast food restaurant.

CAUSE AND EFFECT

PRACTICE 14

1. CO
2. C/E
3. C/E
4. C/E
5. CO
6. CO
7. C/E
8. C/E

PRACTICE 15

1. These instructions show how to use your new iron. Take the iron out of its package/box. As a result of plugging the cord into the outlet/socket, the iron will be turned on. Adjust the temperature gauge. This picture shows high/cotton. Because of the hot temperature used, be careful. The high/cotton setting will have a bad effect on silk. Be careful not to drop the iron into the water, since this will break the iron. Also, you do not want small children to burn themselves. For this reason, keep them away from the iron. Following these directions will help you to enjoy your iron for many years.
2. Each level of education resulted in a higher average salary. Therefore, if you want to earn more money, you should go back to school. You may be able to request a higher salary as a result of a more advanced educational level.

Prediction

Practice 16

1. A
2. B

Practice 17

1. By 2010, the schools will likely spend at least $1,000 less per pupil.
   By 2010, the students will probably decrease their test scores, at least 2%.
2. By 2005, the number of acres of forest logged will likely increase, to between 75,000 and 100,000 acres.
   By 2007, the number of forest-dwelling species will likely decrease, for every type of animal.

SPEAKING MODULE

Quick Study—Question Types

Part 1

Practice A

Answers will vary. Possible answers are given.

1. *What is your name?*
   My name is Mary.
2. *How do you spell it?*
   I spell it M-A-R-Y.
3. *Do you have your identity card? May I see it?*
   Yes, I do. Of course, you may see it.
4. *Let's talk about where you live. Can you describe your neighborhood/neighbourhood?*
   My neighborhood/neighbourhood has lots of apartment buildings. We have a school and a playground. There is also a park in my neighborhood/neighbourhood.
5. *What is an advantage of living there?*
   It's a quiet neighborhood/neighbourhood. That's an advantage.
6. *What is a disadvantage of living there?*
   It is not close to the bus stop or to the train station.
7. *Let's talk about jobs. What kind of job do you have?*
   My job is an office job. I work as a secretary.
8. *What is the best thing about your job?*
   I like the people at my office. They're very friendly.
9. *Let's talk about free time. What is one activity you enjoy doing in your free time?*
   I enjoy cooking in my free time.
10. *How did you become interested in this activity?*
    My mother taught me how to cook. I have loved it since I was a little girl.

PRACTICE B

Answers will vary.

Part 2

PRACTICE C

Place:	the park
Location:	in my neighborhood, 2 blocks away/2 streets away
Transportation:	walking or riding my bike
Appearance:	green grass and playground equipment
Why I like it:	It's peaceful. I like watching the children playing and families having fun.

PRACTICE D

Answers will vary.

PRACTICE E

1. *Do you go alone to this place?*
   Yes, usually I go alone/on my own. Sometimes a friend comes with me.
2. *Are there similar places you like to go?*
   There is a park in another neighborhood. Sometimes I go there, too.

PRACTICE F

Answers will vary.

Part 3

PRACTICE G

1. Most people take vacations to the beach/take holidays by the seaside, a famous city, or a unique location. Many of the places are the same. But now people can travel far away with less trouble. In the past, this was more difficult or impossible.
2. Leisure time is important. It gives people the chance to relax. It refreshes them. It helps people to be ready to do more work in the future.

Target 1—Describing Yourself

PRACTICE 1

Answers will vary.

Personal Information Form

<u>Factual</u>
First Name <u>Stefan</u>
Middle Name <u>Andreas</u>
Last Name <u>Holsen</u>
Age <u>25</u>
Nationality <u>German</u>
Native Language <u>German</u>
Occupation <u>Businessman</u>

<u>Physical</u>
Height <u>5 feet, 8 inches/185 centimetres</u>
Weight <u>175 pounds/8 kilos</u>
Eye Color <u>green</u>
Hair:
Color <u>brown</u> (check one) long__ short <u>X</u> medium length __
(check one) straight __ curly <u>X</u> wavy __
Other characteristics (glasses? beard? etc.) <u>yes, glasses</u>

<u>Emotional</u>
(circle all that apply)
(optimistic) pessimistic easygoing serious (fun loving) (studious) nervous calm
shy confident outgoing (friendly) hardworking (talkative) quiet cheerful

PRACTICE 2

Answers will vary.

Factual
1. My name is Fatma Aksay.
2. My first name is spelled F-A-T-M-A and my last name is spelled A-K-S-A-Y.
3. My name, Fatma, was also my grandmother's name.

Physical
1. I am five feet, five inches tall/182 centimetres tall.
2. My hair is straight.
3. My hair color is brown, but my eyes are green.

Emotional
1. I'm a cheerful person.
2. I'm usually happy and like telling jokes.
3. Sometimes I get nervous, though, when I take tests.

Target 2—Describing Your Family

PRACTICE 1

Answers will vary.

Family Information Form

	Relationship to You	Name	Age	Marital Status	Occupation	Other Information
Parents	mother	Juana	49	married	librarian	
	father	Eduardo	52	married	accountant	
Siblings	younger brother	Teodoro	22	single	student	has a girlfriend
	younger sister	Dora	19	single	student	likes studying languages
Other Relatives	uncle (Dad's brother)	Miguel	47	single	store manager	
	grandparents (all have passed on)					

PRACTICE 2

Answers will vary. (The answers below match Practice 1.)

1. I have four people in my immediate family.
2. I am the oldest child.
3. I have two younger siblings, my brother and my sister.

Target 3—Describing Your Home or Hometown

PRACTICE 1

Home Information Form

Size	medium
Age	fifty years
Number of bedrooms	four
Other rooms	kitchen, living room, dining room, 2 bathrooms
Garden/yard	large size, lots of flowers
Special features	attic
My Bedroom:	
Size	medium
Furniture	wood, painted brown, have a desk and a bed
Colors	white/cream paint on the walls
Art	posters of favorite musicians
Other	computer

Neighborhood[1] Information Form

Name	Flower Valley
Style of houses	older, family homes
Shops/businesses	restaurant, small grocery store/shop, drycleaner, gas/petrol station
Schools	one school for children
Religious buildings	church and a mosque
Other buildings	none
Transportation	bus stop, train stop
Parks/gardens	one park with a playground
Special characteristics	friendly neighborhood, very comfortable

PRACTICE 2

Home: General Description

1. Our home is medium-sized. It is about fifty years old.
2. We have four bedrooms, 2 bathrooms, and some other rooms.
3. Our yard is large, with lots of flowers.
4. We have an attic that we use for storage.

Neighborhood: General Description

1. We live in a neighborhood called Flower Valley.
2. The neighborhood's homes are older.
3. Many of the homes are large and usually families live in them.
4. We have some stores in the neighborhood, so shopping is convenient.

Home: Specific Description

1. Our house has four bedrooms: a large one for my parents and three smaller bedrooms for my brother, sister, and me.
2. My bedroom has brown, wood furniture.
3. I have a bed, desk, and computer in my bedroom.
4. The room is decorated with posters of my favorite bands.

[1]BRITISH: neighbourhood

Neighborhood: Specific Description

1. Flower Valley is a comfortable neighborhood, with very friendly people.
2. We have a restaurant, a small grocery store/shop, a drycleaner, and a gas/petrol station in the neighborhood.
3. I have lived here since I was a child. I walked to school everyday.
4. Everyone in the neighborhood enjoys our park and playground.

Target 4—Describing Your Occupation or School

Practice 1

Answers will vary.

Job Information Form

Company name Translational International

Job title Japanese translator

Length of time at this job 2 years

Duties translate technical materials

Training required for this job computer training, using software, training in technical language

Skills required for this job language skills in English and Japanese, computer skills

Things I like about this job using language

Things I don't like about this job can be tiring; requires a lot of concentration

Future career goals manage a large translation project

Education Information Form

Name of college City University

Major/subject English literature

Classes I am taking now Structure of English, World Literature

Hours per week in class 8

Years to complete degree/certificate 2

Educational goals master's degree

Future career goals teach English and write a book

PRACTICE 2

Answers will vary.

My occupation: Japanese translator

1. I work as a Japanese translator at Translation International.
2. I have worked there for two years.
3. My main duty is translating technical materials.
4. I like using language skills for my work, but sometimes it can be very tiring. Working as a translator requires a lot of concentration.

Target 5—Describing Your Hobbies or General Interests

PRACTICE 1

Answers will vary.

Hobby/Free-Time Activity Information Form

Hobby/Activity #1 playing computer games
How often do you do this hobby or activity? almost every day
Do you do it on your own or with other people? both
Do you belong to a club related to this hobby/activity? no
How did you learn how to do this hobby/activity? from friends and from the instructions that come with games
Do you need special equipment for it? yes, a computer and an Internet connection
What do you like most about it? fun and I can do it any time of the day or night

Hobby/Activity #2 cooking
How often do you do this hobby or activity? twice a week
Do you do it alone or with other people? alone/on my own
Do you belong to a club related to this hobby/activity? no
How did you learn how to do this hobby/activity? watching other people, including TV shows/programmes
Do you need special equipment for it? yes, some cooking equipment
What do you like most about it? I like trying a new recipe and eating the food.

PRACTICE 2

Answers will vary.

Hobby/Activity #1: playing computer games

1. I like playing computer games almost every day.
2. I can play games by myself, or I can go online and play against people who live all over the world.
3. I started playing computer games when I was 10 years old.
4. I like being able to play any time. The computer graphics improve every year, and that makes the games more fun.

Hobby/Activity #2: cooking

1. I like to cook. I usually cook twice a week.
2. It takes time to buy ingredients and try new recipes. I would cook more often if I had more time.
3. I like to watch someone cook on TV. Then I try to make the same food.
4. I love trying my cooking. Sometimes the food is bad, but I still continue cooking.

Target 6—Discussing a Topic

Practice 1

Answers will vary.

Topic 1 Notes

- Cat
- Needed food and water, brushing
- Liked that it was so friendly and easy to care for. Nothing I didn't like about it.
- It's popular because it's easy to care for it.

Topic 2 Notes

- Mom's birthday, age 48
- My dad and my brothers and sisters came.
- Had the party at Mom[1] and Dad's house
- Ate/had a big meal that we cooked for Mom, ate birthday cake and Mom opened her presents.

Topic 3 Notes

- Met Rob when we were 13. Went to the same school.
- Liked to play sports, go to watch games together.
- Were the same age and both liked sports.
- He was my best friend. I didn't have many friends, so he was very important to me.

Topic 4 Notes

- Went to the beach/seaside.
- 2 of my friends went with me.
- Went there for a vacation/holiday, to relax, and to spend time with my friends.
- Went swimming. Saw many different kinds of animals and fish. Went for a long boat ride.

[1]BRITISH: Mum

Practice 2

Answers will vary.

Topic 1

My family had a pet. It was a cat. We named her "Bobo." She needed food and water. Sometimes I brushed her fur. I liked Bobo because she was so friendly. She was easy to care for. I liked everything about Bobo. There was nothing that I didn't like. Cats are popular pets because it's so easy to care for them.

Topic 2

I recently went to my Mom's birthday party. She is now 48 years old. My dad and my brothers and sisters came to the party. It was at Mom and Dad's house. We cooked a big meal. Mom wasn't allowed to do any work. Later we ate birthday cake, and Mom opened her presents.

Topic 3

When I was a teenager, Rob was my best friend. We met when we were 13. We went to the same school. Rob and I liked to play sports together. We watched games together, too. We had a lot in common. We were the same age, went to the same school, and liked sports. This friendship was very important to me. I didn't have many friends. I am lucky that Rob was there and that he was a very good friend.

Topic 4

I recently took a trip to the beach/seaside. Two of my friends went with me. We went there for a holiday/vacation. We needed to relax, and we wanted to spend time together. During the vacation/holiday, we had so much fun. We went to the beach/sea every day and we swam. We took a long boat ride, and we saw many different kinds of animals and fish. We want to return next year.

Target 7—Responding to Follow-up Questions

Practice 1

Answers will vary.

Topic 1

1. Advantage—children have responsibility. Disadvantage—parents do work if children don't
2. Yes, so children can learn responsibility.

Topic 2

1. Celebrate with family and friends, at home or go out.
2. Celebrating the new year.

Topic 3

1. Fix our cars, eat, watch sports.
2. A few good friends, so we're closer.

Topic 4

1. Warm weather, different than where I live.
2. Yes, so I can experience new things. Meet people, learn language and culture.

PRACTICE 2

Answers will vary.

Topic 1

1. The advantage of pets is that children learn responsibility when they own pets. The disadvantage is that sometimes parents must care for the pets.
2. As far as I'm concerned, it is important for children to have pets. Children learn responsibility when they care for their pets.

Topic 2

1. I like to celebrate my birthday by enjoying the day with my family and friends. We might stay at home or go out, but we must be together.
2. I also like to celebrate the beginning of a new year. It is a good way to start the year.

Topic 3

1. I like to fix our cars, eat, and watch sports.
2. Personally I think it's better to have just a few good friends. I want to be closer to a few people. When you have a lot of friends, you don't know each person as well.

Topic 4

1. I'm in favor/favour of visiting places that have warm weather. I live in a cold place, so I like to go to a different climate.
2. As far as I'm concerned, traveling/travelling is a wonderful way to spend time. I like to experience new things. I meet new people and learn about their language and culture.

Target 8—Discussing an Issue in Depth

PRACTICE 1

Answers will vary.

Issues from Topic 1

Def.: For friendship. Dogs are the best pets.
C. & C.: Animals have been useful by doing work and by being companions for people. Nowadays, animals are companions; work is done by machines.

Issues from Topic 2

Def.: Yes. Knowledge gained and more to come. Older people are respected, but everyone wants to be young.
C.& C.: No, they're the same. Older people act younger. Will continue.

Issues from Topic 3

Def.: Kind, loyal, honest. Friends are important, like family.
C. & C.: Men become friends to do activities together. Women have friends who listen to their problems. No, it's same.

Issues from Topic 4

Def.: For business or fun. Too much pollution from cars, cause traffic jams, other problems.
C. & C.: Much more travel now. People can live away from families, but quickly fly to see them. Tourism brings money, but can bring more pollution and strangers.

PRACTICE 2

Issues from Topic 1

Most people have pets for friendship. In my opinion, dogs are the best pets. Animals have been useful to people throughout history. They have been good companions. Also, they did a lot of work, before cars and modern farming equipment. Today most people's attitudes toward animals are different. They value animals for friendship, not their work.

Issues from Topic 2

Birthday celebrations are important in my country. We celebrate the knowledge gained in that year and get ready for the new experiences to come. Older people are respected in my culture, but everyone wants to be young. The birthday celebrations of today and of the past are the same. They all mark the passage of a one-year period. In my opinion, the role of older people in my culture will be the same in the future. But because youth is preferred, older people will continue trying to look younger.

Issues from Topic 3

There are important qualities in a good friend: kindness, loyalty, and honesty. Good friends are like a member of the family. They are there to celebrate the good times and to help you through the bad times. There is a difference between men's and women's friendships. Men become friends because they like to do an activity together. Women become friends to share problems and to give advice. Although there is a difference between men's and women's friendships, the nature of friendship is the same.

Issues from Topic 4

People travel for business or pleasure. We have some transportation problems in my country, such as too much pollution from cars and traffic jams. There is much more travel now, because of planes. It is possible to quickly travel a long distance. This results in advantages and disadvantages. For example, tourism can bring money to a place. On the other hand, tourism can also lead to the construction of more hotels and other buildings, using our few green areas. It can also cause more pollution. These results are negative.

10

EXPLANATORY ANSWERS FOR THE IELTS MODEL TESTS

ACADEMIC MODEL TEST 1

Listening

1. 1.—(A) In Winston's first full exchange, he says he would like to *sign up now* which means he would like to *register for a class today*.
   2.—(C) In the same exchange, he says he wants to register for the classes that begin *next week*.
   3.—(B) Winston says, "I'm planning to take a vacation/holiday in Japan next summer . . ."
2. (B) and (D) either order. The receptionist mentions only three types of courses offered at World Language Academy—Japanese for Tourists, Japanese for Business Travelers, and Japanese for University Students. Two of these courses are included in the answer possibilities (B) and (D). Choice (A) is incorrect because a course is for university students, not professors. Choice (C) is incorrect because the course is for tourists, not tour guides. Choice (E) is incorrect because the speaker talks about native teachers of Japanese as teachers. Choice (F) is incorrect because this type of course is not offered, and Mark is planning on eating, not working in Japanese restaurants.
3. (A) and (D) either order. The student's reasons for learning Japanese are to order food in a restaurant and go shopping. Winston says, "I just want to learn enough to order food in restaurants and go shopping and things like that." Choice (B) *climbing mountains* is mentioned by the receptionist about what she had done in Japan and is therefore incorrect. Choices (C) and (E) confuse *business meeting* and *university course* with the topics of classes offered at the academy. Choice (F) is incorrect because the student does not want to learn with a tutor. Studying with a tutor is mentioned only as a possibility of how he can achieve his goal of learning basic Japanese.

The schedule for Japanese classes is as follows:

Basic: Monday, Tuesday, Wednesday, Thursday 9:00–10:00 A.M.
Intermediate: Monday, Wednesday, Thursday 1:00–3:00
Advanced: Tuesday, Thursday 7:30–9:30
Japanese for Tourists: Monday, Wednesday, Thursday, 5:30–7:30

Morning	Days: Monday–Friday Time: **4** 9:00–2:00 Level: Beginner
Afternoon	Days: Monday, Wednesday, Thursday Time: 1:00–3:00 Level: **5** Intermediate
Evening	Days: Monday, Wednesday, Thursday Time: 5:30–7:30 Level: **6** Beginner Days: **7** Monday, Wednesday, Thursday Time: 7:30–9:30 Level: Advanced
8 Weekend	Days: Saturday Time: 9:00–2:00 Level: Beginner

9. (B) Choice (B) is the correct answer because the student decided to take the Saturday class. It meets from 9:00 to 2:00, and the receptionist says it will have only four or five people in it. Choice (A) is incorrect because the student only has evenings and weekends free, but the student cannot take the night classes they offer because the level is too advanced. Choice (C) is incorrect because the student says that a private class is too expensive for him.
10. (A) Choice (A) is correct because the student asks if he can pay by check, and the receptionist says he can. Choice (B) is incorrect because the student decides to pay by check. The receptionist does say that payment *can* be made by credit card or check.
11. *300.* "In fact, there are more than 300 different species of parrots, and they live all over the world."
12. *green.* "Some species are very colorful/colourful, but, believe it or not, plain old green is actually the most common color for parrots."
13. *one meter.* "The hyacinth macaw, on the other hand, measures one meter/metre from the tip of its beak to the tip of its tail. It's the largest of all the parrots."
14. *social.* "OK, pets. The reason parrots make fantastic pets is that they're naturally social animals."
15. *attention.* "Parrots not only like attention, they need attention."
16. *bored/ignored/lonely/neglected.* "For example, boredom may cause them to pull out all their feathers, and unfortunately, this is quite a common problem. Also, feeling ignored may cause them to scream all day. There have been too many sad stories about neglected pet parrots."
17. *may scream.* "Also, feeling ignored may cause them to scream all day."
18 *(wooden) toys.* "And make sure the toys are made of wood because parrots love to chew."
19. *are messy/have messy habits.* "Another thing to be aware of is that parrots have messy habits. They throw their food everywhere. This is natural behavior/behaviour for them, but it means more work for you. Your parrot's cage will have to be cleaned daily."
20. *seeds.* "In addition to seeds, you should feed your parrot plenty of fresh fruit and vegetables."
21. *several European countries/Europe.* These trains are having a great deal of success in Japan and in several European countries, as well.
22. *1964.* "They've actually been around for a while—since 1964, in fact."
23. *200.* "We usually call a train high speed if it's capable of traveling at 200 kilometers/kilometres an hour or faster."
24. *drive (cars).* "Cars and highways were improved, so more and more people started driving cars."

25. *frequent and affordable.* "Plane service is more frequent and affordable now than it was in the past, so planes, like cars, have become more convenient for people."
26. *congestion.* "But with everybody driving cars and taking planes, we have a lot of congestion."

27–30. (B), (D), (F), and (G) are correct.
- (B) "But, a train trip is much more relaxing than a car trip. You can read, sleep, eat, whatever, while the train carries you to your destination."
- (D) "And of course you're never delayed by traffic jams."
- (F) "Also trains can carry more passengers than planes."
- (G) "They can also offer more frequent service."
- (A) is incorrect because the speaker says that train trips are some times more expensive than car trips. (C) is incorrect because the speaker does not discuss pollution from trains or other forms of transportation. (E) confuses security systems on trains with going through security at the airport.

31. *Germany.* Paragraph 2: "Albert Einstein was born in Germany in 1879."
32. *studying math(s)/mathematics.* Paragraph 3: "He didn't even begin to study mathematics until he was 12."
33. *at age 15.* Paragraph 5: "When Einstein was 15, his family moved to Italy."
34. *1896.* Paragraph 5: " Soon after that, his parents sent him to Switzerland, where in 1896 he finished high school."
35. *1898.* Paragraph 7: "Meanwhile, in 1898, between graduating from high school and getting his job at the Patent Office, Einstein met and fell in love with a young Serbian woman, Mileva Maric."
36. *received/got teaching diploma.* Paragraph 5: "After graduating from high school, he enrolled in a Swiss technological institute. He received a teaching diploma from the institute in 1900."
37. *a Swiss citizen.* Paragraph 5: "He remained in Switzerland and eventually became a Swiss citizen, in 1901."
38. *had a daughter.* Paragraph 7: "They had a daughter in 1902."
39. *1903.* Paragraph 7: "but unusual for the time even for geniuses, they didn't get married until 1903."
40. *1904.* Paragraph 6: "they didn't get married until 1903. Their first son was born the following year."

Reading

Passage 1—The Value of a College Degree

1. False. Paragraph 1 states: "The escalating cost of higher education is causing many to question the value of continuing education beyond high school."
2. True. Paragraph 1 states: "the accumulation of thousands of dollars of debt is, in the long run, worth the investment."
3. True. (Paragraph 4 states: "Most students today—about 80 percent of all students—enroll either in public four-year colleges or in public two-year colleges."
4. Not Given. There is no information about the contrast of public and private colleges.
5. *a lifetime.* Paragraph 3: "According to the Census Bureau, over an adult's working life, high school graduates earn an average of $1.2 million."
6. *$1.6 million/1.6 million dollars.* Paragraph 3: "associate's degree holders earn about $1.6 million"
7. *bachelor's degree holder.* Paragraph 3: "and bachelor's degree holders earn about $2.1 million."
8. *8,655.* Paragraph 4: "a full-time student at a public four-year college pays an average of $8,655 for in-state tuition, room, and board."
9. *tuition.* Paragraph 4: "A full-time student in a public two-year college pays an average of $1,359 per year in tuition."

(C), (D), (E), and (G) are correct.
(C) Paragraph 6 "graduates enjoy, including higher levels of saving"
(D) Paragraph 6 "graduates enjoy . . . more hobbies and leisure activities"

(E) Paragraph 7: "In fact, 'parental schooling levels (after controlling for differences in earnings) are positively correlated with the health status of their children" and "increased schooling" (and higher relative income) are correlated with lower mortality rates for given age brackets.'"

(G) Paragraph 9: "Public benefits of attending college include . . . increased consumption."

Choices (A), (B) and (F) are incorrect. The text does not include a discussion of house size (A), or travel (F). (B) is incorrect because the text gives many reasons why a graduate degree has a positive impact on people ("improved quality of life . . . more open-minded, more cultured, rational greater productivity") but it does not *say* that people are more optimistic about their lives.

Passage 2—Less Television and Less Violence

14. *watched TV*. Paragraph 2: The study found that the third- and fourth-grade students "engaged in fewer acts of verbal and physical aggression than their peers" when they watched less TV.
15. *violently*. Paragraph 2: The study found that the third- and fourth-grade students "engaged in fewer acts of verbal and physical aggression than their peers" when they watched less TV.
16. *6/six months*. Paragraph 3: "18-lesson, 6-month program"
17. *parents*. Paragraph 6: "parental reports of aggressive behavior, and perceptions of a mean and scary world also decreased"
18. *number of hours*. Paragraph 8: "Early lessons encouraged students to keep track of and report on the time they spent watching TV or videos, or playing video games, to motivate them to limit those activities on their own."
19. *avoided TV*. Paragraph 9: "For ten days, students were challenged to go without television, videos, or video games."
20. *less TV*. Paragraph 10 states that "students themselves [began to] advocate reducing screen activities."
21. False. Paragraph 11 states that "This study is by no means the first to find a link."
22. True. Paragraph 14 states that "In the United States and Canada, murder rated doubled."
23. Not Given. Paragraph 14 discusses TV and violence in the United States and Canada, but there is no discussion about which country has more, or if the United States has more than other countries.
24. Not Given. Regarding South Africa, we are given information about how long TV was banned—until 1975 (Paragraph 15)—and that murder rates were steady in the 1940s, but the text does not say when TV was introduced in South Africa.
25. (D)
    In the second to last paragraph, the text states that "watching television of any content robs us of the time to interact with real people," which can be seen as learning an important social skill. (A), (B), and (C) are incorrect because the text does not address the role of TV for adults (A), does not suggest that TV is the *only* cause of violence (B), and does not make any comparisons between the United States and other countries (C).
26. (B)
    In the last line, the authors suggest that "[t]he best solution is to turn it [the TV] off." Choice (A) is incorrect because the authors do not discuss humor[1] in TV programs. Choice (C) is incorrect because they do not talk about watching TV alone or with company. Choice (D) is incorrect because the text says in paragraph 9 that the children were encouraged to keep their TV watching time to under seven hours, but that is not suggested as an ideal amount for the reader.

[1]BRITISH: humour

Passage 3—Issues Affecting the Southern Resident Orcas

27. iii—Declining Fish Populations is the correct answer. Section A discusses the decrease of fish populations which affect the diet of the orcas. In the last line of the first paragraph, "This may be affecting . . .", *this* refers to declining fish populations. In addition, there is no other heading listed that can describe the idea of Section A.
28. ii—Toxic Exposure is the correct answer. The first line of Section B starts with "Toxic substances accumulate . . .," which indicates that the section is about toxic substances. Further reading of the section shows supporting evidence for the topic sentence. Heading (i) is mentioned in the section, but it is not the central idea of the section.
29. vii—Impact of Boat Traffic is the correct answer. Again, the first line of Section C states: "waters around the San Juan Islands are extremely busy due to international commercial shipping, fishing, whale watching, and pleasure boating," and the section goes on to talk about the dangers of various types of boats. The fourth paragraph in Section C mentions "smog" as being similar to the exhaust of idle boat traffic. Also, heading (iv) describes *one* type of boating mentioned in the section.
30. v—Underwater Noise is the correct answer. The first line introduces the idea of "acoustic pollution," suggesting the theme of noise. In the section, there are five additional mentions of "noise," or synonyms of noise: noise, sound, listening, noise, acoustics. Choice (v) is the only logical heading for this section.
31. (B) In section A the text states "90 percent of their [orcas'] diet is salmon." (A) and (D) are both secondary choices for the orcas if there are no salmon, and the orcas must eat from the bottom of the ocean and (C) is true for all orcas, but not for the pods specified in the question—J, K, and L—who eat mostly fish, and the fish they prefer is salmon.
32. (A) Section A states that "salmon have become extinct due to habitat loss." Whales only eat the surviving stocks of salmon after they have already decreased in numbers, so (B) is incorrect; it is *whales* and not the *salmon* that have poor nutrition, making (C) incorrect. Choice (D) assumes that the "winter" is a temperature indicator when it is actually a seasonal adjective and does not describe temperature as being cold.
33. *on bottomfish*. Section A, paragraph 2: "whales may be feeding on bottomfish" becomes "they believe the whales *feed* on bottomfish."
34. *smaller*. Section A says: "their size has decreased" = "they are smaller." The grammar compels you to use the comparative form.
35. *Pollution*. Section B states that orcas are affected more by pollutants than other creatures because they are at the top of the food chain.
36. *(so) popular*. The last sentence of section B says: "because orcas are so popular."
37. *numerous boats/vessels*. Paragraph 1 in section C states that: "On a busy weekend day in the summer, it is not uncommon to see numerous boats in the vicinity of the whales as they travel through the area."
38. *(so) quiet*. Paragraph 3 of section C says: "Kayakers even present a problem here because they're so quiet."
39. *exhaust fumes*. Paragraph 4 of section C says that whales "get a nice big breath of exhaust fumes."
40. *communicating*. Section D discusses how noise pollution contributes to orca communication.

Writing

Writing Task 1

The sales at this small restaurant during the week of October 7 to 13th followed a fairly set pattern from Monday to Friday, and then showed a notable shift on the weekend. The lunch and dinner sales during the week peaked on Friday and then dipped down as the weekend set in.

During the week of October 7–14th, the lunch sales averaged at approximately $2,400. The highest lunch sales occurred on Friday, and the lowest occurred on Sunday. Sunday's lunch sales were approximately $1,000 less than the average lunch sales during the rest of the week.

Dinner sales, which generated at least $1,000 to $1,500 more a day than lunch sales, also remained steady during the week. Just like the lunch sales, the dinner sales peak on Friday and dipped down for the weekend.

Excluding Wednesday and Thursday, the lunch and dinner sales from October 7–11 rose gradually until the end of the business week. Midweek, on Wednesday and Thursday, the sales were slightly lower than they were on Tuesday.

According to the sales report, this restaurant has a steady lunch and dinner crowd. The most profitable day during the second week of October was Friday. Sunday, was the least profitable day, with the full day's sales totaling/totalling less than the Friday dinner sales. These numbers are reflective of a restaurant that is located in a business/financial district where business hours are Monday through Friday.

Writing Task 2

When computers first made their way into the business sector, everyone believed that they would make people's jobs easier. What was not expected was that computers would eliminate jobs. Besides contributing to unemployment, these automated workers often exhibit inadequate job performance.

A number of jobs have been lost as a direct result of new computer technology. Ticket agents in various transportation facilities, from subway/underground stations to airports are virtually nonexistent these days. Bank tellers have been greatly reduced due to automated bank machines. In addition, many call centers/centres that have help lines are almost entirely computerized/computerised. A few years ago I worked as a helper in our local library. Today this position does not exist, because six new computers have been installed. The number of positions lost to computers grows exponentially, and unemployment continues to get worse.

While a computer may easily achieve the main tasks of these jobs, most computers fall short when customers have a unique request or problem. A pre-paid ticket booth does not have insight about the entertainment district and cannot offer friendly directions to a tourist. Similarly, an automated bank machine cannot provide assistance and reassurance to a customer who has just had his credit card stolen. And, more often than not, automated telephone operators cannot answer the one question that we have, and we end up waiting on the line to speak with someone anyway. Every time I go into the library where I worked I notice elderly people who don't know how to use the computers and can't find anyone to help.

In the future, I believe a new business trend will evolve. As computers eliminate jobs, new positions will have to be invented. More and more people will go into business for themselves, and hopefully put the personal touch back into business. I believe that the human workforce will demonstrate that it is more valuable than computers.

Speaking

Part 1

Who is your best friend?
My best friend's name is Mia.

Why do you call this person your best friend?
I call her my best friend because I have known her since my early childhood. She has always been in my life, no matter what else changed.

What makes this friend closer than your other friends?
Whenever I have something to tell someone, I always tell Mia first. It can be good news or bad news. It doesn't matter. I always know that she will be there to listen.

Do you think it's better to have a large group of friends or a few close friends?
I have a few friends other than Mia, but I have never been one to hang out in a large group. Except for maybe in high school when a whole grade/class of kids would hang out/socialize together. But these days I'd much rather have a few close friends who know me very well. I enjoy their company.

Describe what you and your friends like to do.
My favorite thing to do with my friends is just sit in a coffee shop and chat. There's nothing like sitting in my favorite coffee shop with my friends Mia and Jay, just laughing about nothing. We rarely go to movies/films or parties anymore because we're too busy with work and school.

Have you remained friends with people from your childhood? Why or why not.
No, not really. Other than Mia of course. When I started college my parents moved about fifteen minutes away from where I grew up and I kind of/sort of lost touch with everyone. I still see them around sometimes, but we don't have much in common anymore.

How do people choose their friends?
I think we choose our friends based on a comfortable feeling. You know, sometimes people just understand each other so easily and the conversation just flows. Of course, there's usually at least one thing that people have in common, such as work or school.

Part 2

Everyone says I'm a lot like my dad, because we look a lot alike. But, truthfully, I'm a lot more like my mom. Part of the reason my mom and I are so similar is that we spend so much time together. Besides spending one year abroad, I've lived with my mom for my whole life. My parents split up ten years ago, and ever since then my mom and I became very close.

My mom and I have the same taste in a lot of things, such as food, fashion, and literature. We both love to eat spicy food, and we both love to bake sweets. Oh, and neither of us ever start the day without our morning cup of green tea. It was weird when I first realized/realised that I could borrow my mom's clothes. I guess she's always just kept up with modern fashion unlike some of my friends' mothers. We both like long skirts and warm sweaters and neither of us ever wear jeans. My mom and I both like to read as well. Ever since I was little my mother always read to me before bed. Sometimes she still reads out loud to me just for fun.

I guess its natural for a person to share some of the same qualities as one or both of their parents. But I also think that part of the reason we are so alike is just that we became dependent on each other. I'm an only child, so my mom always had lots of time to spend with me.

Part 3

Do you enjoy spending time with relatives? Why or why not?
Yes, I love getting together for family functions because it's nice to catch up on each other's lives and see how people have changed.

Which of your relatives do you spend the most time with?
Well, these days I spend the most time with my mother and my father's mother. I used to spend a lot of time with my grandfather on my mother's side, but he recently passed away.

Who do you spend the least amount of time with?
I spend the least amount of time with my dad and my aunts and uncles. They don't live near me, so I only see them on special occasions.

When do you and your extended family gather?
The only time I get together with my dad's side of the family is at weddings and birthdays. I see my grandmother about once every two weeks when we meet for dinner.

What types of traditions do you and your relatives have?
We used to have a lot more traditions when were kids. For example, every New Year, we would have a big party at my grandfather's house, and all of the kids would collect a lot of money. We also used to have a big summer picnic for all of the birthdays that happened in the summer. I miss those traditions.

Do you think family members are more important than friends?
I think it depends on where you are at in life. At some points in my life, my mom has been the most important person, and at other times I have been closer to one of my friends.

Is there anyone in your life who is not related but is considered part of the family anyway?
My mom has a friend named Sue who I call Auntie Susie. She has been my mom's friend for twenty years, so she has always been in my life. We always invite her to our family gatherings, and she always sends me a birthday gift/present. I consider her my aunt even though she isn't blood related.

ACADEMIC MODEL TEST 2

Listening

Example. (B) Choice (B) is correct because the man is "conducting a survey of shoppers at this mall." He also wants to learn about "people's habits when they shop at the mall." Choice (A) is incorrect because the man is not shopping at the mall; he is conducting a survey. Choice (C) is incorrect because he is not looking for a shop.

1. (B) The man wants to learn about "people's habits when they shop at the mall." The other choices—(A) and (C)—are not mentioned during their conversation.
2. (A) Choice (A) is correct because the man is "interviewing married women, that is women with husbands and children who shop for their families." Choice (B) is incorrect because the man won't talk to "any shopper." Choice (C) is incorrect because the man does not want to speak to children.
3. (B) Choice (B)—26–35—is correct because she says, "I'm 34", which fits into that range. Choices (A) and (C) give numeric ranges that do not match her age.

4. (C) Choice (C) is correct because she says, "I'm here at least twice a week." This statement is the equivalent of choice (C)—two or more times a week. Choice (A)—less than once a month—is incorrect because it is a time period that the man mentions, but the woman does not select that time period. Choice (B)—once a week—is incorrect. It is never mentioned during their conversation.
5. (C) Choice (C) is correct because she says, "The reason I come here so often is for food. I told you I have a large family. I buy all our food at the supermarket here." Choice (A) is incorrect because the woman says, "The clothing stores are quite nice," but she doesn't say that she usually shops for clothes. Choice (B) is incorrect because she says, "I like the book store," but she doesn't say that she usually shops for books.
6. (B) Choice (B) is correct because she spends "about an hour and a half or so." Choice (A)—one hour or less—is incorrect because she doesn't say that she ever spends that amount of time at the mall. Choice (C)—more than two hours—is incorrect because she says, "I'm hardly ever here for more than two hours." So, she is not usually at the mall for that amount of time . . . and the question asks for her usual length of time.
7. (A) Choice (A) is correct because the woman says, "I always drive." Choice (B)—bus—is provided by the man as an option, which she doesn't select. Choice (C)—subway—is incorrect. It is never mentioned.
8. Multiple possible answers:
   (a) Employees are polite
   (b) Give good service
   (c) Very good service
   (d) Polite employees
   The woman likes the shoe store because, "the employees there are so polite. They give very good service."
9. The correct answer is "it's very expensive." The woman says, "[the food] is very expensive. It shouldn't cost so much."
10. Multiple possible answers
    (a) add more parking
    (b) more parking spaces/places
    (c) add parking spaces/places
    (d) add parking
    The woman says, "You should add more parking spaces."
11. (A) Choice (A) is correct because the purpose of the tour is to let people "become familiar with the different activities available at the club." The goal of the tour is to have everyone "decide to become members." Choice (B) is incorrect because the club members already have a membership. They don't need to be convinced to join again. Choice (C) is incorrect because the people who work at the club already know about all of the club's activities.

12–14. Choices (A), (D), and (F) are correct.
Choice (A)—learn to play tennis—is correct because the club does "offer tennis lessons." Choice (D) is correct because the club has "the most modern exercise machines." Choice (F) is correct because club members "have the opportunity to try out for the swim team."
Choice (B) is incorrect because their club store offers only "snacks or drinks." Choice (C) is incorrect because the only expert mentioned is a fitness and technology expert, but not a nutrition expert. Choice (E) is incorrect because "run on a track" is never mentioned.

15–17. Choices (C), (E), and (F) are correct.
Choice (C) is correct because they are told to "supply your own shampoo." Choice (E) is correct because people are told that everyone must "wear rubber sandals in the changing rooms" and since they aren't told where to get the sandals, it is understood that you need to bring your own. Choice (F) is correct because people are told "to supply your own lock."
Choices (A) and (B) are incorrect because the club's locker/changing rooms are kept "well-stocked with basic necessities such as towels and soap." Choice (D) is incorrect because "There are plenty of . . . hair dryers."

18. *by an adult.* "Children must be accompanied by an adult at all times."
19. Multiple possible answers.
    (a) *running.* "No running near the pool."
    (b) *children alone* (see #18).
20. *shower.* People are told, "we ask everyone to shower before entering the pool."
21. *weekly/once a week/every week.* The professor says, "You'll have to write one essay each week." Also, she says, "Every week I'll assign a different type of essay."
22. *350 to 400.*

Essay Type	**Sample Topic**
23 Process	How to change the oil in a car
24 Classification	Three kinds of friends
25 Compare and contrast	Student cafeteria food and restaurant food
Argumentative	The necessity of **26** homework

27. (B) Choice (B) is correct because the professor tells the students that she wants them to "pick your own topics." Choices (A) and (C) are incorrect because the professor says that students will pick their own topics. The professor mentions books, but only when telling students that the topics must be original: "I want them [the topics] to come out of your own heads, not out of any book on essay writing."
28. (C) Choice (C)—Friday—is correct because the professor says each student will "hand [it] in to me the following Friday." Choice (A) is incorrect—Monday—because that is the day that the essay assignment is given, not when it is due. Choice (B)—Wednesday—is incorrect because that day is never mentioned.
29. (C) Choice (C) is correct because the professor says that "your essays will count for 65 percent of your final grade[1]." Choice (A) is incorrect because it doesn't refer to essays: "Other class work will count for 15 percent." Choice (B) is incorrect because it doesn't refer to essays: "Your tests will be 20 percent of the final grade."
30. (A) Choice (A) is correct because the professor tells them, "Please type your essays on a computer." Choice (B) is incorrect because the professor says, "Handwritten essays are not acceptable," which has the same meaning as Choice (B)—write their essays by hand. Choice (C) is incorrect because the professor says, "I don't want to receive any photocopied work."
31. Introduction to Anthropology "This class is Introduction to Anthropology."
32. Tuesday "This class meets every Tuesday evening."
33. women "The men's job is to hunt . . . while the women gather plants . . ."
34. twelve thousand years "Before 12,000 years ago, all humans lived as hunter-gathers."
35. some desert areas/deserts "Today hunter-gather societies still exist in the Arctic, in some desert areas, and in tropical rainforests."
36. rainforests/tropical rainforests (see #35).

Characteristic	**A**	**B**
37 They usually stay in one place.		XX
38 They are nomadic.	XX	
39 They have a higher population density.		XX
40 They have a nonhierarchical social structure.	XX	

[1]BRITISH: mark

37. (B)
Choice (B) is correct because the professor says that farmers are more likely to be sedentary. They can't move often because they need to plant their crops. Choice (A) is incorrect because the hunter-gatherers "travel from place to place."
38. (A)
Choice (A) is correct because the professor says that they tend to be nomadic. Choice (B) is incorrect because farmers can't move often because they need to plant their crops.
39. (B)
Choice (B) is correct because "Farming can support much higher population densities than hunting and gathering can because farming results in a larger food supply." Choice (A) is incorrect because "hunter-gatherer societies generally have lower population densities." Also, the farming society's population density is higher than theirs.
40. (A)
Choice (A) is correct because hunter-gatherer societies "tend not to have hierarchical social structures." Choice (B) is incorrect because farming societies had "hierarchical social structures begin to develop."

Reading

Passage 1—Glaciers

1. (vi—Types of Glaciers) is the correct answer. Paragraph A defines the term *glacier* and describes four specific types of glaciers.
2. (ii—Formation and Growth of Glaciers) is the correct answer. Paragraph B describes the reason why glaciers generally form in the high alpine regions—because "they require cold temperatures throughout the year." The paragraph also describes the retreat of glaciers during periods when melting and evaporation exceed the amount of snowfall.
3. (iii—Glacial Movement) is the correct answer. Paragraph C begins with a clear topic sentence: "The weight and pressure of ice accumulation causes glacier movement." The rest of the paragraph then provides details about this movement.
4. (vii—Glacial Effects on Landscape) is the correct answer. Like the previous paragraph, paragraph D begins with a clear topic sentence directly related to the topic: "glacial erosion creates other unique physical features in the landscape such as horns" and so on. Each feature is described in the following sentences.
5. (v—Glaciers Through the Years) is the correct answer. Paragraph E refers to the glaciers from the Ice Age, the past century, and even looks into the future by referring to studies that glaciologists can conduct now and in the future.
6. False. Paragraph B, first sentence states: "glaciers exist on all continents," and Paragraph B, last sentence states: "The fastest glacial surge on record occurred in . . . the Kutiah Glacier in Pakistan," which is not at the poles.
7. True. Paragraph B, middle sentence states: "While glaciers rely heavily on snowfall, other climatic conditions including freezing rain, avalanches, and wind, contribute to their growth."
8. True. Paragraph B, second to the last sentence states: "With the rare exception of *surging glaciers,* a common glacier flowers about 10 inches per day in the summer and 5 inches per day in the winter." This fits the 5–10 inch range.
9. False. Paragraph C states: "The middle of a glacier moves faster than the sides and bottom because there is no rock to cause friction."
10. Not Given. Paragraph E refers to the last Ice Age and the percentage of glaciers that covered the earth's surface. However, no mention is made of the temperatures then.

11. B Paragraph A explains: "Smaller glaciers that occur at higher elevations are called *alpine* or *valley glaciers.*" Paragraph D refers to "alpine glaciers [occurring] on the same mountain."
12. D Paragraph A states: "*Polar glaciers* . . . always maintain temperatures far below melting." Therefore, these temperatures are freezing, and D is the correct answer.
13. H Paragraph B says: "With the rare exception of *surging glaciers*, a common glacier flows about 10 inches per day in the summer and 5 inches per day in the winter. The fastest glacial surge on record occurred in 1953." So the reader can infer that the term surging glacier is related to the speed of the glacier's movement.
14. A Paragraph D explains: "*Fjords* . . . are coastal valleys that fill with ocean water." Therefore, the reader assumes that fjords form near the ocean and term A (fjord) is selected as the correct answer.
15. G Paragraph D states: "A cirque is a large bowl-shaped valley that forms at the front of a glacier."

Passage 2—Irish Potato Famine

16. F Paragraph F begins by stating the British government's political policy toward Ireland during the famine: "The majority of the British officials in the 1840s adopted the laissez-faire philosophy." The rest of the paragraph provides details about the British government's action (or lack of action) to help Ireland and the impact that had on Ireland.
17. D Paragraph D describes the British tenure system, including how British landowners charged rent and people lived on smaller and smaller parcels of land.
18. B Paragraph B describes how Europeans changed their attitude about potatoes, from saying it "belonged to a botanical family of a poisonous breed" to having the European monarchs order the wide planting of the vegetable.
19. E Paragraph E examines the Penal Laws and the many rights those laws denied the Irish peasants.
20. C Paragraph C describes Ireland's dependence on the potato—as a crop and as a stored food item.
21. I Paragraph B states: "Europeans believed that potatoes belonged to a botanical family of a poisonous breed."
22. K Paragraph B states: "By the late 1700s, the dietary value of the potato had been discovered, and the monarchs of Europe ordered the vegetable to be widely planted."
23. C Paragraph C states: "By 1800, the vast majority of the Irish population had become dependent on the potato as its primary staple."
24. E Paragraph C states: "Those who did manage to grow things such as oats, wheat, and barley relied on earnings from these exported crops to keep their rented homes."
25. G Paragraph D states: "As the population of Ireland grew, however, the plots were continuously subdivided . . . families were forced to move to less fertile land where almost nothing but the potato would grow."
26. A Paragraph E states: "Approximately 500,000 Irish tenants were evicted. . . . Many of these people . . . were put in jail for overdue rent."
27. H Paragraph F states: "Sir Robert Peel . . . showed compassion toward the Irish by making a sudden move to repeal the Corn Laws. . . . For this hasty decision, Peel quickly lost the support of the British people and was forced to resign.
28. F Paragraph F states: "A few relief programs were eventually implemented, such as soup kitchens and workhouses; [but] these were poorly run institutions."

Passage 3—Anesthesiology

29. False. Paragraph 1 states that his book "was the primary reference source for physicians for over sixteen centuries," so it did not fall out of use after 60 A.D.
30. True. Paragraph 2 states: "The mandragora . . . was one of the first plants to be used as an anesthetic." Then the paragraph refers to its use in the Middle Ages.

31. True. Paragraph 3 explains nitrous oxide caused "a strange euphoria, followed by fits of laughter, tears, and sometimes unconsciousness."
32. Not Given. Paragraph 3 refers to laughing gas being used in 1844 to relieve pain during a tooth extraction. However, no details are given about anesthesia/anaesthesia being used for the remainder of the century.
33. True. Paragraph 5 states: "It takes over eight years of schooling and four years of residency until an anesthesiologist is prepared to practice in the United States."
34. False. Paragraph 6 states: "The number of anesthesiologists in the United States has more than doubled since the 1970s."
35. D Paragraph 4 states: "Simpson sprinkled chloroform on a handkerchief."
36. B Paragraph 5 states: "Local anesthetic is used only at the affected site."
37. H Paragraph 2 states: "Dioscorides suggested boiling the root [of mandrake] with wine."
38. F Paragraph 3 states: "laughing gas [also known as nitrous oxide], which he used in 1844 to relieve pain during a tooth extraction."
39. A Paragraph 5 states: "General anesthetic/anaesthetic is used to put a patient into a temporary state of unconsciousness."
40. E Paragraph 3 states that the first anesthetic machine contained an ether-soaked sponge.

Writing

Writing Task 1

Gaining work experience prior to graduation helps university students to succeed in getting their first job. For this reason, some universities insist that all students must complete a Work Experience Requirement. Completing the following six stages results in the requirements' fulfillment.

The process begins with the Application stage. A student reviews an approved list of workplaces and submits applications to places where he would like to work. Next is the Approval stage. When a student receives an acceptance letter, he gives it to the professor for approval. The third stage, Schedule, requires a student to arrange his work schedule. The student should work at least 10 hours/week over 20 weeks. Reports are next. The student must complete a Weekly Report Form and turn it in to the professor every Friday.

The fifth stage, Evaluation, takes place during the final work week. A student participates in an evaluation meeting with his work supervisor, who submits an Evaluation Form. The last stage requires that a student submit a Final Report before the last week of spring semester.

By following these stages and subsequently submitting the final report, the student receives credit from the university.

Writing Task 2—Agree

Families who do not send their children to government-financed[1] school should not be required to pay taxes that support universal education.

[1]American public schools are government-financed, i.e., paid for by local taxpayers.

When families send their children to non-public[1] (that is, parochial and private) schools, they must pay tuition and other school expenses. Spending additional money to pay taxes creates an even greater financial hardship for these families. They must make sacrifices, trying to have enough money to pay for school in addition to other bills. For example, my friend Amalia is a single mother with an eight-year-old son, Andrew. Because they survive solely on her income, money is tight. Amalia works at least 10 hours of overtime each week to cover Andrew's school expenses. This gives Amalia and Andrew less time to spend together, and she is always so tired that she is impatient with him when they do have family time. Clearly, this extra expense is an unfair burden for hard-working parents like Amalia.

While some people may consider parochial or private school to be a luxury, for many families it is essential because their community's public schools fail to meet their children's needs. Unfortunately, due to shrinking budgets, many schools lack well-qualified, experienced educators. Children may be taught by someone who is not a certified teacher or who knows little about the subject matter. Some problems are even more serious. For example, the public high school in my old neighborhood/neighbourhood had serious safety problems, due to students bringing guns, drugs, and alcohol to school. After a gang-related shooting occurred at the high school, my parents felt that they had no choice but to enroll me in a parochial school that was known for being very safe.

Unfortunately, even when families prefer public schools, sometimes they can't send their children to one. These families are burdened not only for paying expenses at another school, but also by being forced to pay taxes to support a public school that they do not use.

Writing Task 2—Disagree

Families who do not send their children to public school should be required to pay taxes that support public education.

Every child in my country is required to attend school and every child is welcome to enroll at his/her local public school. Some families choose to send their children to other schools, and it is their prerogative to do so. However, the public schools are used by the majority of our children and must remain open for everyone. For example, my uncle sent his two children to a private academy for primary school. Then he lost a huge amount of money through some poor investments and he could no longer afford the private school's tuition. The children easily transferred to their local public school and liked it even more than their academy. The public schools supported their family when they had no money to educate their children.

Because the public schools educate so many citizens, everyone in my country—whether a parent or not—should pay taxes to support our educational system. We all benefit from the education that students receive in public school. Our future doctors, fire fighters, and teachers—people whom we rely on everyday—are educated in local public schools. When a person is in trouble, it's reassuring to know that those who will help you—such as fire fighters—know what they're doing because they received good training in school and later. Providing an excellent education in the public school system is vital to the strength of our community and our country.

Our government must offer the best education available, but it can only do so with the financial assistance of all its citizens. Therefore, everyone—including families who do not send their children to public school—should support public education by paying taxes.

[1]American public schools are government-financed, i.e., paid for by local taxpayers.

Speaking

Part 1

Do you have a job? Do you like it? Why or why not?
Yes, I have a job. I work as an enrollment manager for a university. I recruit new students into the program. I like it a lot because I can help people, and I get to meet a lot of new and interesting people. Also I have the opportunity to travel a lot.

Why did you choose this job?
I chose this job because I enjoy travel, and I like meeting people. I have to travel at least 25 percent of the time for my job. I am always talking to people, e-mailing them, or writing articles about our university. It's really interesting.

What kind of education or training did you need to get this job?
I have my MBA (Masters in Business Administration) and that's the same program that I recruit students into. So, having that education really helped me to get this job, because I know what the students need to succeed in our program. Also, I've taken courses in public speaking so I'm comfortable giving presentations about our university.

Why do you like this kind of job?
I like this job because I make a positive difference in students' lives everyday. Also, I spend some time in the office, but I'm on the road a lot, too, seeing different places and moving around. I wouldn't like a job where I had to sit in an office everyday.

How can you prepare yourself to get this kind of job?
To prepare yourself for this kind of job, you need a degree in business administration or public relations or something like that. You don't always need a master's degree, but a lot of universities prefer it. It's also good to have experience working in the admissions office or financial aid office or something like that of a college or university to gain experience in how the process works.

How do people choose jobs?
People choose jobs in many different ways. Some do what their parents did. Others have a great love of something. Sometimes people just look at the money they earn. I think you should know what you enjoy and what you're good at, and choose your profession that way.

Part 2

I recently celebrated New Year's Day. The purpose of this day is to welcome the New Year. I think people celebrate it just about everywhere in the world. I celebrated with my cousins. We try to get together every year to celebrate this holiday, even though some of us live far away now. They're like my brothers and sisters; we grew up together. And that's the reason why this holiday is important to me, because I know I will see my cousins then. We're still young, so we did what young people do. We went to some clubs and stayed out all night dancing. We also met up with some old school friends, so it was like a reunion. We stayed out really late, until about 5:00 in the morning. The next day we went to my aunt's house and had a big family dinner with all the aunts and uncles and cousins, everyone in the family of all ages. We ate/had my country's traditional food and told stories and played games. It was a traditional family party. We do it every year.

Part 3

What are some important holidays in your country?
Some important holidays in my country are New Year's Day, National Day, and Children's Day.

Why do people celebrate holidays?
Holidays are a time to remember important dates and people from our past and to practice our traditions. They're also a time to be with our families, and to relax and enjoy good food.

Do you think holiday celebrations have changed over the years? Why or why not?
Holiday celebrations haven't changed much over the years. The dates are the same, and the reason for each day hasn't changed. Families and friends still meet and spend time together.

Do you think the importance of holiday celebrations has changed over the years? Why or why not?
No, I don't think that the importance of holiday celebrations has changed. These days are still special for everyone. But sometimes it's difficult for people to have time to really enjoy the holiday.

How will holidays be different in the future?
In the future, we may have some new holidays. Also, with so many busy families, some of the holiday traditions may change. Instead of eating home-cooked food on holidays, I think that more and more families will go to restaurants. Then they can do less work and still enjoy the holiday together.

ACADEMIC MODEL TEST 3

Listening

1. *Patty.* In line 9 of the dialogue she says, "It's Patty, that's P-A-T-T-Y."
2. *17.* In line 11, she says, "I live at 17 High Street" and in line 13 she emphasizes this, "SevenTEEN."
3. *apartment.* In line 15, she says, "It's an apartment."/flat."
4. *cell.* In line 19, she says, "It's my cell/mobile phone."
5. (B) In line 23, when asked to describe her glasses, the woman says, "They're round. And they have a chain attached." (A) is incorrect because it only mentions the shape of the glasses, and doesn't say anything about the chain. (C) is incorrect because it indicates square reading glasses, and hers were round.
6. (A) In line 25, the woman says that she "had a window seat." So, she was by the window when she lost her glasses. (B) is incorrect because she was not near a door: "the door [was] at the other end of the car." (C) is incorrect because she "was sitting on the train reading," not in the station.
7. (C) In line 27, she "was [reading] a fascinating article in that new magazine." (A) and (B) are incorrect because those choices are never mentioned.
8. (C) In line 29 she says, "I've come here to visit my aunt." (A) is incorrect because she wasn't going home. In fact, she "left home at five o'clock this morning." (B) is incorrect because she wasn't going to work. She took "a whole week off work to make this trip."
9. (B) In line 31 she says, "At ten o'clock, I think. Yes, that's right." (A) is incorrect because that is the time she left home that morning. (C) is incorrect because in line 31 she says that her train arrived "just about 30 minutes ago. At ten o'clock." So her train arrived at 10 and she is making the lost report at 10:30.

10. (C) In lines 34 and 35, the man asks about what is in her coat pocket, and she finds her glasses then. (A) is incorrect because they were not in her purse/handbag. She does say, "I had my handbag," but her glasses weren't there. (B) is incorrect because she says, "I checked my seat to see if I had left anything on it, but I hadn't."
11. *mainly commercial area.* The downtown is described as "mainly a commercial area."
12. *too far.* The downtown is described as "rather far from the university."
13. *prices are low.* The speaker says that in uptown "The prices there are quite low."
14. *a car.* The speaker says, "you'll need a car if you choose to live there" (in uptown).
15. *University's Student Center/Student Center wall.* The speaker says, "look . . . at the university's Student Center. There is a wall there devoted to apartment ads."
16. *Local newspaper/The Greenfield Times.* He mentions, "The local city newspaper, *The Greenfield Times* ..." lists apartments for rent ads."
17. *bus schedules.* He says the Student Counseling[1] Center (SCC) has "city bus schedules."
18. *roommate matching.* He says the SCC has a "roommate[2] matching service."
19. *inexpensive furniture stores.* He says the SCC can provide "a list of inexpensive furniture stores."
20. *meal.* He mentions that students can sign up "for a meal plan on campus" and that SCC has several different plans.
21. *your health.* The speaker says, "First, bicycling is good for your health."
22. *cheaper than.* The speaker says, "Bicycles are a lot cheaper to use than cars."
23. *pollution.* The speaker says, "Bicycles don't cause pollution like cars and buses do."
24. *bad weather.* The speaker talks about rain and the cold. She says, "So bad weather would be a problem."
25. *a long distance.* The speaker says, "It's difficult to ride your bike if your trip is a long distance."
26. *make bike lanes.* The woman says, "I think the biggest thing is making bicycle lanes on roads."
27. *lock up bikes/lock bikes.* The woman says, "They need a safe place to lock up their bikes."
28. *bicycling maps.* The woman says, "Some cities provide bicycling maps."
29. *helmet.* The woman says, "For safety you should wear a helmet."
30. *waterproof clothes.* The woman says, "For comfort you need . . . waterproof clothes when it rains."
31. *suggested topics list.* In paragraph 1, the professor says, "I have a list of suggested topics . . . and I'd like you to look over it."
32. *final approval/professor's approval.* At the end of paragraph 1, the professor says, "You'll need to get my final approval on your topic."
33. *Gather information.* In paragraph 2, the professor says, "The next thing you'll do is gather information on your topic."
34. *magazines, and newspapers.* In paragraph 2 the professor mentions the "journals, magazines, and newspapers."
35. *encyclopedias/encyclopaedias.* In paragraph 2, the professor refers to the "online encyclopedias."
36. *Write thesis statement.* In paragraph 3 the professor says, "the next step is to write a thesis statement."
37. *body.* Midway through paragraph 4, the professor explains there is an introduction and "then the body."
38. *conclusion.* At the end of paragraph 4, the professor explains there is "finally the conclusion."
39. *Organize/organise your notes.* At the beginning of paragraph 5, the professor says, "you can start organizing your notes."
40. *Revise your draft.* In paragraph 7 the professor says, "the next thing to do is revise your draft."

[1] BRITISH: counselling

[2] BRITISH: flatmate

Reading

Passage 1

1. (B) In paragraph 4, it states that the intradermal allergy test "involves placing the allergen sample under the skin with a syringe."
2. (A) In paragraph 3, it says that the "test is often done on the upper back of children."
3. (C) In paragraph 5, it says that a blood test (the RAST) "is used if patients have preexisting skin conditions."
4. (B) In paragraph 4 about the intradermal allergy test, the text states, "People who have experienced serious allergic reactions called anaphylactic reactions are not advised to have these types of tests."
5. (A) In paragraph 3 about the skin-prick test, the text says, "Results from a skin test can usually be obtained within 20 to 30 minutes."
6. (A) In paragraph 3 about the skin-prick test, the text discusses a controlled hive known as a wheal and flare is described. "The white wheal is the small raised surface, while the flare is the redness that spreads out from it."
7. (C) In paragraph 5 about the blood test, the text states, "The RAST is a more expensive test."
8. eating
   In paragraph 1, the text states: "Allergic reactions are triggered by the contact, inhalation, or *ingestion*."
9. allergens
   In paragraph 1, the text states: "Allergic reactions are triggered by the contact, inhalation, or ingestion of a number of different *allergens*."
10. signs
    In paragraph 1, the text states: "*Symptoms* of allergic reactions range from mild irritation such as itching, wheezing, and coughing."
11. medicines
    In paragraph 1, the text states: "Serious allergic reactions are more likely to result from food, *drugs,* and stinging insects."
12. anaphylaxis
    In paragraph 4, the text states: "Anaphylaxis is an allergic reaction that affects the whole body and is potentially life threatening." This sentence expresses that anaphylaxis is an allergic reaction, and a very severe one.
13. identify
    In paragraph 7, the text states: "After using a reliable testing method, the cause of an allergic reaction is often *identified*."
14. avoiding
    In paragraph 7, the text states: "while those with food allergies learn to safely *remove* certain foods from their diets."

Passage 2

15. (A) Choice (A) is correct because paragraph 1 explains: "the sacred pipe was considered a medium through which humans could pray to The Great Spirit." The text mentions the pipe's "connection to the spiritual world." Choice (B) is incorrect because the reading passage mentions "a gift from the Great Spirit" and "gifts to the earth's first bears," but it does not describe using the sacred pipe in gift exchanges. Choice (C) is incorrect because paragraph 2 says that, "the sacred pipe was built with precise craftsmanship." But there is no mention of it representing traditional handicrafts.

16. (A) Choice (A) is correct because paragraph 2 states: "The bowl of the traditional sacred pipe was made of Red Pipestone. . . . The wooden stem." Paragraph 8 elaborates on the Red Pipestone by explaining that "the quarries must be considered a sacred place" and these quarries, where the pipestone was found, indicate that pipestone is a rock. Choice (B) is incorrect because those are the substances used in mixing tobacco–paragraph 3. Choice (C) is incorrect because there is no mention of red clay in this reading passage.
17. (C) Choice (C) is correct because paragraph 2 states, "In many tribes the man and woman held onto the sacred pipe during the marriage ceremony." Choices (A) and (B) are incorrect because funerals and births are not mentioned.
18. (B) Choice (B) is correct because paragraph 3 states: "tobacco was mixed with herbs, bark, and roots. . . . These mixtures varied depending on the plants that were indigenous to the tribal area." So, the tobacco combined a variety of herbs as well as other plant life. Choice (A) is incorrect because this ceremonial tobacco was not plain. Choice (C) is incorrect because bark was only one of the ingredients in the mixture.
19. (C) Choice (C) is correct because paragraph 8 describes Pipestone, Minnesota. The text refers to its quarries, so this is a source of stone for pipes. Choice (A) is incorrect because there were no battles here. The text states, "Regardless of their conflicts, tribes put their weapons down and gathered in peace in these quarries." Choice (B) is incorrect because the text says that "According to the Dakota tribe, The Great Spirit once called all Indian nations to this location." No mention is made of the Dakota tribe originating from there.
20. *pipe bowl/bowl.* Paragraph 4 states: "In a typical pipe ceremony, the pipe holder stood up and held the pipe bowl in his left hand."
21. *pipe stem/stem.* Paragraph 4 states: "In a typical pipe ceremony, the pipe holder stood up . . . with the stem held toward the East in his right hand."
22. *the East.* Paragraph 4 states: "he sprinkled some on the ground as an offering to both Mother Earth and the East. The East was acknowledged as the place where the morning star rose."
23. *the South.* Paragraph 5 states: "Before offering a prayer to the South. . . . The South was believed to bring strength, growth, and healing."
24. *Mother Earth*
25. *the four directions.* Paragraph 6 explains: "Finally, the stem was held straight up and the tribe acknowledged The Great Spirit, thanking him for being the creator of Mother Earth, Father Sky, and the four directions."
26. *smoke.* Paragraph 7 states: "Each member took a puff of smoke and offered another prayer."
27. *stored separately.* Paragraph 7 explains: "It was important for the stem and bowl to be stored in separate pockets in a pipe pouch. These pieces were not allowed to touch each other, except during a sacred pipe ceremony."

Passage 3

28. 19th century/1800s. Paragraph 2 states: "During the nineteenth century attempts to produce maps of the seafloor involved lowering weighted lines from a boat."
29. *depth.* Paragraph 2 says: "When the hand line hit the ocean floor, the depth of the water was determined."
30. *single-beam sonar.* Paragraph 3 focuses on sonar and says it "was first used to detect submarines and icebergs." So, it was used for detecting objects underwater. The text explains, "By the 1930s, single-beam sonar was being used."
31. *sound waves.* Paragraph 3 states that "By the 1930s single-beam sonar was being used to transmit sound waves in a vertical line from a ship to the seafloor."
32. *1960s.* According to paragraph 4, "The multi-beam sonar . . . was developed in the 1960s."

33. the entire globe/the world/Earth. Paragraph 5 says: "The benefit of using satellites to map the ocean is that it can take pictures of the entire globe."
34. (A) Choice (A) is correct because paragraph 4 says: "The Ring of Fire . . . is famous for its seismic activity."
35. (B) Choice (B) is correct because paragraph 4 states: "The Mid-Ocean Ridge is . . . 1,200 miles wide."
36. (B) Choice (B) is correct because paragraph 4 explains: "The Mid-Ocean Ridge is a section of undersea mountains."
37. (A) Choice (A) is correct because paragraph 4 says: "This area [the Ring of Fire] . . . accounts for more than 75 percent of the world's active and dormant volcanoes."

38–40. (ii) (iii), (v) are correct. Choice (ii) is correct because paragraph 6 states: "Scientists expect bathymetry to become one of the most important sciences as humans search for new energy sources." Choice (iii) is correct because paragraph 6 says: "Preserving the ocean's biosphere for the future will also rely on an accurate mapping of the seafloor." Choice (v) is correct because paragraph 6 states: "Scientists expect bathymetry to become one of the most important sciences as humans . . . seek alternate routes for telecommunication."

Writing

Writing Task 1

Over the past 30 years, the average family has dramatically increased the number of meals that they eat at restaurants. The percentage of the family's food budget spent on restaurant meals steadily climbed. Just 10 percent of the food budget was spent on restaurant meals in 1970, and 15 percent in 1980. That percentage more than doubled in 1990, to 35 percent, and rose again in 2000 to 50 percent.

Where families eat their restaurant meals also changed during that 30-year period. In 1970, families ate the same number of meals at fast food and sit-down restaurants. In 1980, families ate slightly more frequently at sit-down restaurants. However, since 1990, fast food restaurants serve more meals to the families than do the sit-down restaurants. Most of the restaurant meals from 2000 were eaten at fast food restaurants. If this pattern continues, eventually the number of meals that families eat at fast food restaurants could double the number of meals they eat at sit-down restaurants.

Writing Task 2—Agree

"Do as I say, not as I do." This is what society tells us when it punishes murderers with the death penalty. Society tells us that murder is wrong, and in our legal system, murder is against the law. Yet we still see our society kill murderers, and thus we are committing murder ourselves. For this reason, the death penalty should end, and instead murderers should be punished with life in prison.

Society needs to show a positive model of how our lives should be and how people should act. We should always strive to improve our situation, to be at peace and in harmony with others. However, when we kill murderers, we are not working to improve our society. Instead, we are stooping to the criminals' level.

It makes me think about the revenge that came when playing games with my brothers. When we were kids/children, my brother would take my toys, so I would hit him and take my toys back. Then he would hit me harder and take the toys again. Thinking of the death penalty, I imagine a murderer kills someone. Society takes revenge by killing the murderer. This leaves behind the murderer's family and friends, who have tremendous anger inside of them, which they may release onto society. The cycle of killing goes on and on.

Society should not condemn people who are taking the same action that society is taking. Society tells us not to kill, and yet society kills when it exercises the death penalty. Because of this contradiction, we should end the death penalty and instead punish murderers by sentencing them to life in prison.

Writing Task 2—Disagree

I strongly support the death penalty for murderers. In today's society, life is very violent. There are many mentally-ill people committing crimes and almost nothing will stop them. We have interviewed captured criminals who say, "I was going to kill him, but I knew that I could get the death penalty if I did. So I just left him there." Obviously, having the death penalty saves lives and that makes a positive difference to society.

If a criminal does murder someone, and then gets the death penalty, that isn't society's fault. Everyone knows about the death penalty as a punishment for murder. So, the person who murders is really killing himself at the same time he is killing his victim. The murderer has made the choice to die.

It is important to remember that the death penalty is used only for people who have committed very serious crimes. For example, a woman shot a police officer when she was trying to escape from jail. She was already a convicted criminal when she committed murder, and she deserves the death penalty.

People need to accept responsibility for their actions. Punishing murderers with the death penalty is one way that society can help people to realize/realise the consequences of their decisions.

Speaking

Part 1

What kind of food do you enjoy eating?
Most of the time, I enjoy healthy food. I like fish, salad, and vegetables. Sometimes I like something sweet.

What are some kinds of food you never eat? Why?
I never eat fast food. It's so unhealthy that I can't enjoy eating it. Well, sometimes I will eat French fries.

Do you generally prefer to eat at home or at a restaurant? Why?
I usually like to eat at home. It's less expensive than a restaurant, and I can make all of the food exactly the way I like it.

What are some reasons that people eat at restaurants?
Most of all, it's convenient. It's so nice to have someone make the food and clean up everything afterwards.

Describe a popular food in your country. Why do people like this food?
Pasta is a popular food here. It tastes delicious, and the price is good. There's also a lot of variety, because you can always get different toppings on the pasta—cheese one day, or butter, and different sauces. So, people never get bored with it.

Part 2

There is one teacher that I remember very well. I went to school at age five, and she was my first teacher. She taught us English and other subjects too. In fact, she was our only teacher so she taught us everything. She was a very kind person, so patient and respectful. She cared about all of us. I think that I remember her so well because she was my first teacher. She taught me how to tie my shoes and helped me when I couldn't find my mother.

Part 3

What kind of person makes a good teacher?
A person who is smart and caring makes a good teacher. Also, the person should like talking to other people and presenting information.

Why do people choose to become teachers?
There are many reasons, but I think that most teachers want to make a positive difference in others' lives. Many teachers have family members who were teachers.

Do you think education will change in the future? How?
Yes, I think it will change. Technology is a big influence. Now we can take classes online or even have teachers who are online. Instead of only reading about places, we can see them. There are videos from art museums in other countries, for example, so students can immediately see what is really happening.

How does technology affect education?
Technology affects education by offering more opportunities. For example, if you can't travel to a class because of your work schedule, you can take the class online. It's exciting to see how technology changes education, and everything else.

ACADEMIC MODEL TEST 4

Listening

Example: (C) Line 3 has a woman ask, "Tickets? That's our Special Events Department. Let me transfer you." She directs the phone call to that number.

1. (C) Choice (C) is correct because in lines 5 and 7, the man says, "I'm interested in the series you have going on now . . . Actually, I meant the concert series." Choice (A) is incorrect because in line 6, the woman thinks he is interested in the "lecture series on the history of art", but he isn't. Choice (B) is incorrect because he's interested in listening to music at the concert, not attending a lecture.

2. (A) All three choices are mentioned. Choice (A) is correct because in lines 8–11, the woman explains: "there's still a concert tomorrow, that's Thursday." The man asks, "The one tomorrow, is that when they'll be playing the Mozart concerto?" and the woman answers, "Yes, it is." Choice (B) and (C) are incorrect because the man does not want to attend the concert on those days, even though there are performances. In line 8, the woman says, "There's also one [concert] on Saturday, and then the last one is on Sunday."
3. *Milford*. In line 13, he provides his name, "It's Steven Milford. That's M-i-l-f-o-r-d."
4. *1659798164*. In line 17, he gives his credit card number, "1659798164."
5. *32.70*. In line 20, she says: "At 16.35 a piece that comes out to a total of 32 pounds and 70 p/pence."
6. Library
7. Bank
8. Post Office
9. Museum
10. Hotel
11. *56,000*. In paragraph 1, Sheila says: "Ravensburg is the major city on the island, though with a population of only 56,000."
12. *26*. In paragraph 2, Sheila says: "Summer in the city of Ravensburg is warm with average temperatures reaching 26 degrees."
13. *23*. In paragraph 2, Sheila says: "Summer at Blackstone is a bit cooler, with average temperatures of around 23 degrees."
14. *windy*. In paragraph 2, Sheila says: "the weather is often windy because, of course, it's located on the coast."
15. *entertainment*. In paragraph 3, Sheila says: "so if entertainment is what you're looking for, Ravensburg has the advantage there."
16. *very quiet*. At the end of paragraph 3, Sheila says about Blackstone: "It's a very quiet town, which is a disadvantage if you're looking for excitement."
17. *75 kilometers*. In paragraph 4, Sheila says: "Travelers[1] to Blackstone Beach also use the Ravensburg airport, which is about 75 kilometers away."
18. (C) Sheila says, "Some very good deals can be found, however, in the perfume shops."
19. (D) Sheila says, "Jewelry[2] is also popular among tourists, and jewelry shops abound."
20. (E) Sheila says, "Since fishing is the major island industry, no tourist goes home without a package of smoked fish."
For this section, choice (A) is incorrect because Sheila says, "Well, contrary to what one might think, native handicrafts are not a popular item." Choice (B) is incorrect because Sheila says, "there are not many CDs available of the native music, and the ones that are available are quite expensive." Choice (F) is incorrect because Sheila says, ". . . be sure to bring your own fishing gear[3]. Believe it or not, it's difficult and expensive for tourists to buy it on the island."
21. *next Thursday*. In line 6, Janet says, "It's due next Thursday."
22. *40*. In line 8, Janet says, "And it counts for 40 percent of our final semester grade[4]."
23. *TV watching habits/ people's TV habits*. In line 10, Janet says, "I did my research about people's TV watching habits."
24. *library research*. In line 14, Janet says, "Well, after I decided my topic, I went to the library and did some research. I mean, I read about other studies people had done about TV watching."
25. *research method*. In line 16, Janet says, "So after I did the library research, I chose my research method."

[1]BRITISH: Travellers
[2]BRITISH: Jewellery
[3]BRITISH: tackle
[4]BRITISH: end of term mark

26. *questionnaire*. In line 18, Janet says, "Well, I could do either interviews or just send around a paper questionnaire. I decided to use the questionnaire." In line 20, Janet says, "I made up the questions for the questionnaire."
27. *Submit*. In line 23, Harry asks, "So then you just went around and asked people the questions?" Janet answers, "Well, first I had to submit my research design to Professor Farley. He had to make sure it was OK before I went ahead with the research."
28. *Send out questionnaires*. In line 26, Janet says, "So then I had to send out the questionnaire."
29. *Make charts*. After collecting the information, in line 28, Janet says, "I made charts and graphs."
30. *report*. In line 32, Janet says, "Well, I'll have to write a report, too, of course."
31. (A) In paragraph 2, the professor says, "You'll find crows in North America."
32. (D) In paragraph 2, the professor says, "There are several species of crows, for example, in Hawaii."
33. (E) In paragraph 2, the professor says, "And of course you'll find them in other parts of the world, Europe, Asia, and so on."
34. (F) In paragraph 2, the professor says, "And of course you'll find them in other parts of the world, Europe, Asia, and so on."
    Choice (B) is incorrect because in paragraph 2, the professor says, "You'll find crows in North America, although interestingly enough, not in South America." Choice (C) is incorrect because in paragraph 2, the professor says, "There are none in Antarctica."
35. *39–49*. In paragraph 3, the professor says, "[It measures] 39 to 49 centimeters in length."
36. *black*. In paragraph 3, the professor says, "the American crow is completely black, including the beak and feet."
37. *sticks*. In the first sentence of paragraph 4, the professor says, "Crows build large nests of sticks."
38. *trees/bushes/trees and bushes*. In the first sentence of paragraph 4, "Crows build large nests of sticks, usually in trees or sometimes in bushes."
39. *3 to 6*. In paragraph 4, the professor says, "The female lays from three to six eggs at a time."
40. *35*. In paragraph 4, the professor says, "Generally 35 days after hatching they have their feathers and are ready to fly."

Reading

Passage 1

1–4. (A), (B), (D), and (F) are correct. Choice (A) is correct because in paragraph 2, line n (15), it says, "First, K'ang planned to reform China's education system." Choice (B) is correct because in paragraph 2, line n (23), it says, "K'ang also called for the establishment of a national parliamentary government, including popularly elected members and ministries." Choice (D) is correct because paragraph 2 says, "Military reform and the establishment of a new defense[1] system . . . were also on the agenda." Choice (F) is correct because paragraph 2 says, "Military reform . . . as well as the modernization[2] of agriculture and medicine were also on the agenda."

Choice (C) is incorrect because paragraph 2 says, "The edicts called for a public school system with an emphasis on practical and Western studies rather than Neo-Confucian orthodoxy." So, the study of Confucianism was not a focus. Choice (E) is incorrect because paragraph 2 says, "K'ang also called for the establishment of a national parliamentary government, including popularly elected members and ministries." K'ang called for the addition of elections, not the abolition (or end) of elections. Choice (G) is incorrect because there is no mention in the reading passage about initiating foreign trade.

[1]BRITISH: defence

[2]BRITISH: modernisation

5. (F) Choice (F) is correct because paragraph 1 states: "After losing the Sino-Japanese war, the Emperor Guwangxu found his country to be in a major crisis." So, China lost the war with Japan.
6. (B) Choice (B) is correct because paragraph 2 states: "On June 11, 1898, Emperor Guwangxu entrusted the reform movement to K'ang and put the progressive scholar-reformer in control of the government."
7. (L) Choice (L) is correct because paragraph 2 states, "On June 11, 1898, Emperor Guwangxu entrusted the reform movement to K'ang." The text states, "Within days, the imperial court issued a number of statutes related to the social and political structure of the nation."
8. (M) Choice (M) is correct because paragraph 3 states: "There was intense opposition to the reform at all levels of society, and only one in fifteen provinces made attempts to implement the edicts."
9. (A) Choice (A) is correct because paragraph 3 states: "a coup d'etat was organized by Yuan Shikai and Empress Dowager Cixi to force Guangxu and the young reformers out of power and into seclusion."
10. (E) Choice (E) is correct because paragraph 3 states: "After September 21st, the new edicts were abolished."
11. (H) Choice (H) is correct because paragraph 4 states: ". . . anti-foreign and anti-Christian secret societies tore through northern China targeting foreign concessions and missionary facilities."
12. (K) Choice (K) is correct because paragraph 4 states: "an Allied force made up of armies from nine European nations as well as the United States and Japan entered Peking. With little effort, north China was occupied."
13. (N) Choice (N) is correct because paragraph 4 states: "Within a decade, the court ordered many of the original reform measures, including the modernization of the education and military system."

Passage 2

14. (A) Choice A is correct because paragraph 2 states: "A person's breathing stops when air is somehow prevented from entering the trachea."
15. (B) Choice (B) is correct because paragraph 2 states: "The term *central* is used because this type of apnea is related to the central nervous system rather than the blocked airflow." Immediately before this sentence, the passage is describing central sleep apnea.
16. (C) Choice (C) is correct because paragraph 2, states: "The third type of sleep apnea, known as mixed apnea, is a combination of the two."
17. (C) Choice (C) is correct because paragraph 2 states: "The third type of sleep apnea, known as mixed apnea, is a combination of the two and is the most rare form."
18. (A) Choice (A) is correct because paragraph 2 states: "There are three different types of sleep apnea, with obstructive sleep apnea being the most common."
19. False. Paragraph 3, states: "However, like many disorders, sleep apnea can affect children and in many cases is found to be the result of a person's genetic makeup." The paragraph does include risk factors related to sleep apnea, "including being overweight, male, and over the age of forty." So, people with those factors may be more likely to have sleep apnea, but all people can be affected by the disorder.
20. False. Paragraph 3, states: "Despite being so widespread, this disorder often goes undiagnosed."
21. True. Paragraph 3 states: "Often times, it is not the person suffering from sleep apnea who notices the repetitive episodes of sleep interruption, but a partner or family member sleeping nearby."
22. Not Given. This topic is not addressed in this reading passage.
23. True. Paragraph 3 states: "Sleep apnea is also blamed for many cases of impaired driving and poor job performance."

24–27. (A), (B), (D), and (F). Choice (A) is correct because paragraph 5 states: "In extreme cases, especially when facial deformities are the cause of the sleep apnea, surgery is needed to make a clear passage for the air." Choice (B) is correct because paragraph 4 states: "When these treatments prove unsuccessful, sleep apnea sufferers can be fitted with a CPAP mask." Choice (D) is correct because paragraph 4 states: "In many cases, symptoms of sleep apnea can be eliminated when patients try losing weight."

Choice (F) is correct because paragraph 4 states: "People who sleep on their backs or stomachs often find that their symptoms disappear if they try sleeping on their sides."
Choice (C) is incorrect because paragraph 4 states: "Sleep specialists also claim that sleeping pills interfere with the natural performance of the throat and mouth muscles and suggest patients do away with all sleep medication for a trial period." Choice (E) is incorrect because the passage includes surgery as a treatment, but massage is not mentioned. Choice (G) is incorrect because paragraph 4 states: "In many cases, symptoms of sleep apnea can be eliminated when patients try losing weight or abstaining from alcohol." This means that the patient will not drink any alcohol, even moderate amounts as included in item (G).

Passage 3

28. (H) Choice (H) is correct because paragraph 1 states: "the psychological method [which concentrates mostly on intellectual processes, such as memory and abstract reasoning]."
29. (J) Choice (J) is correct because paragraph 1 states: "The main concern of Binet and Simon was to predict elementary school performance independently from the social and economic background of the individual student."
30. (D) Choice (D) is correct because paragraph 2 states: "The Binet-Simon tests are quite effective in predicting school success."
31. (L) Choice (L) is correct because paragraph 2 states: "However, they have been found to be much less predictive of success in post-secondary academic and occupational domains."
32. (I) Choice (I) is correct because paragraph 3 states: "Recent research across the fields of education, cognitive science, and adult development suggests that much of adult intellect is indeed not adequately sampled by extant intelligence measures and might be better assessed through the pedagogical method (Ackerman, 1996; Gregory, 1994)."
33. (C) Choice (C) is correct because paragraph 4 states: "The dilemma for adult intellectual assessment is that the adult is rarely presented with a completely novel problem in the real world of academic or occupational endeavors.[1]"
34. (E) Choice (E) is correct because paragraph 5 states: "From the artificial intelligence field, researchers have discarded the idea of a useful General Problem Solver in favor[2] of knowledge-based expert systems."
35. True. Paragraph 1 states: "they spawned an intelligence assessment paradigm which has been substantially unchanged from their original tests."
36. False. Paragraph 2, states: "The Binet-Simon tests are quite effective in predicting school success in both primary and secondary educational environments. However, they have been found to be much less predictive of success in post-secondary academic and occupational domains." So, even though the tests predict elementary school success, we cannot make a connection between that predictor and a student's college success.
37. False. Paragraph 6 states: "the typical expert is found to mainly differ from the novice in terms of experience and the knowledge structures that are developed through that experience rather than in terms of intellectual processes (e.g., Glaser, 1991)."
38. False. Process structures, not knowledge structures, decline with age. Paragraph 6 states: "various aspects of adult intellectual functioning are greatly determined by knowledge structures and less influenced by the kinds of process measures which have been shown to decline with age over adult development (e.g., Schooler, 1987; Willis & Tosti-Vasey, 1990)."
39. True. Paragraph 7 states: "By bringing together a variety of sources of research evidence, it is clear that our current methods of assessing adult intellect are insufficient."
40. (C) Choice (C) is the correct answer because paragraph 7 states: "When adult knowledge structures are broadly examined with tests such as the Advanced Placement [AP]."

[1] BRITISH: endeavours

[2] BRITISH: favour

Writing

Writing Task 1

Analyzing/analysing the coffee shop's sales report reveals some clear trends in the customers' buying habits. On a typical weekday, the usual morning foods and drinks are bought. More coffee, tea, and pastries are purchased from 7:30 to 10:30 in the morning than at any other time. At 10:30, fewer of these items are purchased; however, the number of sandwiches sold quadruples. The most sandwiches are sold from 10:30 to 12:30.

Later in the day, all items reach their lowest selling point. Three of the four items: coffee, tea, and sandwiches sell their smallest amounts during the 2:30–5:30 block. The fewest pastries are sold from 5:30 to 8:30. However, the sandwiches and drinks sell more briskly from 5:30 to 8:30. It is their second-highest selling time period. This increase occurs when people are leaving work for the day or are working overtime and need to eat something convenient. By reviewing this table, it is clear that the office workers are using the coffee shop throughout the day and following a typical schedule.

Writing Task 2

More and more people rely on their private car as their typical means of transportation. This overreliance on cars causes problems with safety, pollution, and dependence on oil. Solutions to these problems need to be found.

As more people use their own cars, the number of vehicles on the road continues to increase. Greater numbers of vehicles and drivers leads to unsafe driving conditions. People want to reach their destinations quickly, but with so many people on the road, driving quickly can be unsafe. Yesterday, my car was almost hit by a truck/lorry driving much faster than the speed limit.

Another problem is pollution. Instead of having thirty people ride the bus together, each person drives a car. This leads to thirty vehicles spewing pollution into the air. The environment can't handle this large amount of dirty air. Our cities now have smog because the air pollution hangs in the sky.

A third problem is that we depend on oil, but oil is a fossil fuel. When we use all of the world's oil, it will be gone forever. As we drive more vehicles, we use more oil, and eventually none will be left.

To solve these problems, it would be wonderful if people would start to use more busses and trains instead of their private cars. People like their cars' convenience, but if the busses and trains are comfortable and inexpensive, people might use them instead. We also need to investigate how to use fuel more efficiently. Some people are buying hybrid cars, which use gasoline/petrol and electricity, and smaller cars, which have greater fuel efficiency. By identifying the problems and suggesting solutions, we can work to reduce people's over reliance on cars.

Speaking

Part 1

Where do you live now?
I live in a big city, near to my hometown.

Who do you live with?
I have one roommate/flatmate. We met through a newspaper advertisement.

What kind of place do you live in (a house or an apartment/flat)?
It's an apartment/flat.

Do you think it's better to live in a house or an apartment? Why?
For me, it's better to live in an apartment/flat. A house is too expensive. Anyway, even if I had the money for a house, I wouldn't have the time to care for it.

Describe your neighborhood.
The neighborhood/neighbourhood is in a good location. We're close to the bus and train. We have some good restaurants, and it's easy to buy food here. We're downtown/in the city centre, but it's safe.

Do you like it? Why or why not?
I do like our apartment/flat, most of the time. Sometimes the neighbors/neighbours can be noisy and that bothers me.

How do people choose their place to live?
They choose where to live based on location, money, and what is available. If they need a roommate/flatmate like me, they also need to think about that.

Part 2

NOTE: Gift/present

I received a gift that was important to me. It is a set of cuff links and a key chain. My sister gave the gift to me for her wedding. I helped with the wedding, and she wanted to thank me. They are made of silver, and the key chain has my initials on it. I use them for special occasions. I wore the cuff links to an important meeting at work. It is an important gift to me because it is personal. Also, I remember my sister and her wedding when I use the gift.

Part 3

Do you enjoy giving and receiving gifts? Why or why not?
No, I don't enjoy gifts. It's always difficult for me to choose what to give someone. When I receive a gift, I feel bad because the person may have spent a lot of money, but sometimes I don't like it.

Who usually gives you gifts?
My family usually gives gifts to me.

Who do you give gifts to?
I give gifts to my family. Sometimes I give gifts to people at work.

In your country when do people usually give gifts?
There are many times when people in my country give gifts. We give gifts to a person on his birthday, or to people when they marry, or to a baby when she's born. We also give gifts for special occasions.

What kinds of gifts do they give?
There are so many gifts. For someone's birthday, they might give some clothes or a book or music CDs.

Do you think gift-giving customs are different now than they were in the past? How?
No, I think that the customs are the same now as they were in the past. We give gifts for the same reasons that people in the past did. We also give gifts in the same way, usually at a family party if possible.

Do you think they will change in the future? How?
Yes, I think that some customs will change in the future. It seems like new days for gift-giving are added to the calendar. But because of our busy lives, I think that we might give fewer gifts instead of more gifts. Life is too busy.

GENERAL TRAINING MODEL TEST 1

Reading

NOTE: apartment/flat

1. (A) This apartment includes parking.
2. (C) This apartment is near the university.
3. (D) This apartment is big enough for a family and is close to elementary and high schools.
4. (B) This apartment has a pool.
5. (C) This apartment is near the bus lines/routes.
6. (E) This flat offers weekly and monthly rentals.
7. (B) This apartment has a party room.
8. (E) This section says that if there are any problems with the coffeemaker a customer can call the free service line.
9. (C) This section demonstrates how to clean the coffeemaker with vinegar.
10. (D) This section contains the warning that one should only pour coffee beans up to the "full" line.
11. (B) This section states that the coffeemaker comes with a built-in timer for convenience.
12. *Eight ounces*. Section A states: "fill the reservoir with eight ounces of water for each cup of coffee."
13. *Once a month*. Section C states: "Monthly cleaning will keep your coffeemaker functioning properly and your coffee tasting fresh."
14. *Any time*. Section E states that the customer service line is open 24 hours a day.
15. iv. Borrowing Library Materials. This paragraph gives information about how long people can borrow books for and how much they have to pay if they don't bring them back on time.
16. ii. Services for Children. This paragraph discusses picture books, readers, story hour, and a special film series for children.

17. viii. Using Library Computers. This paragraph discusses the library's Internet and computer services. Choice vi. Getting online is incorrect because the paragraph also talks about word processing and keyboarding, which do not necessarily involve using the Internet.
18. vii. Cultural Events. This paragraph discusses some of the cultural events that the library offers including author book signings, concerts, and a film series.
19. i. Places for Meetings. This paragraph provides information about conference rooms that are available to library patrons.
20. v. Employment Opportunities. This paragraph states that there are a number of positions available at the library. It also tells patrons how to apply for employment.
21. *second.* The first paragraph of the *Building Guide* states that room 243 is on the second floor, therefore, Room 245 is also on the second floor. This section states that room 245 is where students can borrow from the multilingual DVD collection.
22. *third.* In the second paragraph of the *Building Guide,* it states that the International Café is on the third floor.
23. *first.* In the second paragraph of the *Building Guide,* it states that the school bookstore is on the first floor. Here students can buy school T-shirts.
24. *third.* The Activities paragraph states that students can sign up for trips in the counselor's[1] office. In the second paragraph of the *Building Guide*, it states that the counselor's office is on the third floor.
25. (C) Choices (A) and (B) are incorrect because the first paragraph of the *Building Guide* states that the language lab is open from 9 to 5 Monday through Friday and 9 to 12 on Saturday.
26. (C) The second paragraph of the *Building Guide* states that there is no fee for counseling services. Choice (A) is incorrect because students can buy school shirts at the bookstore. Choice (B) is incorrect because there is a *nominal* (very small) fee for trip participation.
27. (B) There is a monthly International Banquet. At a banquet, a special meal is usually served. Choice (A) is not mentioned. Choice (C) is incorrect because the Activities paragraph states that trips such as film festivals happen *weekly.*
28. **vii** Paragraph A describes the first subways/underground systems built in Europe in the cities of London, Budapest, Glasgow, and Paris.
29. **ii** Paragraph B describes the first subways in the USA and South America.
30. **i** Paragraph C describes subways built in the second half of the twentieth century.
31. **viii** Paragraph D describes the largest subway systems in the world, measured in terms of total track length and numbers of riders.
32. **vi** Paragraph E gives examples of several subway systems known for the art in their stations.
33. **iv** Paragraph F describes Platform Screen Doors, a safety device now becoming more and more common in subway stations around the world.
34. **E** The Baker Street Station in London honors the fictional detective Sherlock Holmes.
35. **K** The Moscow Metro has more riders than any other subway system.
36. **B** Many subway systems have adopted the name Metro from the Paris Metro.
37. **A** The subway in Hong Kong has four lines that run under Victoria Harbour.
38. **I** The subway in Singapore was the first to be built with Platform Screen Doors. The subway in Hong Kong was the first to add PSDs to a system that was already built.
39. **G** The subway in Seoul has 287 kilometers of track.
40. **H** Buenos Aires has the oldest subway in Latin America.
41. **C** The Washington Metro began running in 1976.

[1]BRITISH: counsellor's

General Training Writing

Writing Task 1

Dear John,

Hello, my name is Irma. I'm Jake Vandelft's cousin. When Jake told me that he had a friend who lived in Toronto, I was excited. I'm hoping to visit Toronto in the summer. I hope you don't mind that I asked for your address. Jake said you probably wouldn't mind answering some questions if I wrote to you.

When I found out that I would get three weeks for a vacation/holiday this summer, I decided I wanted to go to a foreign country/abroad. I've always dreamed of going to Canada. I love watching baseball and I would love to see a major league game in Toronto. The Toronto Blue Jays are my favorite team.

Where should I stay when I visit Toronto? I think it is probably too expensive to stay in a hotel downtown/in the city centre for more than a week. Do you know of any youth hostels? Also, could you tell me about the weather in the summer? I don't know what to pack!

I look forward to hearing from you if you have time to write back. Maybe we can meet for lunch.

Best wishes,
Irma Klein

P.S. Jake said to say hello.

Writing Task 2

On average, today's businessmen and women work more hours than ever. However, modern technology has made the office less of a necessity. Rather than spending every working hour in the office, people can work at home on their personal computers. There are advantages and disadvantages to home offices for both the family and the employer.

The home office gives employees more flexibility with childcare. When a child is sick from school, a parent can put in a few hours of work at home instead of going into the office. Flextime also allows parents to leave work early enough to be home for the children to come home from school. Employees can make up time for their employers by putting in an extra hour or two in the morning or evening from home.

The home office eliminates transportation problems. Sometimes poor weather can make it difficult to get to work. The time it takes for some employees to commute could be better spent on deadlines for their employers from home. When a personal vehicle breaks down or a public service gets shut down, the home office takes the stress out of getting to work.

The home office can be very distracting. Some people find it difficult not to answer personal calls. Others can't explain to relatives or neighbors/neighbours that, even though they are home, they are actually "on the clock." Young children can't be expected to understand the concept of their mother being at work when she is actually in the home, especially if it only happens once in a while. And, when a young child is home, the parent's job is to be a caretaker.

Used sparingly, the home office is a convenient alternative to working at the office. It relieves the stress on busy parents and sometimes saves money and time for the employer. However, rather than killing two birds with one stone, often times neither the job nor the parenting is done adequately out of the home. Even today, the office is really where the work gets done.

GENERAL TRAINING MODEL TEST 2

Reading

1. *The main foyer.* From Dec. 1–4, the Main foyer is being painted.
2. *The main entrance.* From Dec. 5–8, tenants cannot enter the building from the garage.
3. *West Wing elevator/lift.* From Dec. 9–13, the East stairway is being painted. To reach the tenth floor one would have to take an elevator.
4. *East Wing elevator.* From Dec. 14–21, the west and north stairways and elevators are blocked. The east stairway or elevator must be used.
5. *Across the street.* From Dec. 22–27, the parking garage is unavailable. Tenants will get fined if they park on the street, but there is a parking lot/car park across the street that will be made available.
6. *Contact building manager.* Near the bottom of the notice it says, "If you have any questions or complaints, please contact the building manager."
7. *Get a form.* At the end of the notice it says that tenants can request a painting form if they want their apartments/flats painted.
8. *$29.* The invoice shows the last payment made. This bill is for the month of July, so the last bill was for June.
9. *August 21st.* The invoice says: "We must receive your payment in full by August 21st."
10. *£37.50.* EnviroElectric Company charges a £2.50 late fee. The total due is £35. If the payment is not made on time, the late fee will be added to the total due.
11. *East Bradfield.* The mailing address for this company is given below the late fee information.
12. *Visit Bradfield Bank.* The invoice states: "Cash payments may be made by visiting any branch of the Bradfield Bank."
13. Call 385–9387. This number is given for any customer who has questions about a bill.
14. (A) Paragraph 2 states that Evergreen Books is close to the International Student House.
15. (B) Paragraph 2 states that the City Office of Transport where bus schedules are available is city centre/downtown.
16. (B) Paragraph 3 states that there are many theatres in the city centre/downtown.
17. (B) Paragraph 3 states that the finest restaurants in the city are in the city centre/downtown.
18. (C) Paragraph 4 gives examples of places to snack (coffee houses and an ice cream parlor) in the University District.
19. (C) Paragraph 4 states that the University Sport and Health Club has an Olympic-sized pool.
20. (D) Paragraph 5 states that the Art Museum is in the Pleasant Gardens neighborhood.
21. True. Under the heading Dates, it states that summer session registration begins on 19 May.
22. True. Under the heading Tuition and Fees it shows how much less residents pay than nonresidents.
23. False. Under the heading Refunds it states that students can receive all of their money back EXCEPT for the registration fee (£35) if they withdraw before classes start on 2 June.
24. True. Under the heading Refunds it states that students who withdraw during the first week (classes start on June 2nd) will be refunded 50 percent.

25. False. Under the heading Tuition and Fees it says that books cost extra.
26. Not Given. No information is given about how many classes a student can take.
27. False. Under the heading Use of Facilities, it states that summer session students can use the college pool at no cost.
28. *Henge*. Paragraph 2 states that a large circular ditch called the henge was located around the Aubrey Holes.
29. *Aubrey Holes*. Paragraph 2 talks about the series of holes called Aubrey Holes that were dug with deer picks.
30. *Avenue*. Paragraph 2 says that archeologists called the entrance way the "Avenue."
31. *Heel Stone*. Paragraph 2 describes the Heel Stone as being placed along the Avenue.
32. (B) The last sentence in paragraph 3 states that the Beaker people likely, "widened the entrance during this phase in order to show their appreciation for the sun."
33. (A) Halfway through Paragraph 2 is the description of the Slaughter Stone addition in Phase 1.
34. (C) Paragraph 4 contains the description of the bluestones being placed in a horseshoe formation.
35. (B) The second sentence in paragraph 3 describes the wooden posts being added.
36. (A) Paragraph 2 states that the Aubrey Holes were dug with picks made of deer antlers.
37. (C) The second sentence in paragraph 2 states that the bluestones came "all the way from the Preseli Hills." The expression "all the way" means *a long distance*.
38. (C) In the middle of paragraph 4, the addition of the sandstone ring is described.
39. (B) Toward the end of the third paragraph is a description of the Aubrey Holes being filled in: "The original Aubrey Holes were filled in either with earth or cremation remains."
40. (C) In the middle of paragraph 4, the addition of the Altar Stone is described.

Writing

Writing Task 1

September 15/15 September

Dear Sir or Madam,

My friend and I were guests in your hotel last week. We stayed in Room 401 from September the 4th until September the 9th. When I arrived home in Taiwan on the 11th, I realized/realised that I didn't have my watch. The last time I saw my watch was in the hotel room on the morning that we left. I think I may have accidentally left it on the bed.

My lady's watch has a chrome wristband. There is a yellow moon on the face of the watch with a bluish-black background. The brand of the watch is TIMEOUT.

This piece of jewelry/jewellery is not worth a lot of money, but it has sentimental value to me. It was the last gift my grandmother gave me before she passed away. I was wondering if you could ask your staff if they have seen it. Perhaps you could also check in the hotel's lost and found/lost property in case I left it at the hotel restaurant or in a public washroom. Please call me if you find it. I will send you a check to pay for the postage.

Thank you for your help.

Sincerely,

Theresa Lim

Writing Task 2

In the past, children amused themselves without a television. Toys and books kept children occupied, as did the outdoors. Many children today are happy sitting inside and watching TV. Though television is a teaching tool, it also isolates children from important activities.

Children used to get information from books, but now they learn more from TV. Children are often called sponges. They love to learn. Before television became so popular, children learned new words and concepts through storybooks. My mother said I could recite a few books by the time I was two. Some television shows/programmes are designed specifically to teach kids these same things. Though they keep children interested in learning, they don't require children to learn how to read. My little cousins are almost five, and they still can't write their names.

The television keeps children entertained on a rainy day. In the past, children sometimes ran out of ideas if their friends were away or the weather wasn't pleasant. Today they can just flip through the TV channels until something interesting comes on. My uncle says the TV is great because the children never complain they are bored. However, a child that is always entertained has no need to expand his imagination or learn to be creative. My cousins don't have hobbies, and they don't like sports like my brother and I did.

These days, children spend more time with the television than they do their own parents. In busy families, parents turn on the TV to distract their kids so that they can get other things done. My aunt has two jobs, and she is going to school. When she gets home, she doesn't have time to sit and play or read with the kids. Sitting in the same room and watching a program/programme while a parent reads the newspaper isn't my idea of spending quality time together as a family.

The television has changed the way children learn. Though there are plenty of educational shows on television, they don't require active participation from the child. No matter how entertaining a television may be, this machine should never replace books, play, or parenting.

11

APPENDIX

AUDIOSCRIPT FOR THE LISTENING SECTIONS

- Listening Module
- Model Test 1
- Model Test 2
- Model Test 3
- Model Test 4

ANSWER SHEETS

- Listening Module
- Reading Module
- Writing Module

IELTS LISTENING MODULE

Listening Skills

Target 1—Making Assumptions

SECTION 1

Example

W1: Good morning. How may I help you?
M1: Yes, I was wondering, do you have any one-bedroom apartments available?
W1: Yes we do. Were you looking for yourself?
M1: Yes, it's for me.

Narrator: James asks if there are any one-bedroom apartments available, so the correct answer is "one bedroom." Now we shall begin. You should answer the questions as you listen because you will not hear the recording a second time.

Questions 1–10

W1: Good morning. How may I help you?
M1: Yes, I was wondering, do you have any one-bedroom apartments available?
W1: Yes we do. Were you looking for yourself?
M1: Yes, it's for me.
W1: Let me just get some information from you then, for our application form. May I have your name?
M1: Yes. It's Kingston. James Kingston.
W1: And what's your current address?
M1: I live over on State Street. Number 1705 State Street, apartment seven.
W1: And your phone number?
M1: My home phone? It's 721-0584.
W1: Work phone?
M1: 721-1127.
W1: Great. I need to know just one more thing, what is your date of birth.
M1: December 12, 1978.
W1: Thank you. Now, you're interested in a one-bedroom apartment, correct?
M1: That's right.
W1: Did you want just a one-bedroom, or a one-bedroom with a den? We have several of those available, and a study is really nice. Having that extra room gives you space for a small home office or you can use it as a guest room.
M1: I don't think so. I live alone. I don't need an extra room.
W1: Right. Then I'll put you down for a simple one bedroom. With a balcony?
M1: No, I don't need that. I'll tell you what I do need, though, is a parking space.
W1: We have garage parking spaces available for a low monthly fee.
M1: Great. I really need that. Oh, and something else. I need an apartment with lots of closets for storage.
W1: We actually have storage areas in the basement. You can rent your own storage space by the month.
M1: Hmmm. That sounds like a good idea.
W1: All right. So I'll put you down for a storage space in the basement.

M1: Sounds good.

W1: Are you interested in our exercise club? We have an exercise room with several pieces of equipment as well as a sauna.

M1: Is it included in the rent?

W1: It's a available for a small extra fee.

M1: Then I don't think so. I can always go for a walk for free.

W1: All right then, one bedroom, no balcony. . . . I have several apartments you might like. One of them has a fireplace. Would you be interested in that?

M1: Do I have to pay extra for it?

W1: Actually no. That apartment is slightly smaller than our other one bedrooms, so even though it has a fireplace, the rent isn't any higher.

M1: OK then I'll take the fireplace.

W1: There is one drawback to that apartment. It doesn't have a washing machine. You'll have to go out to a laundromat.[1]

M1: Oh. Well, I suppose that doesn't matter. Can I see the apartment today?

W1: Certainly. I can show it to you now. However, we're still painting it, so it won't be available until next month.

M1: I was hoping to move next week, but . . . . maybe I can wait.

W1: And I'll need a small deposit to hold it for you, just 50 percent of the first month's rent.

SECTION 2

Questions 11–20

Now turn to Target 1, Making Assumptions, Section 2, Questions 11–20.

Section 2. You will hear a recording of a tour of an art museum
Listen carefully and answer the questions.

Female tour guide:

Good afternoon, everyone. I'm Lucy and I'll be your guide for today's two o'clock tour of the Jamestown Museum of Art. As a reminder, if you haven't purchased your ticket yet, please do so now. It's 15 dollars for adults and for children twelve and under it costs just 11 dollars. If you're a senior, today's your lucky day because it's Tuesday. That's Senior Citizens Day, so admission is free for all people over 65. However, you'll still need to get a ticket before the tour starts.

All right now, does everyone have a ticket? Yes? Good, then, let's go. We begin our tour here in the Main Gallery. Here you can see our collection of modern art. We're quite proud of this collection, which includes some minor works by major artists, for example, you'll see over there a small Picasso. And on this wall you'll see works by some other well-known modern painters.

Moving ahead to the next room, now we're in the City Gallery. This is the room where we feature local artists, who have painted a variety of subjects. You'll notice here some local scenes, in addition to a few portraits, and right over there you'll see some abstract works. Most of these works are modern, although we have a few older paintings in this room as well.

Straight ahead is the Hall of History. In that room we have a wonderful collection of portraits of famous figures in our city's history. The oldest paintings date back to the 17th century, and there are some quite modern paintings in there as well, including a portrait of our current governor, who was born in this city. Unfortunately, the Hall is closed right now, so we won't be able to visit it today.

[1] BRITISH: laundrette.

Here to our right is the East Room. Isn't this a beautiful room? The view of the garden is just lovely. You'll see there are no paintings in here because this room is devoted entirely to sculpture. That large sculpture in the center is by a well-known local artist, and over here you'll see several pieces by a modern European sculptor. You can see we have quite a number of lovely pieces in this room.

Just beyond the East Room is the gift shop. You may want to visit it after you have finished looking at the galleries. You can buy reproductions of art in the museum's collections, as well as souvenirs of the city, and many other lovely things as well.

All right then, we've visited all the open galleries in the museum. If you would like to return to any area of the museum now and look at the exhibits more carefully, please do so. Remember, the Hall of History is closed for repairs, but it should be open again next month. Also, please don't go up to the second floor. There's nothing up there but offices, and the area is off limits to visitors. Thank you for coming to the museum. Don't forget to visit the gift shop on your way out.

Target 2—Understanding Numbers

Example

M1: Flight 33 leaves from Gate 13 Concourse C3.

Questions 1–5

Question 1

W1: Now, Mr. Wilcox, you can send us a check[1] or, if you pay now by credit card, I can process your order right away.
M1: I'll pay by credit card.
W1: Great. May I have your credit card number then?
M1: It's 8 6 double 7 5 3 2 1 4 8 .
W1: 2 1 4 8. All right then, you should have your order within four business[2] days.

Question 2

M1: The university is very proud of its new theater, which is equipped with a state-of-the-art light and sound system and has a much greater seating capacity than the old one. The old theater had seats for just 250 people while the new one can seat an audience of 500.

Question 3

W1: I'm updating my phone list. Do you know Sherry's phone number by any chance?
M1: I know it by heart. It's 575-3174.
W1: Great. Thanks.

[1] BRITISH: cheque.

[2] BRITISH: working.

Question 4

M1: That room is only three hundred and fifteen dollars a night if you stay for three nights.
W1: Wow! Do you have anything more, uh, economical?
M1: Let me see . . . for next week . . . . Yes, I have another room that is just two hundred and sixty-five dollars a night. For a minimum three-night stay of course.
W1: That's still a lot of money, but I'll take it.

Question 5

M1: Is this the lost luggage office?
W1: Yes. How may I help you?
M1: How can you help me? By finding my luggage that your airline lost.
W1: All right, sir. Calm down. May I have your name and your flight number, please?
M1: My name is Richard Lyons and my flight number is X Y 5 3 8.

Examples

1. S1: seven oh three six five double eight
S2: seven oh three six five eight eight
S3: seven zero three sixty-five eighty-eight

2. S1: seven double four one four nine two
S2: seven four four one four nine two
S3: seven forty-four fourteen ninety-two

3. S1: two oh two double nine eight three
S2: two oh two nine nine eight three
S3: two zero two ninety-nine eighty-three

4. S1: six seven one four five three two
S2: six seven one four five three two
S3: six seventy-one forty-five thirty-two

5. S1: eight two four one five six one
S2: eight two four one five six one
S3: eight twenty-four fifteen sixty-one

6. S1: six three seven oh double five oh
S2: six three seven oh five five oh
S3: six thirty-seven zero fifty-five zero

7. S1: two six five one eight double one
S2: two six five one eight one one
S3: two sixty-five eighteen eleven

8. S1: two eight seven six two one six
S2: two eight seven six two one six
S3: two eighty-seven sixty-two sixteen

9.	S1:	four double five three oh two one
	S2:	four five five three oh two one
	S3:	four fifty-five thirty twenty-one
10.	S1:	three oh five eight four eight oh
	S2:	three oh five eight four eight oh
	S3:	three zero five eighty-four eighty

Target 3—Understanding the Alphabet

Example

M1: Is your name spelled L - i - n or L - y - n - n?
W1: Actually, it's Lynne with an e.

Questions 1–6

1. M1: My name is Tomas, t-o-m-a-s. I use the Spanish spelling.
W1: Oh, without the aitch.

2. W1: I live at 534 Maine Avenue. That's Maine with an "e" on the end.
M1: With an e. Not like Main Street with no "e".

3. M1: Is that Patty, p-a-t-t-y?
W1: No, with an i. P-a-t-t-i.

4. W1: Excuse me. You spelled my family name wrong. It's Roberts. The last letter is s.
M1: Oh, I'm sorry. I thought you said Robertson.

5. M1: All right then, and you live in the city of Springfield.
W1: No, that's Spring<u>vale</u>, v-a-l-e.

6. W1: OK, that's Mr. Nixon, n-i-x . . .
M1: No, no, no. <u>Dix</u>son, <u>d</u>-i-x-s-o-n.

Questions 7–12

7. M1: If you're paying by credit card, I'll need your full name.
W1: Sure. It's Miranda Green. That's m-i-r-a-n-d-a.
M1: A-n-d-a. Great. And what's your credit card number?
W1: 7-oh-4-3-2-1-8.
M1: 2-1-8. OK, you wanted two tickets, right?

8. W1: I'm looking up the number of the Bijou Theater. How do you spell that? With a g?
M1: No, with a j. It's B-i-j-o-u.
W1: B-i-j . . . . Found it. Write this number down for me: 2-3-2-5-4-double 8.

9. M1: Let me just get your name. That was Miss Roberta Johnson.
W1: Not Johnson, Janson. With an a. J-a-n-s-o-n.

M1: S-o-n. Got it. Now I can give you room 203. It's small but has a nice view. That room is only 245 pounds a night.
W1: I'd really prefer a larger room. I don't mind paying for it.
M1: Room 304 is the biggest we have available at the moment. It's 335 pounds a night.
W1: That's fine. I'll take it.

10. W1: All right, Mr. Park. May I have your address?
M1: It's 75 String Street. That's String Street S-t-r-i-n-g.
W1: That's an unusual name for a street. Well, would you like a seat near the front or more towards the middle?
M1: I'd like to be as close to the front as possible. Row B or C would be best.
W1: I can give you row B. Seat number 15 B.
M1: Fifteen B. Perfect.

11. W1: Good evening class. Welcome to Introduction to Economics. I'm your instructor, Dr. Willard. That's W-i-double l-a-r-d. Please don't hesitate to ask for help if you need it. My office hours are Tuesday and Thursday from three to five. My office is here in this building. It's office number 70, on the first floor.

12. M1: Thank you for the opportunity to speak tonight about my passion, wildflowers. If anyone in the audience would like to know more about the subject, I recommend contacting the Wildflower Society. They're at 17-oh-five State Street in Landover. That's L-a-n-d-o-v-e-r. Landover. They issue a number of interesting publications and also host several events each year for wildflower enthusiasts.

Target 4—Listening for Descriptions

Example

W1: It's really easy to get here. Just take the bus to the corner of the High Street and Regent Avenue. Then it's the second house from the corner.
M1: Second house from the corner, OK. It's not the two-story duplex with two doors, is it?
W1: No, that's across the street. Mine's small, it's only one story. There's only one door so knock or ring the bell. I'll be waiting for you.

Questions 1 and 2

Question 1

W1: This is the noon news report for Friday, April 12. Several stores in the downtown area of Jamestown were robbed[1] early this morning. Police are on the lookout for the suspect, who is described as about 45 years of age, bald, somewhat overweight, with a beard. If you see anyone meeting this description, please contact the Jamestown police.

[1]BRITISH: shops in the city centre were burgled.

Question 2

W1: May I help you?
M1: Yes, I'm looking for a present for my girlfriend. It's her nineteenth birthday. I was thinking maybe some jewelry.
W1: I can help you choose something that would look nice on her. What does she look like?
M1: Well, she's very pretty. She has really long dark hair and she's very thin. She almost always wears earrings.
W1: We have many nice earrings to choose from. Or, what about something different? Would she like a necklace?
M1: I don't know. Maybe . . .

Target 5—Listening for Time

Example

M1: The train was almost thirty minutes late. It didn't arrive until five o'clock.

TIME

Questions 1–6

Questions 1 and 2

M1: Good afternoon class. There have been a number of questions about the time for our final exam. As you know, this class regularly meets from two thirty until four Wednesday and Friday. Some of you have realized that during exam week there is a different schedule, thence the questions. Our final exam will be on Wednesday of exam week. It is scheduled to start at one forty-five and should last about an hour and a half, so you'll be out of here at around three fifteen or so.

Questions 3 and 4

W1: Could you tell me what time the train to Chicago leaves?
M1: The next train is at five fifteen.
W1: Hm. That's a long wait. It's only three now. What time does it arrive in Chicago?
M1: The trip is a little over six hours. It arrives at 11:30.

Questions 5 and 6

W1: Hi Cindy. I wanted to see if you could meet me for lunch tomorrow.
W2: Let's see, tomorrow's Monday . . . . I have a Spanish class in the morning . . . . Yes, I think that's a good idea.
W1: OK. Let's meet at twelve.
W2: Well, I have a haircut at 11:30. Better make it quarter past.
W1: Quarter past twelve, great.
W2: I'm so glad we're getting together. I'll be really nervous because I have a job interview in the afternoon. You can help me get ready for it.
W1: You know what's good for nerves? Exercise.
W2: I have my exercise class tomorrow at four. That should help.

DATE

Questions 1–6

Questions 1 and 2

W1: The City Museum of Art was established in the year 1898. It first opened its doors to the public on August fifteenth of that year. There was a spectacular opening celebration, but it wasn't held until later in the year, on December first, to be exact. Now the reasons for the delayed celebration are very interesting . . .

Questions 3 and 4

M1: All right, Mrs. Katz. I need just a bit more information to complete your application. May I have your date of birth?
W1: It's twenty-second September.
M1: Your husband's name is Georges, correct?
W1: Yes, and he was born on seventh July.

Questions 5 and 6

W1: We're thinking about going to Silver Lake this year. When do you think is a good time to go?
M1: Well, most people don't like to go in July or August because it's so hot then. September is too. I think the most popular time to go is October.
W1: Is that when you plan to go?
M1: Actually, no. We can't get away till November this year. We've made our reservations[1] for then, and we're leaving on the seventh.

DAY

Questions 1–6

Questions 1 and 2

W1: Hey, Jim. Are you going to history class?
M1: No, I don't have history today. I have English.
W1: It's Monday. Are you sure you don't have history today?
M1: Yeah. I have English today and Wednesday. My history class is on Thursday.
W1: Just one day a week for history, huh? Not bad.

Questions 3 and 4

M1: We're very glad that you are considering becoming members of the Urban Exercise Club. I'm sure you'll want to sign up for membership after you've enjoyed this afternoon here. Since today's Thursday, you could have a tennis lesson. The tennis instructor is here twice a week, Saturday as well as Thursday. You're lucky it's not Friday. You'll be able to enjoy the steam room. It'll be closed for its weekly cleaning tomorrow.

[1] BRITISH: booking.

Questions 5 and 6

W1: Let me remind you of your assignments for next week. Don't forget that the final exam has been rescheduled, so it'll be on Friday instead of Thursday. And you have an essay due on Tuesday. You should have a lot to study over Saturday and Sunday. Don't forget that I have office hours on Monday afternoon, in case you have any questions.

YEAR

Questions 1–6

Questions 1 and 2

M1: John James Audubon, the famous naturalist and painter of birds, was born on the island of Haiti in 1785. In 1803, he went to live the United States. He was a self-taught painter and supported himself for a while by painting portraits. His famous work, *Birds of America*, was first published in England. Later, in 1842, Audubon published a version of this work in the United States. He died in 1851.

Questions 3 and 4

W1: That was a really interesting lecture on Maria Mahoney. I really admire her for being the first woman governor of our state.

M1: Yes, she was an admirable person. Let's go over our notes. I put down that she was born in 1808.

W1: Not eighteen. Nineteen. She was born in 1908.

M1: Whoops! OK, then, but I have this right. She became governor in 1967.

W1: Are you sure? Wasn't it 1957?

M1: No, 1957 is when she first decided to run for office, but she didn't win an election until 1967.

Questions 5 and 6

M1: The university began construction of the library in 1985. It was expected to take just two years, but by the end of 1987, the library was only three-quarters completed. Finally, by the summer of 1988, construction was finished and the new library opened in August of that year.

SEASON

Questions 1–6

Questions 1 and 2

W1: Tourists visit the region only during certain times of the year. The winters are not harsh, but it rains a lot then and the temperatures are quite cool. Spring is quite a bit less rainy than winter, and the temperatures are warmer, so many tourists like to visit then. Summers are hot and dry, so hot that most tourists stay away. They return in the autumn when the weather is still dry but not as hot.

Questions 3 and 4

W1: Wow, Josh, I can't believe you hiked the whole mountain range. When did you start your trip?
M1: Well, you can't leave too early in the spring, because it's still late winter in the mountains then. Most hikers start in the late spring, and that's what I did too.
W1: And then you hiked all summer. What's summer like in the mountains?
M1: It's not too hot and you can see a lot of wild life, especially later in the summer when the birds start to migrate.
W1: It must have been winter by the time you finished the trip.
M1: Not quite. It was late in the autumn, which is almost as cold as winter in the mountains.

Questions 5 and 6

M1: I'd like to sign up for the beginning Japanese class.
W1: I'm sorry, all our Japanese classes are full. Fall is the busiest time of year here at the language school.
M1: Hm. Well, then, maybe I'll wait until next summer to take a class.
W1: That would be fine, but I recommend enrolling early. Summer is almost as busy as fall.
M1: Really? Well, when is your least busy time of year?
W1: Spring is a quieter time, but we have our lowest enrollment in the winter.

Target 6—Listening for Frequency

Example

W1: Sam works out at the gym several days a week.

Questions 1–6

Question 1

M1: Do you like dancing?
W1: Yes , but I don't go very much.
M1: No?
W1: Well, I go about once a month or so.

Question 2

W1: Do you smoke?
M1: No, I don't.
W1: Really? Not at all?
M1: Mmmm, maybe once or twice a year.

Question 3

M1: Another rainy day. Does it ever stop raining here?
W1: It's the rain forest. It rains every day.

Question 4

W1: Mike says he's a vegetarian. What does that mean?
M1: It means he doesn't eat meat.
W1: No meat at all? Not even on special occasions?
M1: Not even then.

Question 5

M1: How's your class?
W1: It's really hard. The professor loves giving tests.
M1: Really? Does he give a lot of tests?
W1: Oh, yeah. We have one or two a week.

Question 6

W1: Do these geese spend all summer here?
M1: Yes, and all winter, too. They don't migrate.
W1: So you can see them here any season of the year.

Questions 7–12

Question 7

W1: For the first part of my research, I counted the number of shoppers who entered the store between 6 A.M. and 8 A.M.
M1: And you did this every morning?
W1: Yes, every morning for a week.

Question 8

W1: Are you interested in joining the chess club?
M1: Maybe. When does it meet?
W1: On the last Sunday of every month.

Question 9

W1: How often do you have your history class?
M1: Every Tuesday and Thursday.

Question 10

M1: Do you go to the movies much?
W1: I go when I get the chance, but not as often as I'd like. Maybe once or twice a semester.

Question 11

W1: How can I start managing my money better?
M1: First, you need to make a monthly spending plan.

Question 12

M1: While you're student teaching, I'll observe each one of you in the classroom several times.
W1: How frequent will your visits be?
M1: You'll get a visit from me once every two weeks.

Target 7—Listening for Similar Meanings

Example

M1: The survey participants who wrote answers to the questions are all college graduates.

Questions 1–6

Question 1

M1: How many tickets will you need?
W1: There will be three adults and two children in our party.

Question 2

W1: How's your French class? Do you like the instructor?
M1: Yes, she's great, but she gives us a lot of work to do in class.
W1: Then you have to wait weeks before you get your papers back, right?
M1: No, she always checks our assignments on the same day we do them.

Question 3

M1: I've heard that this area of the country is really growing.
W1: Yes, the population is increasing at a rate of about 10,000 people a year.

Question 4

W1: I understand that this area has suffered harsh weather conditions in recent years.
M1: Yes, for example, last year a severe drought killed much of the vegetation in the region.
W1: That must have had a devastating effect on agriculture.

Question 5

M1: If I give you a check for the first month's rent right now, can I move in tomorrow?
W1: I'm sorry, but the apartment won't be available until next week.

Question 6

M1: Let's see . . . I got your address and phone number. Oh, I need to know your occupation.
W1: Put computer programmer.

Target 8—Listening for Emotions

Example

W1: I'm really excited about the chance to debate the team from Oxford.
M1: I'm more apprehensive than excited. In fact, I'm not looking forward to it at all.

Questions 1–6

Question 1

W1: We'll begin the tour of Roselands Park with a bit about the history of the park. Local residents were thrilled when millionaire Samuel Waters announced that he would donate land for the park, including his collection of prized rose bushes. Some of his heirs, quite naturally, were a bit angry when they learned[1] that he had given away so much family property.

Question 2

W1: What's the matter with you? Yesterday you seemed really excited about your science experiment.
M1: That was yesterday. Today I just can't seem to get it to work right.
W1: Oh, don't worry about it. I'm sure it will be fine.
M1: I don't know. I keep trying and trying, but it isn't working the way I planned.

Question 3

M1: Our language lab is equipped with state-of-the-art equipment guaranteed to greatly improve your foreign language skills. Students are often confused when they first use our facilities because it seems complicated at first glance, but it's actually quite simple once you get used to it. Today I'll give you an orientation to the lab, and you'll see how easy it is to use this equipment to complete your class assignments and study for tests.

Question 4

W1: You didn't win the essay contest? Aren't you upset?
M1: Not really.
W1: I'd be really disappointed if I'd worked so hard and didn't even win second or third place.
M1: It's just a contest. It doesn't really matter.

Question 5

W1: In local news, children and teachers at Burnside Elementary School received an unexpected visit yesterday from Mayor Sharon Smith as part of her campaign to focus attention on the plight of city schools. Several school board members accompanied the Mayor. "We had no idea she was planning to visit us," said school principal[2] Roger Simmons. "But naturally we felt quite honored."

[1] BRITISH: learnt
[2] BRITISH: head master.

Question 6

M1: How is your research project going?
W1: Great. It's almost done.
M1: I'm impressed. I always get nervous when I have a big project like that to do.
W1: It's not so bad really. And I'm quite pleased with the results that I'm getting.

Target 9—Listening for an Explanation

Example

Listen to the explanation of how a toaster works.

M1: How does a toaster brown your toast every morning? Like all appliances that heat up, a toaster works by converting electrical energy into heat energy. The electrical current runs from the electrical socket in your kitchen wall, through the toaster plug, to the toaster cord. It travels down the cord to the appliance itself. Inside the toaster are wire loops. The wires are made of a special type of metal. Electricity passes through this metal, creating friction. This friction causes the wires to heat up and glow orange. When the wires have sufficiently heated, your toast pops up ready to eat.

Questions 1–12

Listen to the explanation of how cacao beans are processed.

W1: The rich flavor of chocolate that almost everyone loves comes from the cacao tree, which is grown in tropical regions around the world. The farmer harvests the ripe fruit of the cacao tree, then cuts it open to remove the seeds. These seeds are the cocoa beans from which chocolate is made. The beans are fermented in a large vat for about a week. Then they are placed on trays in the sun to dry. When the cocoa beans are ready, they are shipped off to the chocolate factory. At the chocolate factory, the cocoa beans are turned into all sorts of delicious chocolate treats.

Target 10—Listening for Classifications

Example

M1: The school offers two types of courses. The one during the day is designed for students who are pursuing their academic degree full time. The night courses are designed for students who work during the day and are taking specific courses for an advanced business certificate.

Questions 1–5

Question 1

W1: It's easy to upgrade your ticket from economy class to first class. It costs just a little bit more, and it will enhance your travel experience in several ways. While we have roomy seats in both economy and first class, our first class passengers are also offered pillows and blankets so they can nap in comfort. Snacks are served in economy class, while full meals are served to all first-class passengers. As an economy class passenger you'll be offered the most current magazines for your entertainment, but you'll have to bring your own DVDs if you want to watch movies. In first class, we show complimentary first-run movies.

Question 2

M1: Do you want to go to the movies tonight? There's a great film showing at the Royal Theater.
W1: The Royal Theater? I never like the movies there. They only show violent types like horror and war movies.
M1: So what kind of movie do you like?
W1: Oh, romantic movies and classic movies, like the ones they show at the Deluxe Theater.

Question 3

M1: Although butterflies and moths look very similar, they aren't exactly alike. There are several ways to tell the difference between them. The most well-known difference is that butterflies fly during the day, while moths are night fliers. Additionally, when butterflies rest, they fold their wings back. Moths at rest hold their wings in a horizontal position. The antennae are different also. Butterflies have thin antennae, and moths often have feathery antennae.

Question 4

W1: I have so much to do to get ready for the party. I have to clean the house, cook . . .
M1: You've bought all the food already, haven't you?
W1: Yes, the shopping's done. And I've planned all the decorations, too.
M1: When did you mail[1] the invitations?
W1: Mail the invitations? Oh, no! I guess I'd better do that today.

Question 5

W1: Trees for landscaping your garden can be divided into three categories. Some trees we plant to add beauty to the yard. They are chosen for their beautiful flowers or interesting leaves. These are the ornamental trees. If you live in a sunny location, then you'll probably want to plant some shade trees. These are usually tall, broad-leafed trees. Finally we have the evergreens. Every garden should have at least one to provide a bit of green year round. Most evergreens are cone-bearing trees with needles instead of leaves.

[1]BRITISH: post.

Target 11—Listening for Comparisons and Contrasts

Example

F1: I've been corresponding by mail with a French student.
F2: In English? You don't speak French, do you?
F1: No, unfortunately, but she writes English well. We have a lot in common.
F2: Like what, your age?
F1: Well, I'm actually about two years older than she is. But we do have the same first name.
F2: And you're both students.
F1 Yes, and we are both studying to be doctors, although she wants to be a pediatrician[1], and I want to be a neurosurgeon.
F2: It seems the only similarities are your sex and your given name.
F1: Well, we both like to swim. She likes to dance, too, but you know how little I like dancing.

Questions 1–4.

Question 1

W1: How's your new job?
M1: It's great. Much better than my old job.
W1: Really? That's wonderful. You're earning more money now, aren't you?
M1: Yeah, the salary's a lot higher, but I have to work more hours.
W1: Too bad. I remember you had a really good schedule at your old job.
M1: Yes, I miss that. But the job itself is pretty similar. I have the same kind of responsibilities that I had before.
W1: That makes it easier. Are you still working in the same place?
M1: No, now I have to go to the other side of town. But at least I can still take the bus like I did for my old job.
W1: Well, that's convenient.

Question 2

W1: The new Riverdale Library will have its grand opening next month. The new library, which has been under construction for the past two years, stands on the same site as the old library. But there the similarity ends. The new library is much larger than the old two-story building, boasting four floors of books and two floors of offices, as well as an underground parking garage, which everyone agrees will be a great improvement over the old outside parking lot. With so much space to fill, we have greatly expanded the size of our book collection. You will continue to enjoy the same services as before. Online book renewal, free Internet access, and the Ask-a-Librarian Hotline that you enjoyed at the old library will also be available at our new facilities.

Question 3

M1: I'm interested in joining the health club, but I see you have two types of membership.
W1: Yes, we have both full and associate memberships. The full membership costs almost twice as much as the associate, and many members feel it's worth the extra cost.
M1: What's the difference between them?

[1]BRITISH: paediatrician.

W1: With both types of membership you are entitled to the use of all our club facilities and you can take advantage of all our fitness classes as well. You also get use of the locker room[1] with both memberships, but full members get extra locker room privileges, such as your own locker exclusively for your use and laundry service as well. May I sign you up for a full membership today?

M1: I'm not sure. The associate membership sounds fine to me.

W1: Let me point out that with the full membership you also get a complimentary individualized fitness plan tailored just for you. Associate members may take advantage of this service as well, but they have to pay extra for it.

M1: I'll have to think about it.

Question 4

M1: Toads and frogs begin their lives in similar ways. The eggs hatch in or near water, and the babies, called tadpoles, spend the first part of their lives living in the water. When they become adults, frogs continue to live in the water, while adult toads usually live on the land. When you come across one of these animals, how can you tell whether it's a toad or a frog? The easiest way is to touch its skin. Frogs have smooth skin while the skin of toads is generally rough and bumpy. Their shape is somewhat different also, with toads being plumper and broader than frogs. What is a more typical sound on a summer evening than a chorus of croaking frogs or toads? Both these animals make their croaking sound by inflating a sac in their throat.

Target 12—Listening for Negative Meanings

Example

W1: It was a very dense book, but it wasn't impossible to read.

Questions 7–12

Question 7

M1: The flora and fauna of this region are adapted to the special climate. It hardly ever rains here, even in the winter. Most of the year, there is barely a cloud to be seen in the sky.

Question 8

W1: Your essay writing exam is coming up tomorrow, so I'd like to review some of the testing rules with you now. The good news is that you'll have an unlimited amount of time to write your essay. You won't, however, be permitted to consult a dictionary while[2] writing the exam. Neither can you take anything else into the testing room with you except a pen.

Question 9

M1: I'm in a bit of a hurry. Do you think you can fix the problem with my car today?

W1: I'm sorry, but I'm behind schedule. I won't be able to get to it until the weekend.

M1: Then I'll have to take a bus to work tomorrow.

[1]BRITISH: changing room

[2]BRITISH: whilst.

Question 10

W1: What a restaurant! Never in my life have I tasted such delicious food.
M1: You really think so? But don't you think the service was too slow?
W1: Not a bit. I can't wait to go back there.

Question 11

M1: Botanists and other flower lovers enjoy visiting this area in the spring and summer to see the abundant variety of wildflowers. In the early spring it isn't uncommon to find violets and, later in the season, there is a profusion of wild roses as well. Many also come here seeking the wild iris, although that is more rarely seen in these parts.

Question 12

M1: I have so much homework this week. Not only do I have to write two papers, I have to read four books, too.
W1: Wow. That's a lot.
M1: Yeah, well, at least I don't have any exams to study for.

Target 13—Listening for Chronology

Example

W1: Before you do your research, we'll have an orientation session in the library so you can become familiar with the various sources of information available there. Each student will give a presentation on his or her research topic after all the papers have been submitted. All of this will have to be completed prior to the date of the final exam.

Questions 1–5

Question 1

W1: I'm interested in renting an apartment in this building.
M1: OK, first you'll have to fill out[1] an application. Then, before you submit it, you'll need to get two references.
W1: References?
M1: Yes, from former landlords or your boss or someone like that who can vouch for your responsibility. All right, so you do that, then you'll have to have some money ready for a deposit. As soon as we have an available apartment, we'll notify you, and we'll ask that you pay a deposit to hold it for you.
W1: I have to pay the deposit before signing the lease?
M1: Well, of course we'll refund it if you decide not to take the apartment, but the deposit holds it for you while you look the apartment over and decide whether or not you want it.

[1]BRITISH: fill in.

Question 2

M1: Today we'll take a look at the life of classical composer Wolfgang Amadeus Mozart. Mozart was born in Austria in 1756. His father, Leopold, was a well-known music teacher and published an important text book on violin playing shortly after Wolfgang's birth. Young Wolfgang showed his genius at an early age, beginning to write his own musical compositions at the age of 5. This was one factor that led to his father's decision to take Wolfgang and his sister on performing tours around Europe, beginning in 1762. After a childhood of touring Europe, Mozart visited Vienna in 1781 and decided to settle there. He had been greatly saddened during his tour of 1777 when his mother, who was accompanying him, died while they were abroad. He looked forward to a new life in Vienna.

Question 3

W1: How'd your trip to the beach go?
M1: Fantastic. Well, mostly. Of course, we had to leave home at five in the morning.
W1: Ouch! So early.
M1: Yeah, but, then, by lunch time we were almost there.
W1: So where'd you have lunch? At that burger place, right?
M1: No, we just had a roadside picnic to save time. We'd made our sandwiches the night before we left.
W1: You're so organized.
M1: I guess. Whatever. So anyhow, back in the car after lunch we started arguing about a place to stay. We finally agreed on the White Sands Motel.
W1: I've been there. It's all right.
M1: Yeah, well, it's a good thing we left home early because by the time we got there, there was only one room left at the motel, so we were lucky to get it. We went swimming as soon as we'd checked in.

Question 4

W1: I have to do this research project for my sociology class, and I don't know how to begin.
W2: Is that Professor Miller's class? I took it last year. It's a great class.
W1: Really? Can you help me get started?
W2: Sure, well, I mean, I guess so. Well, I'd say the most important thing is get a partner. It's much easier working with someone else.
W1: So the first thing is to get a partner?
W2: You probably should choose a research topic first, then find a classmate who's also interested in your topic. Then you need the professor's approval.
W1: Approval for what?
W2: No, wait. OK first you and your partner design your research, I mean you write up your questionnaire and decide whom you will interview and all that.
W1: *Then* we get the professor's approval for our research design?
W2: Yes. And then you can start your research.

Question 5

W1: Welcome to Waterside Gardens. We'll begin our tour by walking through the rose garden, just as soon as everyone has shown me his or her tickets. Following the rose garden, we'll view the pond area. We'll visit the greenhouse after everyone who so desires has had a chance to photograph the butterfly garden. It is our most picturesque area. And that's it. I hope you'll enjoy the tour.

MODEL TESTS

MODEL TEST 1

Narrator: IELTS Listening. Model Test 1.

You will hear a number of different recordings, and you will have to answer questions on what you hear. There will be time for you to read the instructions and questions, and you will have a chance to check your work. All the recordings will be played once only.

The test is in four sections. Write all your answers in the Listening Question booklet. At the end of the test you will be given ten minutes to transfer your answers to an answer sheet.

Now turn to Section 1 on page 132.

Section 1. You will hear a conversation between Mark Winston who wants to learn Japanese, and Kathy Green who is a receptionist at the World Language Academy.

First you have some time to look at Questions 1 to 3 on page 132.

Listen carefully and answer Questions 1 to 3.

Questions 1–3

Narrator: You will see that there is an example which has been done for you. On this occasion only, the conversation relating to this will be played first.

Kathy Green: Good Morning. May I help you?
Mark Winston: Yes, I'm Mark Winston and I...

(Telephone rings)

Oh, Excuse me, Mr. Winston. World Language Academy. This is Kathy Green. May I help you? (pause). No this is a private language school, not a travel agency. (pause) No problem at all. Good-bye. I'm sorry, Mr. Winston. Now, may I help YOU?

Mr. Winston: Yes, I hope you can. I'd like to sign up now for a Japanese class next week.

Narrator: The man says he'd like to "**sign up now**" which means "register today" for a language class. The number 2 has been written in the blank. You should answer the questions as you listen because you will not hear the recording a second time. Listen carefully and answer questions 1 to 3.

Kathy Green: Good Morning. May I help you?
Mark Winston: Yes, I'm Mark Winston and I . . .

(Telephone rings)

Oh, Excuse me, Mr. Winston. World Language Academy. This is Kathy Green. May I help you? (pause). No this is a private language school, not a travel agency. (pause) No problem at all. Good-bye. I'm sorry, Mr. Winston. Now may I help YOU?

Mr. Winston: Yes, I hope you can. I'd like to sign up now for a Japanese class next week.
Kathy Green: Classes start next week and we have lots of Japanese classes to choose from. Have you studied Japanese before?
Mark Winston: No, I haven't. I'm a beginner. I'm planning to visit Japan next summer so I want to learn a bit of the language.
Kathy Green: That's great. Japan is a wonderful place to visit. I spent a month in Tokyo last year, actually, and I even climbed Mount Fujiyama.
Mark Winston: Really? That's too much activity for me. I'm just planning to visit Tokyo. I think I'll find plenty to do there.
Kathy Green: You certainly will. All right then let me tell you a bit about our classes. They're all taught by native speakers, and they are all specialists in their field. You can choose a Japanese for Tourists class, Japanese for Business Travelers, or Japanese for University Students. You're not studying at a university, are you?
Mark Winston: No, I graduated a few years ago.
Kathy Green: Well, then, the tourist class is probably best for you.
Mark Winston: Yes, I think you're right. I just want to learn enough to order food in restaurants and go shopping and things like that. When does the Japanese for Tourists class begin?
Kathy Green: Let's see. We have a class for beginners that starts next week. I think there are still a few spaces left. You're in luck . . .we have 15 students enrolled, and there's room for three more.

Narrator: Before you hear the rest of the conversation, you have some time to look at questions 4 to 10 on pages 132 and 133.

Now listen and answer questions 4 to 10.

Questions 4–10

Mark Winston: When does that class meet?
Kathy Green: Every Monday, Wednesday, and Thursday from 5:30 until 7:30.
Mark Winston: That's a bit early for me. I work until 6:00. Don't you have a class that starts later in the evening?
Kathy Green: No . . . not for beginners. The advanced class is Tuesday and Thursday from 7:30 to 9:30, but you've never studied Japanese before, have you?
Mark Winston: No. I don't know anything about it.

Kathy Green: Then you couldn't take that class. Let's see . . . we have an afternoon class on Monday, Wednesday, and Thursday, from one to three. Oh, but that's an intermediate class. What about mornings? We have a beginner's class that meets five days a week, Monday through Friday, from 9 A.M. until 10 A.M. Could you do that?

Mark Winston: No, I work all day. I only have evenings and weekends free.

Kathy Green: Well, we have a beginner's class on Saturday from 9 in the morning until 2 in the afternoon.

Mark Winston: Nine until two? That's a long class.

Kathy Green: We also have private tutors. Actually, I usually recommend private tutors because they give you individualized attention. You are the only student in the class, so the tutor teaches you according to your specific needs. It really is the best way to learn a language.

Mark Winston: It sounds great! I'd learn a lot that way, wouldn't I?

Kathy Green: You really would. And it's very convenient. You can arrange to meet with your tutor at whatever time suits you.

Mark Winston: Fantastic.[1] How do I sign up?

Kathy Green: Well, how many hours a week do you want to study? We usually recommend three to five hours a week for a minimum of four weeks.

Mark Winston: OK. I'll start with three hours a week.

Kathy Green: Great. You can send us a check to cover the first week of classes, or you can pay now by credit card. Three hours of private classes comes out to 300 dollars, plus a 25-dollar registration fee.

Mark Winston: Three hundred dollars? That's 100 dollars a class!

Kathy Green: And it's certainly worth it. You'll be studying with a native speaker of Japanese. And all our tutors are professionally trained in the latest teaching methods. You'll be getting the best instruction money can buy.

Mark Winston: But 100 dollars a class! That's over one thousand dollars for a month of classes. I'm sorry, but I just can't do that.

Kathy Green: Then take the Saturday class. It's only $300 a month. And it's small. There will be only four or five students in it.

Mark Winston: Great. I'll take that class. Can I pay by check?

Kathy Green: Yes. Just bring your check to the first class. See you next Saturday at 9:00.

(Audio fades as last speaker continues to speak.)

Narrator: That is the end of Section 1. You now have half a minute to check your answers.

Now turn to Section 2 on page 133.

Section 2. You will hear a radio interview between Shirley Hobbs the host of the show, Bird Talk, and Iris Pence, an expert of pet parrots.

First, you have some time to look at questions 11 to 13 on page 133.

As you listen to the first part of the talk, answer questions 11 to 13.

(Birds squawking; parrots talking)

[1]BRITISH: Brilliant.

Questions 11–13

Shirley Hobbs: Good afternoon, I'm Shirley Hobbs and welcome to Bird Talk, the show with all the facts about birds. *(Birds squawking; parrots talking)* Our guest today is Iris Pence, owner of Fur and Feathers Pet Store, who will talk to us about a very popular bird—the parrot.

Iris Pence: Thank you, Shirley. First let me clear up a common confusion. I'm not going to talk about one kind of bird because a parrot is not just one kind of bird. There're actually many birds in the parrot family. In fact, there are more than 300 different species of parrots, and they live all over the world. You know, parrots are gorgeous animals, and I think a big reason people are attracted to them is their gorgeous colors. Some species are very colorful, but, believe it or not, plain old green is actually the most common color for parrots. Another thing, parrots can be all different sizes. The smallest parrot is called the pygmy parrot. It's about ten centimeters or so long, so it's small enough to fit in your pocket. The hyacinth macaw, on the other hand, measures one meter from the tip of its beak to the tip of its tail. It's the largest of all the parrots. It's really an impressive bird.

Narrator: Before you hear the rest of the message, you have some time to look at questions 14 to 20 on page 134.

Now listen and answer the questions 14 to 20.

Questions 14–20

Iris Pence: OK, pets. The reason parrots make fantastic pets is that they're naturally social animals. They live in flocks in the wild, so when you bring one of these birds into your home as a pet, it'll treat you like a member of its flock. Parrots really like being with people. But, there's another side to this. Parrots not only like attention, they need attention. So if you plan to get a pet parrot, you have to be ready to spend a lot of time with it. Lonely parrots develop behavioral problems. For example, boredom may cause them to pull out all their feathers, and unfortunately, this is quite a common problem. Also, feeling ignored may cause them to scream all day. There have been too many sad stories about neglected pet parrots. OK, so, if you're thinking about getting a pet parrot, you really have to give it a lot of time and attention. I can't stress this enough.

Of course you can't spend all day with your pet, so one thing to do is make sure it has some toys. A parrot with toys can entertain itself for several hours. And make sure the toys are made of wood because parrots love to chew. Another thing to be aware of is that parrots have messy habits. They throw their food everywhere. This is natural behavior for them, but it means more work for you. Your parrot's cage will have to be cleaned daily. And this brings me to the next point, which is food. Many people think that their pet birds can live on seeds alone, but this isn't true. In addition to seeds, you should feed your parrot plenty of fresh fruit and vegetables. This is true no matter what type of parrot you have. A varied diet will keep your bird healthy and strong.

Now I would like to introduce you to some specific types of parrots and discuss which ones make the best pets . . .

Narrator: That is the end of Section 2. You now have half a minute to check your answers.

Now turn to Section 3 on page 134.

Section 3. You will hear a panel discussion between the panel moderator and two panelists, Dr. Karen Akers and Dr. Fred Williams, both transportation consultants. In the first part of the discussion, they are talking about the future of public transportation.

First, you will have some time to look at questions 21 to 26 on page 134.

Now listen carefully and answer the questions 21 to 26.

Questions 21–26

Moderator: Dr. Williams and Dr. Akers, I want to thank both of you for coming today and sharing your thoughts on the future of public transportation.

(Simultaneous thanks)

Dr. Akers: Glad to be here.

Dr. Williams: Thank You.

Moderator: Let me ask you first, Dr. Williams, traffic congestion is becoming more and more of a problem, and it's spreading. We're used to traffic jams in cities, but now we find traffic problems on many major highways[1] that run between cities. What solutions do you see for the future of transportation?

Dr. Williams: Many transportation experts, myself included, are excited about the potential of high-speed trains. These trains are having a great deal of success in Japan and in several European countries, as well. They've actually been around for a while—since 1964, in fact. The first high-speed train was put into operation that year.

Moderator: What would the speed be exactly of a high-speed train? How would you define "high-speed" train?

Dr. Williams: We usually call a train high speed if it's capable of traveling at 200 kilometers an hour or faster.

Moderator: That's very fast. It would seem to open up a lot of possibilities for transportation between cities.

Dr. Akers: Yes, that's right. Fifty years ago or more, conventional trains were the major form of transportation between cities. Of course, they weren't high-speed trains, but nobody expected that then. Those old trains provided frequent, reliable, and affordable long distance transportation, and most people used them. Then things changed. Cars and highways were improved, so more and more people started driving cars.

Dr. Williams: Cars are a great form of transportation. Everybody loves them because they're so convenient. But we usually use cars for local trips . . . shopping, and going to work, and things like that.

Dr. Akers: That's true. For long distance trips, most people nowadays rely on planes. Plane service is more frequent and affordable now than it was in the past, so planes, like cars, have become more convenient for people. Meanwhile, trains have more or less fallen by the wayside as a common means of transportation.

Moderator: But with everybody driving cars and taking planes, we have a lot of congestion. And not just on the roads. Airports have become very crowded, too.

Dr. Williams: Exactly. We have congestion everywhere now, so we need to look at new forms of transportation.

[1]BRITISH: motorways.

Narrator: Before you hear the rest of the conversation, you have some time to look at questions 27 to 30 on page 135.

Now listen and answer questions 27 to 30.

Questions 27–30

Dr. Akers: And that's where high-speed trains come in. They offer several advantages over both cars and planes. When you take everything into consideration—getting to the train station, boarding the train, and all that—a high-speed train gets you to your destination just about as quickly as a car. So speed isn't really an advantage. Cost isn't always, either. Depending on how many people are traveling with you, a train trip could be more expensive than a car trip. But, a train trip is much more relaxing than a car trip. You can read, sleep, eat, whatever, while the train carries you to your destination. And of course you're never delayed by traffic jams. To my mind, these are great advantages.

Moderator: Yes, I can really see the advantage of the train over the car. But what about planes? Planes are much faster than cars, so that's a big plus for planes.

Dr. Williams: Not necessarily. For trips shorter than 650 kilometers, high-speed trains can actually be faster. Checking in at the airport and going through security takes a long time. You don't have that kind of delay with a train. Also trains can carry more passengers than planes. They can also offer more frequent service. So for your medium distance trips, they really are faster than planes.

Narrator: That is the end of Section 3. You now have half a minute to check your answers.

Now turn to Section 4 on page 135.

Section 4. You will hear a lecture on Albert Einstein. First you have some time to look at the questions 31 to 40 on page 135.

Now listen carefully and complete the timeline in questions 31 to 40.

Questions 31–40

Lecturer: Today I want to talk about the early life of a man whose name is synonymous with genius—Albert Einstein. He is well known, of course, for his work in physics, especially his theory of relativity. This is a term that everyone has heard, but few lay people, . . . and I do not mean to include you in this group, . . . but few non-physicists understand. Equally incomprehensible to most people is why Einstein the genius did so poorly at school. There are some questions, actually misconceptions about his early life, particularly about his lack of success in school that I want to try to clear up for you. Let's look now at some true facts about the life of this famous man.

Albert Einstein was born in Germany in 1879. As a child in school, he had a reputation as a slow learner. Now there were a couple of theories about why he could not keep pace with his classmates. He may have had some sort of learning disability; we don't know for sure. Another theory about his slow learning is that he may have suffered from a condition related to autism.

Whether it was a learning disability or not, Einstein himself believed that his slowness actually helped him develop his theory of relativity. He said that he ended up thinking about time and space at a later age than most children, at a time when his intellect was more developed. He didn't even begin to study mathematics until he was 12. There are popular rumors that he failed his math classes, but this is actually not true.

Mathematics was a late passion; his first was the violin. Like many intellectuals, Einstein had a passion for music. He started his study of the violin during elementary school and continued playing the violin for the rest of his life.

When Einstein was 15, his family moved to Italy. Soon after that, his parents sent him to Switzerland, where in 1896 he finished high school. After graduating from high school, he enrolled in a Swiss technological institute. He received a teaching diploma from the institute in 1900. He remained in Switzerland and eventually became a Swiss citizen, in 1901.

Einstein had a hard time finding a teaching job. In fact he never did find one. A friend's father helped him get a job at the Swiss Patent Office. He began working there in 1902. His job involved reviewing inventors' applications for patents. When he looked over the applications, he often found faults in the applicants' drawings. He would make suggestions so they could improve their designs and better their chances for receiving a patent.

Meanwhile, in 1898, between graduating from high school and getting his job at the Patent Office, Einstein met and fell in love with a young Serbian woman, Mileva Maric. Maric was a mathematician, and Einstein considered her his intellectual equal. They had a daughter in 1902 but unusual for the time even for geniuses, they didn't get married until 1903. Their first son was born the following year. There is no record of whether the two children inherited their father's learning disability.

Narrator: That is the end of Section 4. You now have half a minute to check your answers.

You will now have 10 minutes to transfer your answers to the listening answer sheet.

This is almost the end of the test. You now have one more minute to check all your answers.

That is the end of the Listening section of Model Test 1.

MODEL TEST 2

Narrator: IELTS Listening. Model Test 2

You will hear a number of different recordings, and you will have to answer questions on what you hear. There will be time for you to read the instructions and questions, and you will have a chance to check your work. All the recordings will be played once only.

The test is in four sections. Write all your answers in the Listening Question booklet. At the end of the test you will be given ten minutes to transfer your answers to an answer sheet.

Now turn to Section 1 on page 151.

Section 1. You will hear a conversation between an interviewer and a woman shopper.

First you have some time to look at Questions 1 to 7 on page 151.

You will see that there is an example which has been done for you. On this occasion only, the conversation relating to this will be played first.

Example

M1: Excuse me. Could I have a few minutes of your time?

W1: What do you need?

M1: First, welcome to Lougheed (Lawheed) Mall, the largest shopping center in Vancouver. We're conducting a survey of the shoppers at this mall. We want to learn about when and how often people shop, the stores they prefer, in general, people's habits when they shop at the mall. Would you mind answering a few questions about your shopping?

Narrator: The man says he is conducting a survey of shoppers, so B has been circled. Now we shall begin. You should answer the questions as you listen because you will not hear the recording a second time. Listen carefully and answer questions 1 to 7.

Questions 1–7

M1: Excuse me, ma'am. Could I have a few minutes of your time?

W1: What do you need?

M1: First, welcome to Lougheed (Lawheed) Mall, the largest shopping center in Vancouver. We're conducting a survey of the shoppers at this mall. We want to learn about when and how often people shop, the stores they prefer, in general, people's habits when they shop at the mall. Would you mind answering a few questions about your shopping?

W1: Not at all.

M1: Thank you. Today we're interviewing married women, that is women with husbands and children who shop for their families. So the first question is, do you fit this category?

W1: Yes, I do.

M1: Wonderful. Now, I need to know your age. Are you between the ages of 18 and twenty-five, twenty-six and . . . ?

W1: (interrupting) I'm 34.

M1: Great. OK. Now, how often do you shop here? Less than once a month, at least once a month, once a . . .

W1: I have a big family. I have to buy a lot of things. I'm here at least twice a week.

M1: Well that's just fine. You must be very familiar with the stores here.

W1: I certainly am.

M1: All right then. The next question concerns the things that you buy. What do you usually shop for here?

W1: Just about everything. I've been in all the stores at one time or another. The clothing stores are quite nice, though, frankly, their prices are a bit high, and I like the bookstore too, but . . .

M1: What I need to know, though is, what is the one type of thing you shop for most often? Would it be books?

W1: Oh, no. That's only occasionally. The reason I come here so often is for food. I told you I have a large family. I buy all our food at the supermarket here.

M1: OK. So, the next question is how much time do you usually spend at the mall?

W1: What do you mean? Do you mean every week?

M1: I mean, each time you come here, how long do you spend?

W1: Oh, I'd say about an hour and a half or so. Maybe a little longer, but I'm hardly ever here for more than two hours.

M1: Now there's one last question in this section. How do you usually come to the mall? Do you take the bus, the . . . ?

W1: I always drive.

Narrator: Before you hear the rest of the conversation, you have some time to look at questions 8 to 10 on page 152.

Now listen and answer questions 8 to 10.

Questions 8–10

M1: Fine. OK, the next part of the questionnaire concerns your opinions. You say you've been in all the stores in the mall. In general, in which store would you say you've had the best shopping experience?

W1: That's easy. The shoe store.

M1: That's a big store, isn't it? They have a huge selection of shoes.

W1: They do, but I consider it a good store because the employees there are so polite. They give very good service.

M1: Now, you may have had a chance to eat at our new food court.

W1: Yes, I have, but I don't think I'll eat there again.

M1: Why not?

W1: Well, the food tastes fine, but it's very expensive. It shouldn't cost so much.

M1: I have just one last question. Do you have any suggestions for improvements to the mall?

W1: Yes. You should add more parking spaces. I can never find a place to park. It's really annoying sometimes when . . .

(*Audio fades as last speaker continues to speak.)*

Narrator: That is the end of Section 1. You now have half a minute to check your answers.

Now turn to Section 2 on page 152.

Section 2. You will hear a recording of a tour of a health club.

First, you have some time to look at questions 11 to 14 on page 152.

Now listen carefully and answer questions 11 to 14.

Questions 11–14

Good afternoon. Welcome to the Riverside Health Club. The purpose of today's tour is to let you become familiar with the different activities available at the club. I hope that by the end of the tour all of you will decide to become members.

When you become a member of the health club, you will have the opportunity to participate in a wide range of fitness activities. Over here we have our indoor tennis courts. There are three of them, and if you don't know how to play, we offer tennis lessons throughout the week. Right here next to the courts is the club store. It's quite small, you see, but we have it as a convenience. So if you need snacks or drinks after exercising, you can buy them here.

OK, now this is the exercise room. It's the most well-equipped exercise facility in the city. You won't find old-fashioned weights for lifting here. We have only the most modern exercise machines. All the machines are electronic. They automatically adjust to your weight and fitness level, so you get the workout that's just right for you. The exercise room is run by Peter Jones, who's an expert in both fitness and technology, so he can help you become familiar with the machines. Once you learn how to use them, and Peter makes that easy, they're really great. I work out on them myself just about everyday.

OK. In here we have the swimming pool. We offer different types and levels of swimming lessons. Also you'll notice that the pool is Olympic size, so it's well-suited for competitions. In fact, our swimming team is well-known throughout the city. As a club member, you would have the opportunity to try out for the swim team if you're interested.

Narrator: Before you hear the rest of the tour, you have some time to look at questions 15 to 20 on pages 152 and 153.

Now listen and answer the questions 15 to 20.

Questions 15–20

Over there at the other end are the locker rooms where you can change from your business clothes to your swimsuit or whatever. You can look in them later if you wish. They're very comfortable. We keep them well-stocked with the basic necessities such as towels and soap. You'll have to supply your own shampoo, however. There are plenty of showers so you'll never have to wait your turn. We also have hairdryers for you to use. For safety reasons, we ask that everyone wear rubber sandals in the changing rooms. What else? Oh, you'll have to supply your own lock, of course. That's for your security.

Before we leave the pool area, I'd like to make you aware of some of our rules. The pool is the most popular place in the club, and it's often crowded, so we have rules for everyone's comfort and safety. The most important one, if you have children, please be aware that they are not allowed in the pool area alone. Children must be accompanied by an adult at all times. Naturally there is no running near the pool. The floor is very wet, and it would be easy to get hurt. One last thing, for sanitary reasons, we ask everyone to shower before entering the pool.

All right, I hope you've enjoyed the tour. Are there any questions?

Narrator: That is the end of Section 2. You now have half a minute to check your answers.

Now turn to Section 3 on page 153.

Section 3. You will hear a professor and her students discussing class assignments.

First, you will have some time to look at questions 21 to 26 on page 153.

Now listen carefully and answer questions 21 to 26.

Questions 21–26

W1: In this class we focus on developing writing skills, so one of the most important things we do is practice those skills by writing essays. Today we'll go over the requirements for your essay assignments. You'll have to write one essay each week. They're not very long essays, just about 350 to 400 words apiece. Every week I'll assign a different type of essay, so I thought today we'd go over some of the important essay types. The first type of essay I'll assign will be an essay describing a process. So you'll need to choose something that you can describe step-by-step. Yes, Mr. Smith?

M1: Is that a "how to" essay? I mean, would a topic be something like "How to fix a car?"

W1: Well, you should be more specific. Remember, you have a limited number of words. A better example would be "How to change the oil in a car." Yes?

W2: How about friendship as a topic? "How to make friends." Would that be a topic for a process essay?

W1: It could be, but actually friendship is a better topic for a classification essay, which is the second type I'll assign. In a classification essay you present your idea by organizing it into categories. "Three types of friends" would be a good topic for a classification essay. The third essay type you'll write is compare and contrast. So, obviously, for your topic you'll pick two or more things to compare.

M2: (*laughing*) Like comparing the food in the student cafeteria to the food in a real restaurant.

W1: Why not? That could actually be quite a good topic. But it really doesn't matter which topic you choose, as long as you develop your argument well. The next essay type is argumentative, in which you'll present an opinion and prove or defend it.

M1: I like to argue.

W1: Then you should do quite well with an argumentative essay. When writing this type of essay, be sure to state your opinion in a clear, straightforward sentence. For example "Homework is necessary" could be a thesis statement. Yes?

Narrator: Before you hear the rest of the conversation, you have some time to look at questions 27 to 30 on pages 153 and 154.

Now listen carefully and answer questions 27 to 30.

Questions 27–30

W2: Will you give us the topics, or do we pick our own?

W1: I'd like you to pick your own topics. That way you can write about things that interest you. But be sure your topics are original. I want them to come out of your own heads, not out of any book on essay writing. So, any original topic is fine as long as it fits the assigned essay type. Are there any more questions? Yes?

M2: When are the essays due?

W1: Every Monday I'll make a new essay assignment, which you'll have to hand in to me the following Friday. Another question?

W2: Will the essays count toward the final grade?

W1: Of course. The essays are the most important thing we do in this class. All together your essays will count for 65 percent of your final grade. Other class work will count for 15 percent and your tests will be 20 percent of the final grade. One more thing. Please type your essays on a computer. Handwritten essays are not acceptable, and I don't want to receive any photocopied work either.

Narrator: That is the end of Section 3. You now have half a minute to check your answers.

Now turn to Section 4 on page 154.

Section 4. You will hear a professor give a lecture. First you have some time to look at questions 31 to 36 on page 154.

Now listen carefully and answer questions 31 to 36.

Questions 31–36

Good evening. I'm Professor Williams and this class is Introduction to Anthropology. This class meets every Tuesday evening from 6:45 until 8:15. Please be on time for each class session. This evening we'll begin with a discussion of hunter-gatherer societies. This is an important topic because at one time all humans were hunter-gatherers. What are hunter-gatherer societies? They are groups of people that survive by hunting animals and gathering plants to eat. Typically in these societies the men's job is to hunt large animals while the women both gather plants and hunt smaller animals. Before twelve thousand years ago, all humans lived as hunter-gatherers. Now there are relatively few groups of people living this way, but there are some. Experts estimate that in about 50 years or so all such groups will have disappeared. Today hunter-gatherer societies still exist in the Arctic, in some desert areas, and in tropical rainforests. These are areas where other forms of food production, namely agriculture, are too difficult because of the climate.

Narrator: Before you hear the rest of the conversation, you have some time to look at questions 37 to 40 on page 154.

Now listen carefully and answer questions 37 to 40.

Questions 37–40

In history, many hunter-gatherer societies eventually developed into farming societies. What are some of the basic differences between hunter-gatherers and farmers? The first is that hunter-gatherers tend to be nomadic. They travel from place to place. Once they have used up the food in one area, they have to move on to the next place to find more. Farmers, on the other hand, are more likely to be sedentary. They can't move often because, of course, they have to stay in one place long enough to plant their crops and harvest them.

Another difference is that hunter-gatherer societies generally have lower population densities. Farming can support much higher population densities than hunting and gathering can because farming results in a larger food supply. So you'll find smaller groups among hunter-gatherers. Another very important difference is in social structure. A characteristic of hunter-gatherer societies is that they tend not to have hierarchical social structures. They usually don't have surplus food, or surplus anything, and if they did they would have no place to keep it since they move around so often. So in a hunter-gatherer society, there is little ability to support full-time leaders. Everybody has to spend their time looking for food. These societies are more egalitarian than farming societies, where we see hierarchical social structures begin to develop.

Please bear in mind that everything I have said so far this evening is of a general nature. Next we will look at some specific examples of hunter-gatherer societies to see how these general concepts translate into reality.

Narrator: That is the end of Section 4. You now have half a minute to check your answers.

You will now have 10 minutes to transfer your answers to the listening answer sheet.

This is almost the end of the test. You now have one more minute to check all your answers.

That is the end of the Listening section of Model Test 2.

MODEL TEST 3

Narrator: IELTS Listening. Model Test 3.

You will hear a number of different recordings, and you will have to answer questions on what you hear. There will be time for you to read the instructions and questions, and you will have a chance to check your work. All the recordings will be played once only.

The test is in four sections. Write all your answers in the Listening Question booklet. At the end of the test you will be given ten minutes to transfer your answers to an answer sheet.

Now turn to Section 1 on page 169.

Section 1. You will hear a conversation between a lost and found agent, and a woman who has lost something.

First you have some time to look at Questions 1 to 4 on page 169.

You will see that there is an example which has been done for you. On this occasion only, the conversation relating to this will be played first.

Example

W1: (*excited and impatient*) Is this the lost and found department?
M1: Yes, this is Lost Property. Did you lose something on the train?
W1: Yes, I did. I lost something very valuable, and it's very important that I get it back.
M1: All right, calm down. We'll fill in a lost item report form. Now, when did you lose the item?
W1: Just now. Today. A few minutes ago.
M1: Today's Monday, OK, right.

Narrator: The item was lost today which is Monday, so "Monday" has been written in the space. Now we shall begin. You should answer the questions as you listen because you will not hear the recording a second time. Listen carefully and answer questions 1 to 4.

Questions 1–4

W1: (*excited and impatient*)Is this the lost and found department?
M1: Yes, this is Lost Property. Did you lose something on the train?
W1: Yes, I did. I lost something very valuable, and it's very important that I get it back.
M1: All right, calm down. We'll fill out a lost item report form. Now, when did you lose the item?
W1: Just now. Today. A few minutes ago.
M1: Today's Monday, OK, right.
W1: Can't you hurry? Can't you send the police to look for it or something?
M1: Now just relax. This will only take a minute. May I have your name, please?
W1: It's Patty, that's P-A-T-T-Y, last name Brown, like the color.
M1: Patty Brown. All right, Ms. Brown, your address?
W1: I live at 17 High Street.
M1: Seventy or seventeen?
W1: SevenTEEN.
M1: Is that a house or a flat?
W1: Oh. It's a flat, an apartment. Number 5. And the city is Riverdale.

M1: Just one more thing. I need a phone number.
W1: 305-5938.
M1: Is that home or office or . . .
W1: It's my mobile phone. That's the best number to use because you can always reach me there.

Narrator: Before you hear the rest of the conversation, you have some time to look at questions 5 to 10 on page 169.

Now listen and answer questions 5 to 10.

Questions 5–10

M1: OK. I'll need a description of the lost item. What exactly did you lose?
W1: I lost my reading glasses. But you know I bought them in Italy, they're Italian designer glasses and very expensive.
M1: I see. And can you describe them? Are they square or round or . . .
W1: They're round. And they have a chain attached. You know, those chains on glasses so you can hang them around your neck.
M1: Where were you when you last had them?
W1: I was sitting on the train reading. I had a window seat. The train was just about to enter the station. I heard the door at the other end of the car open, so I looked up from the article I was reading to see what the noise was.
M1: So you had your glasses on then because you were reading?
W1: Yes, that's right. It was a fascinating article in that new magazine, you know the one, I can't remember the name now but anyhow . . .
M1: Which train were you on?
W1: Oh, dear. I don't remember the number, but it was the train from Riverdale. I've come here to visit my aunt. I've taken a whole week off of work to make this trip. I left home at five o'clock this morning, and I'm very tired.
M1: I'm sorry to hear that. Several trains have arrived from Riverdale this morning. What time did your train get here?
W1: Oh, just about 30 minutes ago. At ten o'clock, I think. Yes, that's right.
M1: So the last time you had your glasses was when you were reading on the train?
W1: Yes, and when I got off the train, I had my hand bag and my suitcase, and I checked my seat to see if I had left anything on it, but I hadn't.
M1: And what's that in your coat pocket?
W1: What's what? Oh . . . oh, my glasses! Oh my goodness! I can't believe they were there the whole time.

(*Audio fades as last speaker continues to speak.)*

Narrator: That is the end of Section 1. You now have half a minute to check your answers.

Now turn to Section 2 on page 170.

Section 2. You will hear a recording of a talk about student housing.

First, you have some time to look at questions 11 to 14 on page 170.

Now listen carefully and answer questions 11 to 14.

Questions 11–14

M1: Good morning. Welcome to Day 2 of Student Orientation Week. The subject of the first talk today will be off-campus housing. This is of interest to those of you who don't want to live in student housing and are not familiar with our city. I'll give you some tips about where to look for housing and how to go about it.

OK, first let's talk about where to look for an apartment. There are some places that I don't recommend. The obvious place to look, you might think, would be in the neighborhood of the university. However, that's probably not a very good idea because, unfortunately, this is one of the more expensive areas of the city to live in. The downtown area is a popular place to visit; however, that's not a good place to look for housing, either, because it's mainly a commercial area. There are very few apartments there. It's also rather far from the university. So where does that leave us? I can recommend a couple of good places to look. Many students rent apartments in the uptown neighborhoods. The prices there are quite low, and many buses go there so it's very easy to get to the university from there. The Greenfield Park neighborhood is also popular. It's closer to the university, but not many buses run in that direction, so you'll need a car if you choose to live there.

Narrator: Before you hear the rest of the talk you have some time to look at questions 15 to 20 on page 170.

Now listen and answer the questions 15 to 20.

Questions 15–20

M1: All right, so let's say you've decided on a neighborhood. Next you have to find out what apartments are available. There are a number of places where you can look for apartment ads. The best place to look is at the university's Student Center. There is a wall there devoted to apartment ads. You can also look in the university newspaper. It comes out every Friday, which gives you the weekend for apartment hunting. The local city newspaper, *The Greenfield Times*, also lists apartment for rent ads. Again, Friday and Saturday are the best days. That's when you'll find the most ads. Finally, of course, you can look on the Internet. There are several Internet sites devoted to apartment rental ads in this area.

The staff at the Student Counseling Center is always ready to help you in your apartment search. They have available city maps as well as city bus schedules to help you get around to the various neighborhoods. If you would like to find someone to share an apartment with you, the Counseling Center has a roommate matching service. Most students find that having roommates is the most economical way to rent an apartment. The Center can also provide you with a list of inexpensive furniture stores. We all know how expensive it can be to furnish an apartment, but it can also be done in a more economical way. Also you might want to consider signing up for a meal plan on campus. If you don't like to cook or are too busy, well, you still have to eat, right? If you live off campus you can still eat in the university student dining rooms. We have plans for buying meals by the week, month, or semester. The Student Counseling Center can give you all the necessary information on that.

Narrator: That is the end of Section 2. You now have half a minute to check your answers.

Now turn to Section 3 on page 170.

Section 3. You will hear two students talking about their assignment.

First, you will have some time to look at questions 21 to 25 on page 170.

Now listen carefully and answer the questions 21 to 25.

Questions 21–25

M1: Have you decided what you're going to write your paper on? The one for Professor Anderson's class?

W1: The topic is transportation, right? I've been thinking about writing about bicycles as a way to solve our transportation problems.

M1: Really? I usually think of bicycling as a sport or recreational activity.

W1: Around here, that's what most people think. But in some parts of the world bicycles are an important form of transportation for many people. I think we have a lot to learn from them.

M1: So, what are you going to say in your paper?

W1: I'm not sure. Maybe you can help me figure some of it out.

M1: Sure. OK, well, I'd say if you want to persuade people to use bicycles more often, you have to start by thinking about the advantages and disadvantages.

W1: You're right. Let's see . . . well, I think the advantages are obvious. First, bicycling is good for your health.

M1: Yes, that's true. And another thing is that bicycles are a lot cheaper to use than cars.

W1: Or any other form of transportation, when you think about it. You don't have to pay a fare every time you ride your bike, like you do when you take the bus or the train.

M1: OK, another one is that bicycles don't cause pollution like cars and buses do.

W1: Yeah, that's a really important one. Bicycles are a clean form of transportation.

M1: OK, so what about the other side? What are some disadvantages, some reasons why people might not want to use bicycles?

W1: One thing I thought of is weather. Who wants to ride a bike in the rain? Or if you live where the weather is cold all winter, it would be hard to use a bicycle regularly. So bad weather would be a problem.

M1: Bad health would be too. Some people just aren't strong enough to ride bikes very much. You have to be in good shape.

W1: Yes, especially if you live far from your job or wherever you have to go. So that would be another problem, distance. It's difficult to ride your bike if your trip is a long distance.

Narrator: Before you hear the rest of the conversation, you have some time to look at questions 26 to 30 on page 171.

Now listen and answer questions 26 to 30.

Questions 26–30

M1: OK, so using a bike might not work for everyone, but for a lot of people it would. How can people be encouraged to use bikes for transportation?

W1: I think there's a lot cities can do. I think the biggest thing is making bicycle lanes on roads. It's really dangerous riding a bike where there's a lot of traffic, so special lanes just for bicycles would make things a lot safer.

M1: That's a great idea.

W1: Yeah, they already do that in some cities. And another thing is to make safe places for people to leave their bikes. I mean like at subway stations. A lot of people ride to the subway station and then take the subway to work. They need a safe place to lock up their bikes all day so they don't get stolen.

M1: That seems important.

W1: Yes, and another thing I've read about is maps. Some cities provide bicycling maps that show all the good routes. They show people how easy it is to get around by bike.

M1: OK, but what about equipment? Don't you need a lot of special stuff to ride a bicycle?

W1: I don't think so. For safety you should wear a helmet, and at night you should have lights or wear reflective tape so cars can see you. For comfort you need light clothes, and waterproof clothes when it rains. But that's all I can think of. Really, it's easy and inexpensive to get started riding a bike.

M1: I think you'll write a great paper. You've already persuaded me to get a bike.

Narrator: That is the end of Section 3. You now have half a minute to check your answers.

Now turn to Section 4 on page 171.

Section 4. You will hear a professor explaining an assignment to the class. First you have some time to look at the questions 31 to 40 on page 171.

Now listen carefully and answer questions 31 to 40.

Questions 31–40

W1: Good afternoon everyone. Today we'll talk about the most important assignment you'll do in this class, which is write a research paper. I'll start by going over the process step by step so you'll know exactly what I expect of you. All right, let's begin at the beginning. The first step is to choose a topic. I have a list of suggested topics related to the content of this class, and I'd like you to look over it to find a topic that interests you. Then, since they are somewhat general, I'd like you to narrow your topic choice down to something more specific. You'll need to get my final approval on your topic before you begin your research.

The next thing you'll do is gather information on your topic. There are two major places to go for that. At the library you'll have reference books and other types of books available, as well as journals, magazines, and newspapers. Don't forget to look at atlases and other similar sources too. They contain a lot of useful information. Then of course there is the Internet, where you'll find online journals and newspapers, as well as online encyclopedias, and much more.

After you have gathered some information and had the chance to start thinking about your topic, the next step is to write a thesis statement. This is a critical part of the process because the bulk of the paper will be about using your information to defend your thesis statement. I will be happy to help you with this, and, actually, with any other part of your writing process if you need it.

Now then, let's say you have your thesis statement and you have your information. How do you get started writing? It can seem overwhelming with all your ideas and notes floating around. Writing an outline will help you to start getting focused. Make sure your outline includes three important things: first your introduction, where you state your thesis, then the body, which is the bulk of the paper and where you make the arguments to support your thesis, and finally the conclusion. Here you'll restate your thesis and summarize your arguments.

So now that you have your outline, you can start organizing your notes. Organize them according to the outline. As you go along you'll start seeing what information is important to emphasize, what information you may actually not want to include, what you need to find out more about, etc. So organizing your notes helps you understand your information better and start to analyze it.

The next step is to write your first draft. If you have developed a good outline and organized your notes well, then this should not be too difficult. Following your outline, present your information and analysis of it.

Then, of course, the next thing to do is revise your draft. Read it over carefully, checking to make sure that you have explained your ideas clearly and presented your information correctly. You may want to reorganize some of your information at this point, too.

Finally, you'll type your final draft on the computer. Make sure that you check it for punctuation and spelling errors before you hand it in.

OK, that's a general outline of how to go about writing a research paper. Now let's talk about the proper format for footnotes and bibliographic entries.

Narrator: That is the end of Section 4. You now have half a minute to check your answers.

You will now have 10 minutes to transfer your answers to the listening answer sheet.

This is almost the end of the test. You now have one more minute to check all your answers.

That is the end of the Listening section of Model Test 3.

MODEL TEST 4

Narrator: IELTS Listening. Model Test 4.

You will hear a number of different recordings, and you will have to answer questions on what you hear. There will be time for you to read the instructions and questions, and you will have a chance to check your work. All the recordings will be played once only.

The test is in four sections. Write all your answers in the Listening Question booklet. At the end of the test you will be given ten minutes to transfer your answers to an answer sheet.

Now turn to Section 1 on page 186.

Section 1. You will hear a man buying tickets over the phone.

First you have some time to look at Questions 1 to 5 on page 186.

You will see that there is an example which has been done for you. On this occasion only, the conversation relating to this will be played first.

Example

Sound effects in italics.

F1: Good morning. Municipal Museum of Art. Information Desk.
M1: Yes, I'd like to find out about tickets for . . .
F1: Tickets? That's our Special Events Department. Let me transfer you.

Narrator: The woman says she will transfer him to the Special Events Department, so C has been circled. Now we shall begin. You should answer the questions as you listen because you will not hear the recording a second time. Listen carefully and answer questions 1 to 5.

Questions 1–5

Sound effects in italics.

F1: Good morning. Municipal Museum of Art. Information Desk.
M1: Yes, I'd like to find out about tickets for . . .
F1: Tickets? That's our Special Events Department. Let me transfer you.

(*telephone ringing*)

F2: Special Events.
M1: Yes, hello. I'm interested in the series you have going on now . . .
F2: Oh, you mean our lecture series on the history of art.
M1: Actually, I meant the concert series.
F2: Oh, yes, of course. It's already begun but there's still a concert tomorrow, that's Thursday. There's also one on Saturday, and then the last one is on Sunday.
M1: The one tomorrow, is that when they'll be playing the Mozart concerto?
F2: Yes, it is.
M1: Then I'd like two tickets for that, if they're still available.
F2: Yes, we have some tickets left. Now, I'll need your name.
M1: It's Steven Milford. That's M-i-l-f-o-r-d.
F2: Since you want tickets for tomorrow there isn't time to mail in a check. You'll have to pay by credit card.
M1: That's not a problem.
F2: Then I'll need your credit card number.
M1: Oh, of course. It's 1659798164.
F2: . . . 8164. Got it. OK you wanted two tickets, right?
M1: Yes.
F2: At 16.35 apiece that comes out to a total of 32 pounds and 70 p. You can pick up your tickets at the door.

Narrator: Before you hear the rest of the conversation, you have some time to look at questions 6 to 10 on page 186.

Now listen and answer questions 6 to 10.

Questions 6–10

M1: Fine. Um, could you tell me how to get there? We're coming by train.
F2: Certainly. It's very easy. When you get out of the train station, you'll see the library right across the street. Just walk down to the corner . . .
M1: Do I go right or left out of the train station?
F2: Oh, sorry. Go right, walk down to the corner. Right there on the corner you'll see a bank and across the street on the opposite corner is the post office. There are some office buildings across the street, too. Anyhow, you just go right at the corner, pass the car park and you'll see the museum right there in the middle of the block. If you get to a hotel, you've gone too far.
M1: So right at the corner and pass the car park but not the hotel. All right I think I've got it.
F2: Great. Make sure you're here by 7:30.

(*Audio fades as last speaker continues to speak.*)

Narrator: That is the end of Section 1. You now have half a minute to check your answers.

Now turn to Section 2 on page 187.

Section 2. You will hear a recording of a radio show about tourism to Raven Island.

First, you have some time to look at questions 11 to 17 on page 187.

Now listen carefully and answer questions 11 to 17.

Questions 11–17

M1: Good afternoon and welcome to Travel Time. Our guest today is Sheila Farnsworth, director of Raven Tours travel agency. She'll talk to us about travel to Raven Island.

F1: Thank you, George. Raven Island is becoming quite a popular tourist destination, and with good reason. The prices are still low, and there's so much to enjoy there. Most tourists to Raven Island usually spend their time in one of two places. Ravensburg is the major city on the island, though with a population of only 56,000, it's not large by most standards. But for those who enjoy a more urban style vacation, Ravensburg is where they go. For those looking for a bit of peace and quiet, Blackstone Beach is a favorite destination. This town, located on the island's northern coast, has a population of just 12,000 people.

The weather on Raven Island is always nice, especially during the summer. Summer in the city of Ravensburg is warm with average temperatures reaching 26 degrees or higher, and the weather is always pleasantly sunny there during July and August. Summer at Blackstone is a bit cooler, with average temperatures of around 23 degrees, and the weather is often windy because, of course, it's located on the coast.

Ravensburg has a lot to offer visitors. Its clubs and theaters are well-known, so if entertainment is what you're looking for, Ravensburg has the advantage there. The disadvantage to this is that, particularly during the summer theater festival, the city can become quite crowded with entertainment seekers. Blackstone Beach, on the other hand, is famous for its many fine seafood restaurants, considered to be the best on the island. So if you like seafood, that's the place to go. Unfortunately, eating seafood is the major activity in Blackstone. It's a very quiet town, which is a disadvantage if you're looking for excitement.

How can you get there? The Ravensburg airport is actually located a bit out of town. It's 25 kilometers from the city, but frequent bus service, taxis, and car rentals make it quite easy to get downtown. Travelers to Blackstone Beach also use the Ravensburg airport, which is about 75 kilometers away. There are three buses a day from the airport to Blackstone or you can rent[1] a car, of course.

Narrator: Before you hear the rest of the talk, you have some time to look at questions 18 to 20 on page 187.

Now listen and answer the questions 18 to 20.

Questions 18–20

F1: Because of the low prices on Raven Island, many tourists travel there with shopping on their minds. What are some of the best bargains available on the island? Well, contrary to what one might think, native handicrafts are not a popular item. And although Raven Island has a beautiful musical tradition, there are not many CDs available of the native music, and the ones that are available are quite expensive. Some very good deals can be found, however, in the perfume shops. Raven Island Scents, a local factory, produces several fashionable perfumes, which they sell at reasonable prices. Jewelry is also popular among tourists, and jewelry shops abound. Since fishing is the major island industry, no tourist goes home without a package of smoked fish. If you want to try fishing yourself, however, be sure to bring your own fishing gear.[2] Believe it or not, it's difficult and expensive for tourists to buy it on the island.

[1] BRITISH: hire.

[2] BRITISH: tackle.

Narrator: That is the end of Section 2. You now have half a minute to check your answers.

Now turn to Section 3 on page 187.

Section 3. You will hear two students talking about a class project.

First, you will have some time to look at questions 21 to 23 on page 187.

Now listen carefully and answer the questions 21 to 23.

Questions 21–23

M1: Hi, Janet.
F1: Harry. What's up?
M1: You know that research project we have to do for Professor Farley's class? Have you started it yet?
F1: Started it? I'm almost done.
M1: Really? I'm having trouble. Do you think you could help me?
F1: You're going to need a lot of help. It's due next Thursday.
M1: I know.
F1: And it counts for 40 percent of our final semester grade.
M1: I know! So I could really use your help. So, what topic did you choose?
F1: I did my research about people's TV watching habits.
M1: You mean which programs they watch?
F1: Yeah, and how often they watch. It was really interesting.

Narrator: Before you hear the rest of the conversation, you have some time to look at questions 24 to 30 on page 188.

Now listen and answer questions 24 to 30.

Questions 24–30

M1: So, how'd you get started?
F1: Well, after I decided my topic, I went to the library and did some research. I mean, I read about other studies people had done about TV watching.
M1: How did that help you?
F1: Oh, it was really important. It gave me lots of ideas about what questions to ask. So after I did the library research, I chose my research method.
M1: What did you choose?
F1: Well, I could do either interviews or just send around a paper questionnaire. I decided to use the questionnaire because I could get information from a lot more people that way.
M1: And then what?
F1: I made up the questions for the questionnaire.
M1: And who did you give it to?
F1: Well, that's what I had to do next, choose my subjects. You have to think about if you want data from people of a certain age or certain professions and things like that. I decided to ask people like myself—university students.
M1: So then you just went around and asked people the questions?
F1: Well, first I had to submit my research design to Professor Farley. He had to make sure it was OK before I went ahead with the research.
M1: Did he make you change anything?
F1: No, he pretty much liked it the way it was. So then I had to send out the questionnaire. I just put it in all the students' mailboxes. A lot of them responded. I got a lot of results—pages and pages.
M1: Well, what did you do with all that information?

F1: Well, I did what Professor Farley told us to do. I made charts and graphs. That helped me figure out what all that data meant.
M1: Charts and graphs, huh? Hmm, I'll have to look at my class notes.
F1: Yes, you'd better. The professor outlined the whole process for us.
M1: So then you'll just hand in those charts and graphs on Thursday?
F1: Well, I'll have to write a report, too, of course. I mean, the professor wants to see our interpretation of the results. That's the whole point, don't you see?
M1: Yeah, I guess. If I get started now, do you think I'll finish on time?
F1: Maybe, if you don't have anything else to do this week.

Narrator: That is the end of Section 3. You now have half a minute to check your answers.

Now turn to Section 4 on page 188.

Section 4. You will hear a professor giving a lecture on the American crow. First you have some time to look at the questions 31 to 40 on page 188.

Now listen carefully and answer questions 31 to 40.

Questions 31–40

M1: Today I'll talk about the American crow, also known as the common crow. This bird has a bad reputation, and many people consider it to be a pest, but the American crow and many of its cousins in the corvid family are actually among the most intelligent of all the birds.

There are about 40 species in the crow family, and they can be found in most parts of the world. You'll find crows in North America, although interestingly enough, not in South America. While crows live in cold areas of the far north close to the Arctic region, there are none in Antarctica. They also like warm regions. There are several species of crows, for example, in Hawaii. And of course you'll find them in other parts of the world, Europe, Asia, and so on.

The American crow is one of the 15 species of crows found in North America, and is also one of the most common. It's not a small bird, measuring 39 to 49 centimeters in length. Unlike some of its cousins—the magpie, for example, which is black and white, or the blue jay which is blue with white and black markings—the American crow is completely black, including the beak and feet. Because of their intensely dark color, some people dislike crows, or better said, fear them. Another reason people dislike crows is because they associate these birds with garbage. Crows love garbage and are often seen hanging around dumpsters behind restaurants and grocery stores. In addition to garbage left behind by humans, crows eat seeds, grains, eggs, fish, and carrion. They'll eat just about anything. One of their absolute favorite foods is corn.

Crows build large nests of sticks, usually in trees or sometimes in bushes. For safety reasons, they almost never nest on the ground. Mostly they nest alone but in some places they have been seen nesting in colonies. The female lays from three to six eggs at a time. The eggs hatch in about 18 days. The babies stay in the nest for around a month. Generally 35 days after hatching they have their feathers and are ready to fly.

Next we'll talk about some studies which have demonstrated the extreme intelligence of these animals.

Narrator: That is the end of Section 4. You now have half a minute to check your answers.

You will now have 10 minutes to transfer your answers to the listening answer sheet.

This is almost the end of the test. You now have one more minute to check all your answers.

That is the end of the Listening section of Model Test 4.

NOTE: Please photocopy the Answer Sheets on page 339 to 344 to use for Model Tests.

IELTS Listening Answer Sheet

		✓ ✗
1		1
2		2
3		3
4		4
5		5
6		6
7		7
8		8
9		9
10		10
11		11
12		12
13		13
14		14
15		15
16		16
17		17
18		18
19		19
20		20

		✓ ✗
21		21
22		22
23		23
24		24
25		25
26		26
27		27
28		28
29		29
30		30
31		31
32		32
33		33
34		34
35		35
36		36
37		37
38		38
39		39
40		40
	Listening Total	

IELTS Reading Answer Sheet

Module taken:

Academic ▭ General Training ▭

		✓		✗
1		▭	1	▭
2		▭	2	▭
3		▭	3	▭
4		▭	4	▭
5		▭	5	▭
6		▭	6	▭
7		▭	7	▭
8		▭	8	▭
9		▭	9	▭
10		▭	10	▭
11		▭	11	▭
12		▭	12	▭
13		▭	13	▭
14		▭	14	▭
15		▭	15	▭
16		▭	16	▭
17		▭	17	▭
18		▭	18	▭
19		▭	19	▭
20		▭	20	▭

		✓		✗
21		▭	21	▭
22		▭	22	▭
23		▭	23	▭
24		▭	24	▭
25		▭	25	▭
26		▭	26	▭
27		▭	27	▭
28		▭	28	▭
29		▭	29	▭
30		▭	30	▭
31		▭	31	▭
32		▭	32	▭
33		▭	33	▭
34		▭	34	▭
35		▭	35	▭
36		▭	36	▭
37		▭	37	▭
38		▭	38	▭
39		▭	39	▭
40		▭	40	▭
	Listening Total			

Writing (Academic and General Training) Answer Sheet

Module: ACADEMIC ☐ GENERAL TRAINING ☐ (Tick as appropriate)

TASK 1

-2-

Writing (Academic and General Training) Answer Sheet

TASK 2 **-3-**

-4-

NOTE:
The enclosed Audio CD contains audio for the Listening Module exercises (Targets 1–13) and the Listening Module in IELTS Model Test 1.

Please refer to the Audioscript in the Appendix for the Listening Modules for Model Tests 2, 3, and 4.

CD Tracks:

Tracks 1 and 2:	Target 1—Making Assumptions
Tracks 3 and 4:	Target 2—Understanding Numbers
Tracks 5 and 6:	Target 3—Understanding the Alphabet
Track 7:	Target 4—Listening for Descriptions
Tracks 8–12:	Target 5—Listening for Time
Tracks 13 and 14:	Target 6—Listening for Frequency
Track 15:	Target 7—Listening for Similar Meanings
Track 16:	Target 8—Listening for Emotions
Track 17:	Target 9—Listening for an Explanation
Track 18:	Target 10—Listening for Classifications
Track 19:	Target 11—Listening for Comparisons and Contrasts
Track 20:	Target 12—Listening for Negative Meanings
Track 21:	Target 13—Listening for Chronology
Tracks 22–29:	Model Test 1—Listening Module